D0873878

THE MARBLE FOOT

by the same author

BAUDELAIRE AND THE SYMBOLISTS
CAROLINE OF ENGLAND
FOUR PORTRAITS
JOHN RUSKIN: THE PORTRAIT OF A PROPHET
HOGARTH'S PROGRESS
SHAKESPEARE: THE POET AND HIS BACKGROUND
ALEXANDER POPE: THE EDUCATION OF GENIUS
THE SIGN OF THE FISH
CASANOVA IN LONDON
THE SINGULAR PREFERENCE
available in one volume
BYRON: THE YEARS OF FAME
BYRON IN ITALY

THE
MARBLE FOOT

PETER QUENNELL

An Autobiography
1905-1938

COLLINS
ST JAMES'S PLACE, LONDON
1976

William Collins Sons & Co. Ltd
London · Glasgow · Sydney · Auckland
Toronto · Johannesburg

First published 1976
© Peter Quennell 1976

ISBN 0 00 216509 0

Set in Monotype Bembo
Made and printed in Great Britain by
William Collins Sons & Co. Ltd Glasgow

To My Wife

Pour l'enfant, amoureux de cartes et d'estampes,
L'univers est égal à son vaste appétit.
Ah! que le monde est grand à la clarté des lampes!
Aux yeux du souvenir que le monde est petit.

Charles Baudelaire: LE VOYAGE

When one subtracts from life infancy (which is vegetation),
– sleep, eating, and swilling – buttoning and unbuttoning
– how much remains of downright existence? The summer
of a dormouse.

Byron, JOURNAL, Tuesday, December 7th, 1813;

I

WHEN MY FATHER FIRST CALLED ON MY MOTHER'S FAMILY, he is said to have been wearing a check cut-away coat, a garment that disconcerted my grandfather, and offended or, at least, surprised my uncles. They were also taken aback by his boisterous sense of humour and by his somewhat loud voice. In his early thirties, he was a tall, spare, broad-shouldered and extremely long-legged man, with a bright eye, decisive masculine features and a darkish curling forelock. He talked incessantly. Yet, despite the noise he made and the general commotion he aroused, even that self-centred household must surely have agreed that he had much to recommend him. His morals were sound; he was a notably hard worker; and he had already established a reputation among rising English architects. He soon dazzled my nineteen-year-old mother; and perhaps she was doubly dazzled because their original meeting had so nearly failed to come about. Earlier that day, she remembered, she had been feeling ill and overtired, and had decided she must refuse an invitation to her cousins' little party. Then she had changed her mind. She was a naturally sociable character; her cousins, the Paynes, who lived in a far more extravagant style than the quiet, impecunious Courtneys, liked entertaining young people; and one of the guests they had collected that night was the gay and ebullient Charles Quennell. He and my mother waltzed throughout the evening; and, as he bade her good night, he asked if he might pay her a visit at her father's house, The Postern, a modest house for all its romantic name, upon the fringes of suburban Bromley.

Having renewed their acquaintanceship, they were enchanted to discover just how many tastes they had in common. My mother attended a near-by art-school; my father, a keen member of the Junior Art Workers' Guild and a staunch supporter of the post-Ruskinian Arts-and-Crafts movement, not only planned buildings but had designed a variety of domestic objects for a progressive London firm – chairs, tables, bookcases, bedsteads and simple but handsome garden-seats, made of solid English oak instead of late-Victorian cast iron. He, therefore, suggested that, since they were both artists, they should collaborate on the production of a wall-paper; and amid its arabesque, my suspicious uncles noted, he wove a frieze of interlacing hearts. My father was an obstinate and strong-willed man; but, although he had determined to marry my mother, it proved difficult to convince my grandfather that his elder daughter had yet reached the age when she might reasonably think of leaving home. At last he permitted them to announce their engagement; but he still postponed the wedding-day; whereupon my father adopted a stratagem that slowly weakened his resistance. The moment had come, he proclaimed, to consider buying furniture; and, as his own parents' house was overcrowded, he hoped that my grandfather would allow him to store his purchases within the moderately spacious Postern. Like a series of Trojan horses, piece after piece – 'good eighteenth-century stuff' he had picked up at sales – was manhandled across the threshold, until it grew more and more difficult to move about the rooms and passages. My grandfather then gave way; the date of the wedding was fixed; and my father and mother were duly married on May 19th 1904.

A few old photographs depict the wedding-reception. Here Charles Quennell, a slim, alert figure, now in an elegant Edwardian frock-coat, gazes down with an air of protective pride upon my enraptured, yet unsmiling mother. He is self-assured; she is faintly tremulous. Another photograph reveals the crowd of wedding-guests parading around The Postern's narrow lawn, among whom I think that I can distinguish my paternal grandmother, delighted temporarily to command the stage, lifting the stern profile of an ancient Roman matron beneath a small bedizened bonnet. Her husband I cannot see; no doubt he has put his hands into his pockets, and ambled swiftly out of range. A lazy man, devoted to cricket and fishing, he possessed few social graces; and I doubt if he found much to interest him in this busy assemblage of new relations.

There was always a distinct difference between the Quennell and Courtney families. Both, however, were very far from rich; and both, should they choose to do so, could claim to have known 'better days'. On his marriage to Clara Keziah Toswell, my grandfather, Alan Courtney, had been a fairly prosperous shipbroker. He and his brother-in-law had worked in partnership; and for a time they had succeeded. But Alan Courtney's associate was an idler and a spendthrift. Unknown to my high-minded grandfather, he had long mismanaged their concerns. The business was finally declared bankrupt; and, while his improvident partner, scenting catastrophe, had made over all his assets to his wife, my grandfather, who had taken no such precautions, found himself completely ruined. Yet he had refused to accept defeat, and, having first obtained an appointment as a humble City clerk, from which he slowly fought his way back to a more remunerative position, had spent the rest of his existence – or the larger part of it – paying off his liabilities.

During those laborious years, my patient grandmother died; a grave and gentle-faced woman with a crown of beautifully braided hair, she had caught a fatal chill sitting in rain-damp clothes at the bedside of a sick friend. My mother was then about thirteen; and a hush immediately descended upon the household at The Postern. But it was not an altogether cheerless hush. My mother had a younger sister, Joyce, and five brothers, of whom the eldest, Basil, had wedded and moved away some time before she met my father. Among themselves, like the young Brontës, they led an intensely active private life; and my mother afterwards enjoyed describing their various elaborate games. They had never been dull, she said – how strange it was to observe that her own children sometimes yawned and spoke of boredom! Now they would construct an immense kite, which, one stormy autumn day, was driven off course and crashed into a distant greenhouse; now build railway systems where discarded billiard-balls – they were allowed few toys – took the place of locomotives; now stage full-length plays in a miniature theatre, with pasteboard actors and a home-made muslin curtain.

Except for Claude, the most mechanically-minded member of the family, all the Courtneys were 'artistic'. They sang part-songs, accompanied by Philip, the most musical, who was both performer and composer, and indefatigably drew and painted. It was a busy life; and even my austere, preoccupied grandfather had his own absorbing week-end pastime; with the help of Claude, he was building the model, four or five feet long, of an ocean-going liner. During my childhood, this craft was still on the stocks; and I remember the sharp rasping note of grandfather's foot-driven lathe as, one after another, he fashioned the parts of its perfectly proportioned engines. He was a reserved parent, but attentive and dutiful; and only now and then did his inherited puritanism cast a sudden chilling shadow. There had been an occasion, for instance, when my mother and uncles were seated contentedly around a table, each illustrating a chosen subject. One of my uncles had selected 'The Dance of Salome', and was portraying the dancer as a Middle Eastern houri, in voluminous silken pantaloons and a small embroidered jacket, between which he permitted to appear a narrow strip of naked skin. My grandfather had entered the room, taken a coldly considering view of his children's various works, then picked up a brush, charged it with a lurid purple and, silently leaning over the artist's shoulder, painted out Salome's midriff. No less silently he had turned and gone his way. My uncle accepted the implied reproach, and hastened to destroy his drawing.

Such a show of Victorian moral bias would not in any way have shocked my father; he was himself a staunch moralist, and liked and understood my mother's family, though, having a keen sense of the ludicrous, he sometimes laughed at individual members. Thus my dandified Uncle Philip, with his delicate touch on the piano, his crisp fair hair, his manicured finger-nails and neatly poised gold-rimmed pince-nez, my more masculine father was never tired of teasing. My uncle wore scent; he would come down to breakfast, my father complained, positively 'reeking like a badger'; and, once when my father was on a visit to The Postern and caught that early-morning fragrance, he flipped a piece of bacon-rind across the table-cloth at my uncle who happened to be sitting opposite, but cleverly ducked, so that it struck the breakfast-room wall where it left a large and greasy stain, which the whole family, by dint of desperate scrubbing, contrived at the last moment to wipe away, just before my grandfather's firm and measured footsteps had resounded on the stairs above.

The atmosphere of my father's own home was a good deal less enlivening. My maternal grandfather had slowly paid off his debts, and restored his household to some degree of middle-class domestic comfort. My father's family, on the other hand, still bore the disfiguring traces of their early struggles; and those struggles would seem to have been largely caused, not by the kind of undeserved mishap that had almost overwhelmed the Courtneys, but by my grandfather's professional incompetence and his naturally easy-going disposition. It was my grandmother who had rescued the Quennells from ruin, and she who had insisted that her children must receive a proper schooling. As a young woman, she had learned to distrust men; for her father, 'The Wicked Gunsmith' – the nickname that his grandson first invented – had been a tyrant and a rake. A daguerreotype portrait, lightly hand-coloured, encased in a small pinchbeck frame, and no doubt intended to be worn as a brooch or locket, displays his gross, commanding features. His heavy cheeks, which the photographer has tinted pink, his curly topknot and the profusion of cylindrical curls carefully arranged above the ears, give him a macabre resemblance to a huge ill-tempered baby. His lips are pursed, their corners turned down; his broadcloth waistcoat supports a massive watch-chain; his plumpish fists are strong and square.

To judge from the nickname my father bestowed on him, he must have manufactured sporting guns. Otherwise I am totally ignorant of the life and works of this formidable ancestor, except that he is reputed to have kept a mistress, whom he one day brought home, suggesting that she and his wife and daughter should henceforward share the same house. Not surprisingly, my great-grandmother and her only child thereupon removed themselves, and presently set up a small girls' school in some genteel suburban region – I think the neighbourhood they chose was Blackheath. Their establishment prospered; my grandmother, Emma Rebecca Hobbs, with her clear head and her sharp, authoritative ways, made an admirable educationalist; and she might have continued to prosper, had she not met and married a charming, carefree young man. Evidently, it was a love-match; my grandmother seems to have been obliged to pay most of the expenses of the ceremony. Henry Quennell was neither prosperous nor industrious. Bred in the building-trade – he was the son of a builder employed by the Duchy of Cornwall – he had little taste for hard work, and preferred to sit at the Oval, watching the day's cricket, rather than superintend his business.

In his autobiographical sketch *A Little Learning*, Evelyn Waugh asserts that 'mankind . . . is stubbornly curious of genealogy', and proceeds to list some of the late-eighteenth-century lawyers and clerics who had helped to make him what he was. I have been less fortunate; on both sides of my family beyond the third generation, I am equally ill-instructed about my ancestors' Christian names, the surnames of the women they married or the places of their birth. But I believe that my great-grandfather, the father of Henry Quennell, had migrated to London from the Home Counties. In the Elizabethan and Jacobean ages, there were numerous Quennells, mostly yeoman farmers, scattered around southern England, the least undistinguished being a certain Thomas, who lived at Lythe Hill, close to Chiddingfold, Surrey, and, on his death in 1571, left a characteristic sixteenth-century will, bequeathing the bulk of his estate to his wife, Agnys – 'six of my best kine (except one cow named Lusty)', half a dozen oxen, two 'ambling mares', heifers and hogs, and a large variety of household-stuff, ranging from 'my three best beds' with bolsters, pillows and sheets, to 'all my pewter vessel' and 'half of my bacon at the beam'. Thomas Quennell was clearly a solid yeoman, industrious, methodical and fond of good food. His brother Robert succeeded him at Lythe Hill; and in the seventeenth century, on the outbreak of the Civil Wars, Robert's eldest son, Peter Quennell, became a Royalist ironmaster. Until the Parliamentarians closed his works by violence, he continued to manufacture 'gunns and shott for supply of his Majestie's stores'* in the southern Black Country, and, thanks to the services he had done the King, is said to have been granted a simple and pretty, if somewhat unimposing coat of arms. Thomas Quennell's last direct descendant, however, was not a man who required armorial

* See *Wealden Iron* by E. Straker, 1931.

16

bearings. A subject of Queen Victoria, he spent his summer on the roads, where he earned his livelihood by breaking stones, and passed his winters in the workhouse.

To revert to the Henry Quennell I knew, when my father married, he and my grandmother were living at a house conveniently near the Oval cricket-ground, in a thoroughfare named Foxley Road. Kennington, which abuts on South Brixton and North Lambeth, is not a very cheerful neighbourhood; but the row of slate-roofed yellow-brick houses, built in 1824, that my grandparents inhabited, though today it is squalid and run-down, has still a certain architectural grace. David Cox,* the celebrated water-colourist, had once inhabited the same row; and the adjacent streets are scattered with the former homes of late-eighteenth- and early-nineteenth-century merchants. Since they departed, the entire district had gradually lost its character; factories and warehouses had closed in; and, when my mother first visited Kennington, she found it a 'rough' and unattractive place. Life at Foxley Road proved to be very different from the mild existence of The Postern; and my father's unmarried sister, Edith, met her with a dark and jealous scowl. But she admired my grandmother; and my grandmother, who adored her eldest son, obviously returned her liking.

By her children my grandmother was called 'The Mater'; while their father, though his paternal virtues were not always much in evidence, they affectionately styled 'The Pater'. She was as strong as he was self-indulgent, as purposeful as he was idle. Sometimes his idleness had reached so dangerous a point that my grandmother was obliged to leave her bed before his workmen had arrived, tuck up her skirts and herself perform some of the preliminary tasks – pounding mortar and mixing cement – that had to be got through in the building-yard before the day's work could be started. My grandfather presumably remained asleep; they must, I assume, have had some bitter quarrels. But the fiercest dispute they ever fought out between them had concerned the education of their family. My grandfather announced that, as any form of 'private' education was plainly quite beyond his means, his

* A pupil of Blake's friend, John Varley, Cox (1783–1859) lived in London from 1827 to 1841.

children should be sent to a local elementary school. My grandmother struck back, defending her three sons, and their right to achieve a dignified, a 'gentlemanly' position in late-Victorian society. She cowed my grandfather; he finally succumbed; my father and his two brothers were sent to the kind of schools that did them credit. The stand that she took determined my father's future, in some degree perhaps my own existence. We were saved for the English middle classes, for the state of life that Daniel Defoe declared was 'the best State in the World', since it was neither 'exposed to the Miseries and Hardships, the Labour and Sufferings' that usually afflict the poor, nor 'embarrass'd with the Pride, Luxury, Ambition and Envy of the upper part of Mankind'.

So long as he lived, my father would honour the debt that he owed his obstinate, devoted mother, remembering how close his family had come to final submergence in the proletarian underworld – a world that he saw every day as he walked the London back-streets. During his later life, he told me that, although he respected the author's genius, he could not bear to open Dickens's novels. They reminded him far too vividly of his youth; of the 'grey little people' – his own expressive phrase – and 'grey little streets' that had formed the sombre background of his childhood. Hence his habitual caution, the curious economies he practised, his life-long fear of some unforeseeable, irremediable disaster that might one day descend on him and drag him down. The aspect of my father's temperament that had first delighted my mother was his unfailing dash and gusto. He danced admirably, attended bohemian parties given by such members of the artistic *avant-garde* as Byam Shaw and Walter Crane, and rode to hounds, bravely and competently, across the switchback slopes of Exmoor, yet also found time to assist in the charitable activities of an East End boys'-club. My mother had expected to share these pursuits – at least, the party-going and the riding; she had enjoyed occasional jaunts upon her cousins' old pony. But she soon discovered that, according to my father's view, a man's pursuits before he took a wife should undergo a radical change once he had entered into marriage. After the ceremony, he very seldom danced; accepting an invitation to a party, given by a London friend, meant that he and my mother might fail to catch the last train home, and that he would probably be confronted with an exorbitant hotel bill. He could no longer afford to hunt, he declared, and never rode a horse again. The riding-boots, that had suited his legs so well, lay collecting dust, until they were finally thrown out among other household rubbish, at the bottom of a cupboard.

There had been premonitory signs of this depressing change that my mother failed to notice. As she grew old, her memory became vague; but, even at an earlier period, it was surprisingly elastic; in one mood she would choose to relate a story; in another, deny with an indignant toss of the head, that she could ever have told me such a tale. Usually, I credited her previous version of the anecdote – how, for example, while they were still engaged, my father had taken her out to spend a day in London. He had raised his umbrella; and she had imagined that he was signalling a hansom-cab, an irresistibly attractive means of transport with its rapid pace and high-perched driver. But she then noticed that he was calling an omnibus, on to which he climbed briskly and unselfconsciously, as soon as he had handed in my somewhat saddened mother, who, of course, was already far too docile to admit her disappointment. Yet more unexpectedly, when they planned their honeymoon – it was to take them down to Cornwall – my father announced that nothing could equal the country omnibus as a method of travelling around England. They would drive from inn to inn, and from sight to sight, behind a team of sturdy horses, through hawthorn lanes and ancient market-towns, enthroned upon its spacious roof. And so they did, one happily clement season, my mother wearing a large straw hat and the wide sleeveless, all-enveloping mantle in those days called a 'dust-coat'.

When they returned, it was to an ugly little house that they had rented near Bromley, at which they remained until the house that my father had himself designed was ready for their occupation. The name of the rented house I do not know; but there, under the wavering and elusive Sign of the Fish, I entered the world on March 9th 1905; and there I first had my photograph taken, held in the monthly nurse's arms and enveloped in a thick shawl – I had been carried out into the back garden – while my mother, heavily shawled herself, contemplated my almost invisible head with an air of wondering, admiring, if slightly apprehensive tenderness. Soon afterwards we moved to our proper home, at the top of a steepish slope looking across a valley towards wooded Chislehurst. That suburb had had an interesting history. Madame de Lieven, during her famous residence as Russian ambassadress to the Court of St James's, had been the occupant of Camden Place; and later, it became the English home of the exiled Empress Eugénie, who, in its drawing-room, used to perform her celebrated '*révérence de l'Impératrice*', the deep curtsey of ineffable grace and distinction with which she bade her courtiers good night. The commemorative obelisk she raised to her tragic son, the Prince Imperial, bearing his family device, the Napoleonic bees, rose – and still rises – among the silver birches on the Common.*

The suburb of Bickley, however, in 1905, was a comparatively modern growth. A few Victorian mansions were scattered around the neighbourhood; but almost all the buildings it had recently acquired were the trim and well-appointed products of my father's drawing-board. Nearly every building we saw on our walks was designed by him and raised beneath his eye, his employer being an active Jewish builder who had earlier 'developed' parts of Hampstead. Their collaboration continued throughout my childhood; and I remember picnicking with my nurse in a flowery meadow full of buttercups, meadow-sweet and cow-parsley, and, as we left, seeing a cart arrive, which rolled heavily across the grass and discharged a load of bricks. It occurred to me – and the thought was saddening; even then I had learned to regret the past – that I should never picnic there again. Otherwise I greatly enjoyed watching brand-new houses spring up. All the houses that my father planned had a certain family resemblance; each was solidly constructed of red brick, and – with many ingenious variations – exhibited a sober neo-Georgian frontage. Behind each

* More recently, the eccentric novelist Ronald Firbank had passed a happy childhood at Chislehurst – in a house opposite the church where both the Prince and Napoleon III had originally been buried; and his biographer tells us that he never ceased to regret this period of his existence, which inspired many of his adult stories. See Brigid Brophy: *Prancing Novelist*, 1973.

lay a tolerably large garden, covering about an acre, surrounded
not by an old-fashioned brick wall but by a creosote-painted
wooden fence.

In 1906, my father published his first book, a handsome folio
volume, entitled *Modern Suburban Houses*, which includes a highly
characteristic preface, setting forth his main principles. Here he
writes both as a professional architect and as a lover of the country.
Since 'the development of Building Estates' could not be avoided,
'it should be a matter of interest to many that where the town
must encroach on the country it should be done in a seemly
manner – for instance, good trees, old hedgerows, any little
irregularity of shape . . . should be allowed to remain. This [my
father shrewdly adds] is not sentiment, but business – a good tree
will often sell a house . . .'

He is also sensible and informative about the type of house his
clients needed, and the kind of life that it would shelter. 'The
accommodation generally required [he observes] is the usual
three reception rooms' – drawing-room, dining-room and a
smaller apartment, a study or 'Smoke Room', where the master
of the house could keep his papers, and the children do their
home-work. Servants are not ignored; nowadays, when it was
difficult to obtain satisfactory servants, 'and more difficult to
retain them', the kitchen must have spacious windows; and he
notes that, although 'a Sitting Hall with a fireplace' made an
enjoyable adjunct that most householders appreciated, 'their
sense of economy and dread of their servants is such that they
would not dream of lighting a fire there!' Even more characteristic is the interest my father shows in the quality of the
materials employed – his preference for 'sand-faced red bricks
instead of the wire-cut and pressed variety', and his affection for
'the pleasant purple grey stocks from Guildford and Petersfield'
that, 'if enlivened with red brick dressings', produced so handsome
an appearance. My father was a man who loved quality – the
quality of really sound workmanship, which, he felt, was the
concrete expression of almost every moral virtue – and who sought
to translate his vision of the Good Life, chaste, domestic, warmly
philoprogenitive, into terms of well-laid bricks-and-mortar.

These basic principles he successfully exemplified in the construction of his own house. Before its main entry extended an open lawn, raised terrace-like above the road, supported by a low retaining wall and bisected by a stone-paved path; but to the left, behind a row of palings, he had enclosed the magnificent beech trees that gave the house its name, and around their feet had planted a 'wild garden' with fritillaries and daffodils. Naturally, the façade was neo-Georgian; and the windows of Four Beeches all had leaded panes and decorative wrought-iron latches. Around the square hall ran a wooden gallery, out of which the bedrooms opened. The stairs were broad; and on one newel-post sat a replica of Alfred Stevens's famous lion; while the hall windows, above the staircase, contained medallions of Pre-Raphaelite stained glass, designed by my father's friend, Paul Woodruff, to represent Earth, Air, Fire and Water. Woodruff, I think, had also designed the plaster ceiling, embossed with thistles and Tudor roses, of the room we called the Studio. This was our drawing-room and my parents' working-room combined. Folding doors could be pulled across to divide it into separate sections, so that, theoretically at least, if my mother entertained, my father need not leave his desk. In fact, the doors were very rarely closed; and some rich but faded Persian carpets and a modern chintz-clad sofa, eighteenth-century chairs and tables, a small Jacobean chest of drawers, an Italian walnut cabinet, blue-and-white Delft tobacco-jars, labelled 'Pompadour' and 'Spanjoly', and a brass Cromwellian clock, a solid drawing-board just beneath the garden window and a gaunt écorché figure, made up an agreeably miscellaneous background.

Miscellaneous, too, were the pictures that hung on our walls – Japanese prints, including some good examples of the work of Hiroshige; reproductions of Botticelli, Carpaccio and Benozzo Gozzoli, in the 'Arundel' series, made before photographic techniques were employed to reproduce the Old Masters; one or two striking woodcuts by William Nicholson; and, more unexpectedly, a number of macabre scenes from Alfred Rethel's 'Dance of Death'.* Stranger still was a drawing that decorated the lobby

* Alfred Rethel, a German historical painter, who worked principally at Frankfurt, also produced a succession of large pictures, representing *Daniel in the Lions' Den* and *The Guardian Angel of the Emperor Maximilian*.

just behind the front door, in pen-and-ink on yellow paper. The artist, I learned, had been one of my father's friends; his name I have long ago forgotten; but he appeared to have recorded his impressions of a particularly hideous nightmare, and showed a solitary pilgrim struggling against the wind down a narrow crooked causeway, while from the gulfs that yawned to left and right rose a threatening cohort of gigantic crabs. Why had my father placed it there? My mother, I believe, must have subsequently destroyed it. But then, why did he find space for the alarming fantasies of Rethel – 'Death the Enemy' fiddling at a masked ball, while his cholera-stricken victims are stretched supine around his feet; Death riding across the fields, his scythe slung across his bony shoulder; and 'Death the Friend', tolling the vesper-bell, as the aged bell-ringer sits dead in his chair beside the belfry window? These pictures, not only the German artist's but those of Gozzoli and Carpaccio, with their wealth of mysterious details, afforded me incessant pleasure; and into each of them I plunged delightedly, seeking to determine, for example, the nature of the roundish objects – large pebbles or lumps of horse-dung – each set off by a neat rosette of grass, that, in the frescoes at the Palazzo Riccardi, Gozzoli has scattered beneath the hooves of his Medicean cavalcade; or to enumerate the strange variety of St Augustine's favourite ornaments. Wasn't it odd that the bronze statuette of a naked heathen goddess should stand amid the other *objets d'art* he had collected on his study-shelves?*

Compared with the pleasantly furnished Studio, the dining-room, which had rough-cast walls and green-tiled window-ledges, made a decidedly austere impression; and my mother's family used sometimes to suggest that Four Beeches was not a very comfortable house; that it provided few cushioned armchairs, and that a host of piercing draughts swept through its rooms. A modern visitor no doubt would also have criticized the remarkable harshness of the lighting. My father had an instinctive distaste

---

* The original picture in the Scuola di San Giorgio degli Schiavoni, Venice, once regarded as a representation of St Jerome, has now been rechristened 'The vision of St Augustine'. While writing to Jerome, at the moment on the point of death, Augustine beholds a vivid celestial light shining through the casement of his large and beautifully furnished cell at Hippo.

for luxury, and abhorred undue concealment; and, just as in the houses he built he seldom troubled to arrange that what he called 'the necessary Lavatory accommodation' should occupy a part of the plan where it was either inaudible or inconspicuous – there was nothing at all unpleasant, he felt, about the homely rumbling of a cistern – so he would hang a single electric bulb above the centre of a room, whence, from beneath a milk-white porcelain shade, it cast a bleak and chilly glare.

None of these drawbacks disturbed my own enjoyment of the place in which we lived. I was extremely happy at Four Beeches, inhabiting a long nursery that ran the whole length of the house immediately below the roof, which my father had equipped with benches carpentered on the same lines as those of an eighteenth-century rustic tavern. Another amusingly old-fashioned touch, it had a two-leaved stable-door. Across the lower leaf he one day dropped a rough-coated, wall-eyed mongrel puppy, which he had bought from a countryman for a couple of shillings; and 'Blue-Eye', soon shortened to 'Blooey', remained my ugly devoted companion until, some thirteen or fourteen years later, I finally went away to Oxford and, as he had meanwhile grown malodorous, decrepit and warty, my parents took advantage of my absence to have poor Blooey put down. Ruskin describes the 'very small, perky, contented, Cock-Robinson-Crusoe sort of life' that he had led in early childhood. Such was my own existence. I especially loved the garden; for, on either side of the lawn, which stretched from the Studio windows to the black-painted fence that closed our prospect, stood a pair of ancient hollow elms; and in the left-hand tree, amid its wide-spread branches, about ten or fifteen feet above the ground, my father had built a solid, well-railed wooden platform, to which one ascended through a trap-door; while a rope-ladder dropped into the roomy dungeon, smelling of earth and mildew and decayed bark, that lay immediately beneath the boards. Having retired to 'The-House-in-the-Tree', I had a magnificent view of the lawn, and of my parents in their deck-chairs, and could sometimes overhear tantalizing snatches of their more private conversations.

Was I a pleasant child? During her pregnancy, my mother said, she would often indulge in agreeable daydreams of the kind of son that she awaited. She had already decided that I was to be a son; and she pictured me merry, red-headed, talkative, constantly 'running around and making new friends'. A false dream, as she herself admitted. I was 'always a *difficult* child', she sighed, though, of course, she loved me dearly; and at an early stage she began to suspect that I was showing signs of undue 'cleverness', which did not exactly accord with her dream-picture of the gay, mercurial, red-headed imp. Once more I refer to an early photograph; and a curious photograph it is, taken, I imagine, when I was three or four years old. Seated on an upturned basket, I am looking side-ways at the photographer, giving him or her a slightly mistrust-ful, perhaps a faintly hostile glance. My eyebrows are tilted; the line of my mouth droops; and, beneath the blond fringe that partly covers it, the shadow of an infantile frown seems to be gathering across my brow. Maybe I was squinting against the sun; possibly my six-buttoned black boots had been causing me discomfort. I am surprised, indeed, that my mother or my nanny should have expected me to wear them; for otherwise I am dressed in a decidedly picturesque style – in a smock-frock copied from the sturdy uniform, made of substantial unbleached linen, still worn by old-fashioned country labourers at the conclusion of the nineteenth century.

It is not, I think, a particularly childish face; and some of my early sayings that were afterwards repeated to me suggest a rather doubtful, even a mildly cynical attitude towards the world in which I found myself. Thus a friend described how she had seen me grasping the bars of my nursery play-pen – evidently I was then too young to be allowed the unhampered freedom of the floor – and heard me intoning for my visitor's benefit a refrain that touched her sentimental heart. 'What we *want*,' I repeated, 'and what we *get* are *two different things*!' This, I assume, was one of my nanny's wise old saws, brought out if I made some un-reasonable demand; but I put into the words such a poignant strength of feeling that they appeared to represent my own con-victions. I was also regarded as an oddly self-centred child, never fond of sharing with other children any toy I really valued. A little girl cousin, for example, whom I was obliged to entertain in my nursery, once spilt a favourite pot of paint. Besides wasting my

25

paint, she had spoiled her new dress. My aunt betrayed some agitation. Whereat I approached her in a manner that I meant to be both courteous and diplomatic, assuring her that it was 'not my *best* paint', and was astonished to hear my civil remark dismissed as a piece of deliberate impertinence.

Until my fifth year, I had no companion in my pleasant, roomy nursery, with its raftered roof and dormer-windows; nor, when an infant sister appeared, did I welcome her arrival. I enjoyed my comparative solitude; I was not a gregarious child. I had friends, of course – a pair of Scottish twins, an adventurous boy and girl, who lived just across the fence at the bottom of our garden, as well as a less bohemian family, related to a past Lord Mayor, inhabitants of one of the largest houses that my father had designed, a stone's throw from the steps of Four Beeches. Meetings with unknown children, however, at crowded children's parties often ended in humiliation. I would stand and sulk; my silver-buckled patent-leather shoes seemed to have developed leaden soles. 'Won't you dance with my little boy?' demanded my anxious mother, leading me up towards a little girl; and 'No, I *won't!*' the little girl would reply, turning her back and waywardly mincing off. I began to be bored in company, though seldom in solitude, at a very early age; and, if I were taken to a strange house and left to enjoy myself among a gaggle of prospective playmates, my ennui and loneliness soon became so intense that I lost all sense of time; I was condemned, I felt, to an eternity of silent, self-absorbed despair. Was it not possible I might *never* reach home? I imagined spending my whole existence in this grimly unfamiliar place, cut off from every object I loved and every human shape I recognized.

Imagination, then as now, was both my Heaven and my Hell; and, once I had learned to read, at the age of four or five, not only its enchanting pleasures but its excruciating pains acquired, of course, a double strength. I found I could read one day on the dining-room floor, while I was turning over some old yellow-bound copies of that venerable magazine, *The Boy's Own Paper*, which my father had bequeathed to me, and which serialized the novels of Jules Verne, illustrated by a series of extremely vivid wood-engravings. The story I scrutinized was not by Jules Verne, but the work of some unknown author who described an African caravan, journeying to the sound of camel-bells from oasis to oasis. Suddenly, the printed words I painfully spelt out melted into a smooth continuous narrative, whence a procession of fascinating images emerged and wound its way across my mental landscape. My grandfather had given me *Robinson Crusoe* to celebrate my fifth birthday; and, about the same period, I acquired a stout green-clad repository of fact and fiction entitled *The Children's Encyclopaedia*, a mixture of history and fairy stories, cautionary tales, popular verses and simplified scientific essays, edited under the aegis of Lord Northcliffe by an expert journalist named Arthur Mee. It provided its reader with hours of deep enjoyment, but also helped to provoke some terrifying visions. I learned of 'light-years'; of the vast distances that divided even the closest of the stars and planets; of the huge abysses of space, surrounding the Earth, in which we somehow hung suspended.

Having once entered my imagination, the idea of endless Space and illimitable Time began to haunt me as I slept; and I suffered from a recurrent nightmare in which I seemed to have been trans-fixed a million-million miles above the globe, and the hideous impossibility of conceiving such a figure reduced me to a state of wild distraction. Simultaneously, my arms had dwindled to writhing threads, though each supported a bunch of enormous rocky fingers;* until my struggles to escape eventually broke the bond, and I would wake, sweating and shrieking, and see my mother at my bedside. My dreams and nightmares sometimes appeared so real that it occurred to me that, when I believed I was awake, I might in reality be fast asleep. Arthur Waley writes of the Chinese sage Chuang Tzǔ, who, having dreamed that he had a butterfly's wings, thenceforward could never quite make up his mind whether he was a sage who had dreamed that he was a butterfly or a butterfly dreaming that it was a sage. Similarly, I would play with the morbid notion that my accustomed daily life might prove to be a pleasant dream,† and that I might open my eyes

---

* This nightmare I subsequently recognized in the fantasies of various modern Surrealist artists.
† More than half a century later, I was to hear my own six-year-old son voice almost exactly the same fears.

to discover that, instead of my kind English nanny, I had a hideous dark-skinned *ayah* – a dreadful personage I had glimpsed around the neighbourhood accompanying her Anglo-Indian charges.

Heaven is more difficult to describe than Hell; the pains of a childish imagination are less elusive than its pleasures. A long series of poets, from Vaughan and Traherne to Blake, Wordsworth, Coleridge and Baudelaire, have described the 'sense of wonder and novelty' with which a child surveys the world; and both Coleridge and Baudelaire believed that an ability to 'carry on the feelings of childhood into the powers of manhood' was, above all else, 'the character and privilege of genius'.* This, I suppose, must be a splendid gift granted to men of genius alone. But, although my own experiences were comparatively unfruitful, I, too, once saw the world I lived in through the eyes of an adventurous traveller, alarmed, astonished, entertained, delighted by its smallest as well as by its largest details, and equally pleased with the flowers – bearing such odd and romantic names, snapdragon, columbine, larkspur, Solomon's seal – that peopled our herbaceous borders, and with an old brick, strangely mottled and misshapen, that I found beside a garden path. I, too, had moments of visionary exaltation – when I walked out to greet the celestial brilliance of an early summer morning, or when I left a neighbour's Christmas party and looked up the silent snow-clad road (on which I half expected to see the fresh tracks of a reindeer-sledge) that curved away towards Four Beeches.

My sense of exaltation reached its highest point, however, during our annual visits to the sea. I can no longer distinguish clearly between our various seaside holidays. But very often we occupied a decrepit farmhouse on the quiet East Anglian coast; and always, as soon as we had finished our breakfast, I suffered the same exquisite impatience to be allowed to get down to the beach, while my adult companions dawdled interminably back and forth, filling baskets, folding rugs and collecting shawls and hats and shoes. Though not far off, the sea remained invisible, hidden behind a stubble-field and a range of lofty sand-dunes; and, once we had passed the field, we had to spend precious minutes climbing those hot, slippery ridges and brushing through thickets of

* *Biographia Literaria.*

bent-grass (encrusted, I remember, with the fragile cocoons of a small bright-winged black-and-scarlet moth*) before we scaled a sharp rise that commanded the beach, and beneath us lay the vast and dragonish ocean – a monster so many-coloured, so endlessly changeful, so impulsive in its moods and vagaries, that my chief thought, as I breasted the sand-hills, was to discover just what it had been 'up to', what extraordinary miracles it had accomplished, since I last went home to bed.

Would a high tide be charging and tumbling against a shingly bank beyond the dunes? Or had it retreated over acres of hard-ribbed sand towards the remote margin that divided sea and sky, where, fretting and sparkling under the early-morning sun, it formed a single band of incandescent light? It had had far to go. Off this part of the Norfolk coast, the sea-bed slopes down very gently; and my father and uncles would push their shrimping-nets – huge nets several feet wide – to and fro across its corrugated floor, wading back at length to discharge their catch on the sands, and separate glassy bewhiskered shrimps and prawns from the other sea-trove they had swept up, tiny flatfish, perfectly shaped yet delicate as pieces of porcelain, and no larger than a half-crown, or minute squids, a transparent opaline grey, which knotted their tentacles around a finger.

Except for ourselves, the whole enormous beach (since then, I believe, disfigured by the rapid growth of an adjacent seaside town) was very often almost empty. That, of course, was some sixty years ago; and, in those days, the masts of a sailing ship would frequently appear upon the dark horizon – a pyramid of white canvas that emerged above its rim with a peculiar ghost-like stealth and smoothness. But, if the beach at Hemsby provided my keenest pleasures, I can recollect one moment of devastating gloom that I happened to experience there. I have already mentioned the poet Thomas Traherne, whose *Centuries of Meditations*† give us a marvellously vivid account of his own exalted childhood, when every object that furnished his daily life possessed a super-natural grace and lustre. Yet elsewhere in his book he describes

---

* A friend has identified this moth as the Six-spot Burnet (*Zygaena filipendulae*).
† First published from the original manuscript in 1908. Traherne (*c.* 1637–74) was a devout and learned clergyman.

just such a moment of acute spiritual malaise as, later, would sometimes descend upon the youthful William Wordsworth:

> Another time in a lowering and sad evening, being alone in the
> field, when all things were dead and quiet, a certain want and
> horror fell upon me, beyond imagination. The unprofitable-
> ness and silence of the place dissatisfied me . . . from the utmost
> ends of the earth fears surrounded me . . . I was a weak and
> little child . . .

My own malaise, which this passage recalls, had a very different
origin. I was not alone; it was caused, not by the absence of
human companionship, but by the presence of my father. I was
playing beside a pool at the edge of the sea, when he walked up
and suggested that we should together build a fleet. In his pocket
he carried some walnut-shells and a piece of sealing-wax, with
which he began fixing match-sticks to the shells by way of masts.
His kindness disturbed me. I became aware that there was something subtly, indefinably wrong about his well-meant zeal and
patience; and that our respective attitudes – mine, trying to look
more pleased than, alas, I really felt; his, exhibiting an enthusiasm
that, I suspected, was probably half-assumed – put us both into a
false position. I was embarrassed on his behalf. Why should a
large grown-up person – his grown-upness emphasized by the
slightly feral odour of a massive adult body – have troubled to
join me in my lilliputian games? I feared, too, that he might
notice my lack of interest; and with these fears, as I watched him
hard at work, was presently mingled a secret sense of pity – for
the colossus who had deliberately humbled himself in his futile
efforts to amuse a child. The 'certain want and horror', of which
Traherne speaks, gradually invaded my imagination, and drew
a veil across the sky. Even the clear pool, where he was launching
his nutshell craft, became a sad and slimy puddle.

Children suffer almost as much as adults from boredom, gloom
and malaise; but they are particularly susceptible, I think, to the
pangs of disappointment. With them 'looking forward' is still a
favourite pursuit; they build up an imaginative picture of the
experiences that lie ahead – how they will behave on such-and-
such an occasion, and enjoy the treats they have been promised.

Should reality fall short of the vision, even in the smallest detail, romantic hopes may turn to grief and rage. Thus, again at the seaside, I observed the grown-ups shaping a heap of sand into something that I took to be a lion. My excitement grew; but, once they had modelled its paws and flanks, they proceeded to add a monstrous human head, flattened, lowering and repulsive. Here, they told me, was an ancient Egyptian sphinx. I had never seen a sphinx before; and I regarded it as merely the King of Beasts irremediably spoiled and degraded. I shed bitter tears; and, though I was afterwards persuaded to have my photograph taken glumly straddling the creature's spine, I was not sorry, next day, when I saw that the tide had obliterated it overnight.

During early childhood we have neither virtues nor vices; and, until I had reached the age of four, I was a self-contained amoral-ist, absorbing every sensation that I experienced and every ob-servation that I made, like one of those quietly gluttonous sea-anemones I admired and teased upon the beach. When I was four, however, my existence abruptly changed: in September 1909 I learned I had 'a baby sister', and found myself dragging my feet, beside the repainted perambulator that had originally been mine alone, up and down the asphalt paths of Bickley. Sometimes an appreciative neighbour would arrest our dismal progress, examine the faintly squeaking infant and ask me if I wasn't *proud* of her; at which, 'No, I'm not; I hate her', I would immediately respond. I spoke the horrid truth. I was savagely jealous of my sister; the easy-going amoralist had become a moral culprit; and, to make my feelings even less attractive, they sprang not so much from a fear that I might lose my parents' affection as from a deep-rooted distrust of change. Now that a stranger had entered my pleasant nursery, my whole *hortus conclusus* of habits and pastimes must inevitably be laid waste. Nor was my antagonism short-lived. It persisted in differing shapes throughout my youth; and I was almost grown-up before it had finally vanished, and my ill-used sister had become at last a friend.

Meanwhile, I had learned the powers of love. When my grand-mother died, my mother's devoted nurse took over the running of The Postern. 'Nanny' was a somewhat remarkable personage, wrinkled, small and rheumy-eyed, who had originally gone into

31

service with a Kentish gentleman-farmer, and often described his prosperous crowded household – where the butler had sought her hand in marriage – and the regular round of feasts and jollities that had marked the passage of the seasons. She sang old nursery-rhymes that I have never heard again;* and, on my visits to The Postern, she would order the kitchen-maid to catch half a dozen flies, and drown them in a glass of water. The inanimate flies were then scattered across a plate of table-salt, which had the miraculous effect of restoring them to life and enabling them, after they had scraped and groomed themselves, to spread their wings and dart away. This strange scientific experiment I followed with unfailing interest. But Nanny also offered me more conventional treats; and one evening she escorted me to the Crystal Palace, to see the latest Christmas pantomime. It was there I fell in love, and first suffered the exquisite agonies of a wild romantic longing.

We had already arrived at the transformation-scene; Bengal-lighting bathed the stage, all rosy pinks, celestial blues and dreamily dissolving yellows; and behind gauzy veils, which slowly melted and lifted, a mysterious and beautiful young woman, *'un être, qui n'était que lumière, or et gaze'* – I assume she was the Fairy Princess –moved out between the canvas drops, her face radiantly trans-figured by the changing colours of her background. I felt a sharp pang; I was keenly aware of the distance that divided us; I longed – how I could not imagine – to incorporate my life with hers. I knew that I should presently forget her face; and the prospect of forgetting and losing her – of returning to my own colourless existence – made my anguish doubly poignant. We were near the end of the pantomime; and perhaps, if the curtain had gone down, I should have borne my loss more bravely. But, at this moment, Nanny jerked my elbow and said that the time had come to catch our train. Having caught it and dismounted on a dark platform, we finished our journey in a decrepit four-wheeler, rattling through suburban streets. I remember the acrid smell of the cab and the salty taste of tears, as they drenched my nose, found their way into my mouth or, slipping around its corners, wet my chin.

* A particularly interesting song concerned the Fox, 'Jack Hoffreypot', and the Goose, 'Combimio'.

Later, I had a comparatively placid relationship with an eleven- or twelve-year-old girl named Beryl, who lived in our immediate neighbourhood. I was three or four years younger; but, as her brother and I were school-friends, I was frequently admitted to their garden. A tall, thin child, whose long thin legs were always cased in tight black stockings, Beryl had a pale and lengthy face, framed by dark curls of the kind that old-fashioned nannies used to roll about their fingers. I adored her beauty; and we sometimes exchanged kisses – at least, she permitted me to kiss her cheek; and I told my mother that I intended to give Beryl my finest Eastern conch-shell. I was in love with her, I unluckily explained; whereupon my mother, looking puzzled and cross, displayed an unusual lack of sympathy, declaring that 'little boys didn't fall in love', and that such a gift would be extremely foolish. I was undeterred; I continued to love Beryl, who aroused an emotion that was both sentimental and aesthetic; and, as often happens, my passion for my beloved herself soon included her surroundings. I associated her image both with the scent of the syringa bushes that overhung the gravel walks, and with some absurd verses painted on a wooden seat – in a garden, the author assured his readers, one was always close to God's heart – that then represented my idea of poetry. I was only wretched should Beryl leave my side and, linked affectionately to a friend of her own sex, wander off to 'tell secrets'. I detested the habit, suspecting that they were involved in feminine mysteries far beyond my comprehension, and began to assume that the feminine character is naturally devious and secretive, and there are large areas of the beloved's life that the lover cannot penetrate. This disturbing belief, since the days of my love for Beryl, has very often caused me pain.

My sentimental education, however, was to be temporarily interrupted. Once I had passed through the hands of a governess – the admirable Miss Figgis, with her enamelled Victorian brooch, brown, high-necked garments, dyed hair and neatly-drawn central parting – I was enlisted at a private school in Chislehurst. There 'girl' was a term of abuse; 'you *girl*', we shouted derisively if a little boy showed signs of shedding tears. The atmosphere of St Alfred's was roughly masculine; and it was conducted by two unmarried brothers, whom, using their Christian names, we called 'Mr John' and 'Mr Jonathan'. They were an odd pair; Mr John, a gaunt and elderly parson, having snow-white locks but thick black eyebrows over keen dark eyes; Mr Jonathan, the younger and shorter of the two, swart and square and hook-nosed, not unlike, it would presently occur to me, Jane Eyre's Mr Rochester. Mr John was parsonic and persuasive; Mr Jonathan, intensely passionate, the only man I have met who would literally 'foam at the mouth' should his violent temper be excited. Each was a devoted educationalist; each, as I look back on them, unmistakably a paederast, though their emotional leanings, which were more or less controlled, may have done more good than harm. Mr Jonathan had handsome favourites, and sometimes spent his holidays teaching them to sail or swim; Mr John's treatment of his pupils was indifferently affectionate. He liked to sit beside a boy on the horse-drawn vehicle that took us to the playing-fields, and allow his fingers – long and square-tipped, heavily stained with blotches of red ink – to creep inch by inch up his companion's thigh.

Both our headmasters taught us capably; and for a time I did them credit. I learned so well, indeed, that it was thought that one day I might secure a scholarship at Winchester; and, simultaneously, I became an energetic athlete, enjoyed football and was described on my school report as 'a promising full-back'. But my progress was intermittent; while I remained at St Alfred's, I was subject to sudden losses of energy, crises of physical and nervous fatigue, during which, from a high position in my form, I drifted down into the lowest rank, and sat surrounded by far younger boys, only distinguished from them by the gift I was supposed to possess of writing brilliant English essays. I was tolerated, however, and rarely bullied; and I cannot pretend that my school-days were altogether miserable. At St Alfred's, both Mr John and Mr Jonathan seem to have decided to protect me. I was spared, for example, all the horrors of a 'lamming', the supreme humiliation inflicted on a boy who had 'let his house down'.

The school, I must explain, was divided into houses; and each boy, according to his work and behaviour, received a weekly share of good and bad marks. Should his *pessimes* exceed his *optimes*, it affected the whole house's score; and other members were encouraged to exact vengeance, slapping, punching and cuffing him, until he fled in tear-stained misery. Our headmasters countenanced, no doubt they had founded, these stupidly vindictive rites. Mosaic disciplinarians, they did their best to inject us with a haunting sense of sin. Some boys were irremediable sinners – chief among them being a squat and sullen child, who, to crown his record of idleness and dirtiness, and of constant mean revolts against authority, was caught defiling the enamel drinking-mugs that hung in rows above the cloakroom sink, and desecrating the sacred butt from which Mr John daily drew his shaving water. The culprit was then expelled and packed off to a special school – the kind of school, our masters informed us, where he need expect no mercy.

As a day-boy, I divided my life between St Alfred's and my parents' house. Although my sister's intrusion had slightly dimmed its beauties, I retained a warm affection for my own home, and took a keen interest in the frieze of grown-up personages who filed processionally across my view. Most were relations; my father was not gregarious; and we seldom entertained. Nor did my parents often go abroad; their journeys to a modest Swiss resort, and to Vienna on an architectural conference, were such remarkable events that they assumed an almost legendary value. I was never tired of listening to the story of how my father had lost control of a bob-sleigh, hurtled off the run and severely grazed his jaw, or to my mother's accounts of the Austro-Hungarian capital, and of the gallant young white-uniformed officers she had watched trotting round the Ringstrasse. Ours was a small world, rigidly circumscribed by the limitations of our class and period. Upper-class people, we knew, were 'fast' and extravagant; and, when we read in magazines about the beautiful Lady Diana Manners and the exhibitionistic Mrs Asquith, we dismissed them as beings of a completely alien species. Like other middle-class families, we formed a self-sufficient unit; and our few visitors, apart from relations, were either fellow architects my father had known since his youth, or one or two friends whom my mother had made when she was working at her art-school.

My father would greet them with loud expressions of bonhomie; but they were not encouraged to prolong their stay.

Our relations, on the other hand, he suffered more or less gladly; and between Four Beeches and the not-far-distant Postern there was a fairly regular exchange of visits. My Courtney uncles and my unmarried Aunt Joyce provided absorbing subjects for critical examination. They became the text-book in which I studied life, and first learned to appreciate some of the vagaries of human conduct. A favourite subject was Uncle Philip. At an early age he had been drafted into a London bank that had a large number of Far Eastern branches, just as his eldest brother, Basil, had been shoved into a mining business, and Claude relegated to the Corn Exchange. Philip did not demur; and, although he had no financial gifts, wherever he was posted – in Japan, Malaysia or a Chinese treaty-port – he used his musical talents to advantage, organizing operettas and concerts, even gaily costumed minstrel-shows. He would return on holiday, looking roseate and prosperous, once at least accompanied by a sleek Malaysian body-servant, distribute lacquered trifles, pieces of Satsuma-ware and embroidered Mandarin coats, and show us photographs of himself against the background of a large exotic garden, wearing a solar topee and sometimes arm-in-arm with a string of little native boys. His personal dandyism increased his prestige as an adventurous world-traveller; I admired the beautifully-cut suits, the crisp golden curls and polished finger-nails that my father had found so annoying; and I was puzzled and grieved, on one of his earlier visits, to see my carefree uncle suddenly reduced to a state of deep confusion and distraction.

Backwards and forwards across the sunlit lawn paced my uncle and my mother. From the House-in-the-Tree I failed to catch their words; but I understood that my uncle was suffering deeply, and my mother tentatively consoling him. The nature of the crisis at length became clear; my uncle had proposed marriage to a very 'nice' girl, but had later broken off their engagement in a mysterious and dramatic fashion. According to my father's account – and I suspect that he gave his story a deliberately ribald twist – having spent a week-end among the betrothed's family, Philip had burst into his future mother-in-law's bedroom an hour or two before breakfast, declaring that he must immediately leave the house and, then and there, 'go home to Nanny'. This seemed the only explanation or excuse that he was capable of providing; but my father concluded, with a sardonic smile, that 'poor old Philip' had been somehow badly frightened.

The strange story had an equally curious ending. After several years of silence, during which he resumed his celibate life in a distant Eastern city, he proposed again, was promptly accepted and settled down to a calm and happy marriage. He and I had meanwhile fallen out. Our previous friendship, I imagine, had been vaguely sentimental. But, at the end of a holiday in England, when he came to bid me goodbye, I happened to be recovering from a childish illness and lay comfortably abed reading. I had chosen an excellent book. Seated opposite, my uncle began to address me in solemn and pathetic phrases. He was going. He might not soon return. Should I forget my old uncle? Though moved, I now experienced a secret quiver of embarrassment; and, simultaneously, I remembered the book that I was holding propped against my knees. As my uncle grew more and more pathetic, the temptation to lower my eyes towards its pages became increasingly compulsive, until I gave way, dropped my line of vision and carried off a single sentence. Deeply ashamed, I then looked up at my uncle and did my best to produce the kind of response that I knew he was expecting. In vain; the magnetic charm of the book – both for its own sake and as a means of escape from his tenderly reproachful glances – proved stronger than all my good intentions. My uncle rose, repeated his farewells and left me to my selfish pleasures.

Yet I respect my uncle; he actively enjoyed himself; and having lost his wife (who died of some Eastern fever) and retired in pensioned dignity, he devoted the remainder of his days to gratifying his own eclectic tastes. Though he had begotten an only son, he put most of his savings into the purchase of a small but adequate annuity, which enabled him year after year to embark upon a well-found cruise that wafted him around the Mediterranean or as far afield as the Pacific. At home, besides prosecuting his interest in amateur theatricals and composing light music, he joined a suburban nudist colony, where he refreshed himself for many seasons, indignantly resigning, however, when a brand-new block of flats threatened to overlook the nudists' pleasance, and they were requested in future to adopt some kind of rudimentary garb. My uncle had also joined the St John Ambulance Association. He rose, I believe, to high rank; and, during the summer months, if he were not abroad at the time, he would move down to a popular seaside resort and pitch his official tent upon the sands. There, sporting a trim black-and-white uniform, a pair of neat white gloves tucked beneath a shoulder-strap, he would deal efficiently with cuts and bruises, jellyfish-stings and serious cases of sunburn, but, as evening descended, regain the Grand Hotel and round off the day listening to a ladies' string-orchestra, or meeting holiday acquaintances, in the gilt-and-marble Palm Court.

His passion for genealogy was another distinctive trait. He could unfold the exact lineage and family relationships of almost any royal person; and, at one moment, he and my Uncle Claude spent much of their time trying to establish a definite link between an obscure half-pay officer named Captain Courtney (now buried in a Chelsea graveyard) and the notorious Duke of Cumberland, who had fathered him, their octogenarian great-great aunt alleged, 'on the wrong side of the blanket'. They did not succeed; as a prospective ancestor, the wicked Royal Duke (who was rumoured to have seduced his sister and murdered his valet*) proved impossible to pin down. Nor, despite the fact that they bore the same crest, a *dolphin, embowed, proper*, could they trace the connection they had hoped to find between the Courtneys of Bromley and the Courtenays, Earls of Devon, a family that Edward Gibbon describes as the most illustrious in the whole of Europe. My Uncle Philip therefore consoled himself by reverting to the present age; and, using a small pen – he had an extremely neat script – and the finest hand-made paper, designed an elaborate family tree, embellished with a meticulous record of our birth-dates and alliances. This developed smoothly so long as his

---

* The latter rumour, though current at the time, has been conclusively dismissed. The only evidence for her allegations that Great-great-aunt Millicent could provide was that the Duke of Cumberland seemed to have taken some interest in Captain Courtney's father, and once procured him a minor post at Court.

nephews and nieces were children. But, when they grew up, they contracted a deplorable habit of divorcing and remarrying; and he was hard put to it to accommodate our matrimonial revolutions – unfortunately, I was the chief offender – within the framework of his calligraphic page. To my mother he commented bitterly on the trouble we had given him.

Although some of his pursuits were undoubtedly foolish, I cannot regard my uncle as in any sense a failure. I have always felt an affection for determined hedonists; and he alone among his kinsmen seems to have understood his own needs, and to have followed his personal inclinations with a certain dash and energy. If Philip was probably the happiest of the Courtneys, the oddest and, no doubt, the most original was my unmarried Aunt Joyce. Six years younger than my mother, sallow, gaunt and long-limbed, she had the kind of androgynous handsomeness that might have suited a Renaissance sibyl. Besides designing and painting in the manner of the latter-day Pre-Raphaelites, she also wrote romantic prose. She had derived her literary style from the works of Anthony Hope, whose *Prisoner of Zenda* and *Rupert of Hentzau* then occupied a prominent place in every English circulating library. Under his spell she embarked on the composition of a lengthy and elaborate narrative. But, although the background of her tale was picturesquely Ruritanian, it had developed with the passage of time into an autobiographical fantasia, the heroine being a beloved friend of the novelist's, a sultry and intense young woman; while the hero, a gallant young soldier, evidently symbolized my aunt herself. The relationship that her book commemorated had already troubled and alarmed her family; and, noticing that, as they sat side-by-side below my refuge in the tree, my aunt and her friend were apt to hold hands, I, too, had felt a little puzzled.

Such relationships were seldom discussed at the time; and the conclusions a modern spectator might draw would probably be far too cynical. My aunt, I believe, remained entirely innocent; and, when her friend suggested they should set up house together, she seems to have refused with some alarm. It is clear that in her romantic dreams she customarily took a young man's part; but all the emotional outlet she needed she found on the plane of the imagination. Thus, from a short story, the book she produced grew into a massive volume, beautifully bound, every hand-written page bearing numerous embellishments – whole pictures, decorative head-lines and magnificent initial letters. Now and then I was permitted to examine the text, or, at least, to read a chosen paragraph. My aunt's untutored prose-style did not make for very easy reading; but one of her images, because I thought it extraordinarily vivid at the time, I have remembered ever since. As her hero and heroine rode through the autumnal woods, she likened the dead bracken underneath the trees to 'the rusted armour of a fallen legion'. My aunt died, in early middle age, a victim of shock, we were told, after one of those 'successful' operations which so often cost the patient's life. Her grasp on existence seems to have been strangely weak; and she left behind few traces. Her pictures were scattered or lost. No publisher having agreed to print her book, the bulky manuscript was given to her woman friend, who immediately vanished.

Most Victorian and Edwardian families included an un-marriageable daughter; and among my father's siblings we had Aunt Edith, as ill-adjusted a young woman as Joyce Courtney, but considerably less talented. My grandfather and grandmother had meanwhile removed from London to an Edwardian house in Dorset. There my grandfather kept chickens; and thence, his fishing-rod strapped to the carrier of his bicycle, he frequently rode into neighbouring Bournemouth. Only Aunt Edith was left at home. True, many efforts had been made to persuade her to adopt some independent calling, as a 'companion' or a governess. But, again and again, if she were sent away, she would quickly reappear, bringing a lugubrious tale of the woes and injustices that she had undergone beneath a stranger's roof. So at home she was obliged to stay, awkward, obstinate and ill-tempered, with her rough red cheeks, her clumsy chapped hands and her scraped-back dark hair. She loved me; and I welcomed her brusque affection. But for a child there is something peculiarly dreadful about displays of adult wretchedness; and I shall never forget how one day I entered her bedroom, and discovered her clad in a suit of woollen underwear – the kind of garment then called 'combinations' – sobbing bitterly and unrestrainedly. Her stone-coloured carapace, which moulded her hips and bosom, gave her an unearthly resemblance to some rough-hewn ancient statue.

I liked my grandparents' household, and was fond of my grandfather, as, in a cloth-cap, his shirt-sleeves rolled up, he moved contentedly around his plot, feeding his Buff Orpingtons with muscular sweeps of the arm, or carrying back empty buckets to the kitchen. The whole kitchen reeked of chicken-food and of boiling rabbit-mash; and the garden smelt of the small conifers that bristled in a miniature forest, through which ran a fascinating labyrinth of secret paths, just behind the pens and hutches. In an unreclaimed bog, at the bottom of the road, I watched, for the first and last time, a sundew, at the edge of a black pool, opening its fine-toothed jaws to grasp a fly; and I remember that the squelching marsh-soil had a strangely acid scent. But what I most enjoyed were our expeditions to Bournemouth, and the days we passed upon the pier and beach. My grandfather was a silently sociable companion; and I had gained his respect because, during our first visit to the sea, I cast out my leaded line across the breakers – or perhaps it was my grandfather who made the cast – and was suddenly rewarded with a sharp electric tug. I had caught a sea-bass, a fierce little plunging and snapping fish, which I hauled in hand-over-hand towards the shingle.

As I have said before, my paternal grandfather was a lazy, unassuming man; but I greatly preferred him to my high-nosed, straight-backed grandmother, who usually wore a Victorian amethyst brooch, a neat lace fichu and a mauve or violet dress, and whose thin lips were often contracted into a faintly supercilious smile. She walked upright; my grandfather, whom age had begun to bow, trudged or ambled, like a friendly yet crafty beast in one of Beatrix Potter's tales. Though I was happy at Ferndown, there as elsewhere I occasionally suffered, particularly when the sun sank, from overwhelming bouts of homesickness; and I was always glad of my mother's arrival to take me home again to Bickley. She appeared as love and wisdom, charm and elegance personified. During this period, my possessive affection for my mother was completely unshadowed. Still young – on the outbreak of the World War, an event that would transform her whole life, she had not yet reached her thirty-first birthday –

she joined with youthful zest in my various pursuits and plans, and, later, admired and patiently collected everything I wrote or drew.

Those were 'the good years', my mother used to say, as she pensively reviewed her first decade of marriage, and remembered the harsh and difficult period that had very soon succeeded it. Life ran quietly and smoothly at Four Beeches; and she had all the leisure she could use. Besides a nanny, we kept two or three servants, the cook and the parlour-maid receiving an annual wage, which they seem to have accepted gladly, of less than £50 each, and wearing the caps, starched collars and neat white aprons that their employers had provided. Our nanny – a good-looking, black-eyed young woman, afterwards 'got into trouble' by her betrothed, a somewhat anaemic-looking carpenter – wore her own distinctive uniform, and tied the velvet strings of her small blue bonnet beneath a sharply pointed chin. Thus my mother had very little house-work to distract her from her painting. Tradesmen's carts regularly bowled up with the goods that she had ordered. But once a week my mother would visit the bank at Bromley, where an assistant, who held a copper shovel, poured a miniature flood of sovereigns and half-sovereigns, as bright as if they had just been minted, through the open mouth of a brown-paper bag; and she would then make her way either to the draper's or to the grocer's shop. The grocer's was prettily named Puckeridge; the draper's emporium was of the dusty, old-fashioned kind that H. G. Wells – during his childhood he had been brought up at Bromley – vividly portrayed in *Kipps*. Overhead stretched an elaborate network of wires; and along these wires bills and receipts, travelling away towards the cashier and down again towards the customer, hurtled energetically to and fro.

For such expeditions we travelled by 'the Brake', a vehicle that a modern dictionary describes as 'a large open wagonette with four wheels'. Plying for hire between Bickley and Bromley, it was drawn by two gigantic horses; and, seated on the driver's box, I would observe their massive dappled rumps rolling heavily beneath my eyes, and await the moment when one or other of them would shrug its flanks, raise its short-cropped tail and majestically relieve itself. Though my father purchased in rapid succession several modern motor-cars, including a three-wheeled 'runabout', which he steered with the help of a horizontal rod, ours was still a largely horse-drawn age. From the big nineteenth-century villas around Chislehurst emerged elegant high-wheeled carriages, each bearing a top-hatted, top-booted coachman and a grave, erect young footman; and en route for Bromley we passed a roadside forge, at which – always an absorbing spectacle – local cart-horses were regularly shod. Their scorched hooves emitted a delicious pungent fragrance; and no less attractive were the thud and clank of the hammer, and the sight of a radiant red-hot bar, dropped on to the polished surface of the anvil to be gradually shaped and flattened, while the rough metal threw off fiery flakes beneath the shoe-smith's ringing blows.

Memory, however, is a strictly selective process; and, if my mother remembered her early married life as a period of unalloyed contentment, she omitted some dramatic crises. There was much that she chose to forget; much that, as time passed, she could only half recall. Marriage was an 'excellent mystery', wrote the authors of the English *Book of Common Prayer*. Every marriage has a slightly mysterious side; and it becomes doubly mysterious when the married couple concerned are the authors of one's own existence. My parents were happily married. Yet both, when they entered the married state, had been, my mother assured me, completely inexperienced; and she herself was at once innocent and profoundly ignorant. Nature, or Providence, alone had guided them; and, as my mother explained in a communicative mood – she was warning me against the dangers of illicit passion and advocating the joys of a harmonious marriage – just where the relationship might have been expected to fail, it had proved triumphantly successful. They had achieved, in that sphere, an almost perfect union; and their conflicts were not on a physical but on a purely temperamental plane.

My mother was receptive and imaginative; my father, stubborn, limited and self-willed. She had grown up amid a cheerful, affectionate family. He had had a hard and anxious youth; for, although he had attended a respectable London school, there had been no question of his parents' finding the means to send him to a university; and, as soon as he had left school, his working-life began. It was a rough life; he had learned his business doing a foreman's job on the sites of new buildings. Often his work took him to the City of London, where he had watched the workmen, who were digging out foundations, suddenly unearth the mass of human bones that filled a seventeenth-century 'plague-pit'. Labourers, or navvies, were then a separate race, with red hand-kerchiefs knotted around their necks and corduroy trousers strapped below the knee; and my father described seeing one of the sewer-rats that haunted every piece of waste land leap up a navvy's trouser-leg; at which the man had grasped it through the folds of the heavy stuff and quickly crushed it to death inside his iron palm.

My father completed his apprenticeship at the offices of two different London firms; but, in 1896, when he was only twenty-four, having recently been awarded the National Gold Medal for Architectural Design (South Kensington) and the Silver Medal of the Royal Institute of British Architects, he had set up his own office at No. 17 Victoria Street; and there Fred Taylor, a well-known poster-artist, portrayed him in a stylish chalk-drawing – a lean, long-legged, shirt-sleeved figure perched upon a high stool, unfinished plans scattered across his desk and an old-fashioned telephone just behind him, amid drifting eddies of tobacco-smoke. As a young architect, his range was uncommonly wide; and, besides his domestic work, he designed the West End showrooms of a prosperous photographic firm, the mausoleum of a dis-tinguished theatrical knight, the chapel of Cambridge House, a Cornish church-tower and two complete churches, one High-Anglican and the other Roman Catholic, the first, St John's, Upper Edmonton, being certainly his masterpiece. Inspired by Westminster Cathedral, which was still in an unfinished state and had not yet acquired its present meretricious incrustations, here he employed a part-Gothic, part-Byzantine style; and the result was a severely plain yet beautifully proportioned building that con-tinues to dignify the tumble-down streets of a decaying London suburb.

Thus my father advanced into middle-life, active, enthusiastic and apparently well-satisfied with the course of his career. He enjoyed his work, loved his two children, and continued to cherish my adoring mother. As a young woman, if not beautiful, she had a nobly handsome presence, regular features, clear eyes and a somewhat heavy Grecian chin. So long was the mane of red-gold hair, piled in braided tresses round her head, that, when she removed the hairpins and let it tumble down, she could sit easily upon her own tresses. She had also a splendid upright carriage, which she retained until her old age. Yet, in every photograph taken at this period, she reveals not only a look of dignity and gravity, but an uncertain and slightly vulnerable air – an expression of wondering, faintly bewildered innocence, which she seems to be endeavouring to conceal beneath an attitude of adult poise. She attracted men and was pleasantly aware, I think, of the attraction she exerted. But she was naturally virtuous and pure-minded; and my father was both a demanding and a strictly faithful husband. For him, though he was virile and attractive himself, once he had chosen the perfect wife, other women had ceased to exist from an amatory point of view; and, because he loved my mother and knew that she loved him, his method of displaying his love was often less romantic than she might perhaps have hoped. He seldom paid her a direct compliment, rarely noticed or troubled to praise her clothes, and dispensed with all the *petits soins* that, Casanova tells us, are the best way to an impressionable young woman's heart. Since she was sure of his love, my mother thought he implied, there was no need to draw particular attention to a single aspect of her being.

She lacked my father's energy, and found it difficult to follow the rapid series of enthusiasms that chased one another through his mind. Now we were to leave England *en famille*, and transfer ourselves to the United States. Now he became a disciple of 'hay-box cooking', a form of cookery said by its originator to condense the natural goodness of the food, which involved packing a covered dish into a box of damp hay, and then allowing the fermentation of the hay to produce the necessary heat. Later again, he took up 'deep breathing'; and for some weeks, the instant they left their beds, he would assemble his whole household at a widely opened window and bid them breathe regularly in and out. My father, as I have suggested elsewhere, had a powerful personality. But he imposed his wishes less by commanding obedience than by quietly and firmly assuming that my mother shared his views; while opposition he preferred to overwhelm by silently ignoring it. Personal problems he disposed of in the same high-handed fashion. Despite the fact that he had a warm, affectionate nature, his gift of imaginative sympathy could not be extended beyond certain limits. 'No' was a word of which he made frequent use; my mother dreaded the repetition of that calmly crushing syllable. Once he had said 'no', a curtain ran down, behind which he retreated to his own work.

Yet, although he was a self-centred man, my father could not have been described as crudely selfish. Everything he did was done with the best intentions. Because he felt that my mother needed support, he tenderly controlled her movements, until it was he who ordered the progress of their life, and she who followed his neatly established pattern. In the process, however, he deprived her of various amusements that had helped to sweeten her existence. Like her brother Philip, she had derived a keen pleasure from amateur theatricals. But my father, who did not enjoy seeing his wife, even as Shakespeare's Rosalind, being courted by another man, soon persuaded her to give them up. Similarly, during the earlier days of their marriage, her portraits of children had had a ready sale, and she used now and then to visit country houses at which she passed the week-end, and executed charming pictures – on Bristol-board, in delicately tinted pencil – of aristocratic little boys and girls. She enjoyed her excursions into this unfamiliar world, with its elegant surroundings and pleasantly carefree mode of life, and the large talkative luncheon parties where even lace-coiffed dowagers could be seen freely smoking cigarettes – a habit that at first surprised her, but that she soon herself adopted. My father, alas, was unimpressed; not only did he object to being left alone, but he believed a woman's place was in the bosom of her family. My mother reluctantly submitted, and declined all further invitations.

When the moment of revolt at last came, she had been married eight or nine years. She fell ill; and there ensued a long succession of crises that overshadowed our entire existence. I remember separate episodes in sharply painful detail; but their order now escapes me. Did our troubles begin when we embarked with

46

Uncle Philip on a voyage to Madeira? No doubt my mother's health was already causing anxiety, and my father had been warned that she required a change of climate. At all events, we boldly set out from Southampton; but, before we had cleared the Channel (which was only moderately rough), my mother had succumbed to so severe a bout of sea-sickness that the ship-doctor declared that her heart might suffer if we crossed the Bay of Biscay, and that we should immediately be put ashore. Her collapse was puzzling; for, although, during her middle age, we continued to believe that she had a weak heart – and at intervals she still experienced what were vaguely diagnosed as 'heart-attacks' – the specialist who attended her in her old age assured me that, although other organs were fast failing, her heart remained particularly strong.

We obeyed the doctor's instructions, however, and disembarked at Le Havre. There, for the first time, I stepped on to foreign soil, an extraordinarily interesting adventure. I recollect a tall gaunt African, stalking down the quayside wearing long linen robes and a round embroidered cap, while a crowd of ragged street-urchins scurried after him and threw stones – 'In his own country', remarked my father, 'he is probably a chieftain or a prince'; and, yet more vividly, a hideous scene we glimpsed as we were driving to the station. A labourer pushing a heavy cart suddenly slipped forward between the shafts he held, and a torrent of bright blood shot from his open mouth and streamed away across the wet grey cobbles. Looking back, we saw that he had fallen to his knees. I was alarmed and moved, yet not disgusted. The tragedy aroused that 'sense of pity and terror' which I afterwards learned to recognize in the works of the great dramatic poets.

Our destination was Rouen, where we spent some days, near the Cathedral, at the venerable Hotel de la Poste. Since those days, I am told, the bombardments of the Second World War have largely obliterated the ancient quarters that once surrounded the Cathedral precincts; but I was then delighted by the tall half-timbered houses that bulged out above dark dividing lanes, and by a green-lipped fountain perpetually gurgling beneath the gilded face of an immense clock. No less romantic, as we explored the Cathedral itself, were the dusty red hats of defunct cardinals that hung before its solemn windows. When, soon afterwards, I began to write verse, Rouen provided me with many of the subjects that I did my best to fix in rhyme. Evidently, I was growing up; and on our return journey, as we traversed the sunny Channel, I made what I believe was my earliest attempt to become a modern poet. My theme, strangely enough, was boredom. I described a Byronic hero, who seems to have suffered from an overpowering lassitude, and was 'bored as bored could be' by the spectacle of human life. My mother admired this effort, but was disconcerted by its pessimistic trend. Little boys ought not to be bored, she said, just as, earlier, she had told me that sensible little boys should not pretend to fall in love.

On our way home, we briefly paused at Brighton; and there I witnessed a disturbing clash between my mother and my father. She wished to travel by a miniature railroad to a dismal 'beauty-spot' called Black Rock. My father refused; he was growing tired of our unprofitable holiday. So he allowed us to travel alone; and my mother confided to me that she thought my father 'selfish'. It was a criticism he did not deserve; but my mother's employment of the horrid adjective – one of the most damning in our domestic vocabulary – produced a strong effect upon my mind. Predictably, I took my mother's side; that my father might perhaps err was an unexpected piece of news; and, once I had heard him criticized, I gradually acquired the knack of distinguishing his weakest points. Nor, when we had returned home, did he quite regain his previous stature. General confusion prevailed at Four Beeches. My mother's disorders had entered a new phase; an atmosphere of suffering pervaded the house; and I listened horror-struck to the piteous wails she uttered while she was being carried to her room. The doctors, who today would no doubt have decided that her malady had a psychosomatic origin, talked in a large, unhelpful way of 'nerves'. To my mother it was a terribly real affliction; and, long after she had been restored to complete health, she described 'the yellow waves of illness' that, from her bed, as soon as she awoke, she would feel rolling towards her up the stairs.

A 'rest-cure' was the next solution that her hard-pressed doctors offered. She was, therefore, transported to a country nursing-home, at which the bedridden patients were required to drink unlimited quantities of fresh milk, and thus blanket their recalcitrant nerves beneath folds of superfluous adipose tissue. My mother obeyed, and rapidly gained weight. But she also developed a slightly exaggerated affection for one of her nurses, that seemed to cause my father deep anxiety. She was unwilling to leave her haven; and, when my father wrote begging her to return, she indignantly refused his pleas, again accusing him of 'selfishness', a word she underlined in red ink. Such was my father's distress that he showed me the angry phrase, and pointed out the underlining. This kind of domestic opposition, which I doubt if he had ever encountered before, threw him completely off his balance. Though, earlier, he had shown few signs of faith, he now began to read the Bible, particularly the Old Testament, and said that he derived especial solace from the *Book of Isaiah*. He had always admired a fine dramatic image; and the Prophet's comparison of Jehovah's protective power to 'the shadow of a great rock in a weary land' he thought peculiarly moving.

At length he won the day; and my mother gave in. She was no match either for his masterly affection or for his resolute strength of purpose; and he immediately descended on the nursing-home and, like a planet recapturing a vagrant satellite, swept her back into his sphere. She would never revolt again; and soon afterwards the background of our family life underwent a sudden catastrophic change. The crisis described above appears to have taken place during the earlier part of 1914; in July rumours of international conflict already filled the newspapers; and I remember a Prize Day where I heard Mr Jonathan, as he entertained a group of parents, telling them that, although the news seemed grave, he still hoped to spend his summer holidays revisiting the Rhine and its picturesque old castles. In 1914 my father, now forty-two, had reached the summit of his professional career. His last important commission – the design of Aultmore House, a grandiose Inverness-shire country seat, ordered by an affluent Scottish merchant, who derived his large fortune from a department-store in Moscow – was among the most profitable that he had yet secured. If not rich, he was now definitely well established, and had earned a solid reputation. Since 1912 he had thrice been elected to the Council of the Royal Institute of British Architects, the governing body of the architectural world.

In one respect, my father was a singularly ill-fated man – he had had little sense of timing; and he chose the autumn of 1915, when his professional prospects were singularly bleak, to resign from the Council of the Institute. The incident remains obscure;* but my mother often informed me that he had acted with the very highest motives, standing up bravely and determinedly for what he believed to be 'the right thing', and thus deliberately forfeiting the advantageous position that might have helped him through the war-years. Certainly the War had brought him close to ruin; new houses were no longer in demand; and any kind of domestic building, should the cost exceed a diminutive sum, was soon officially prohibited. As my father's private savings had not been large, and he had a wife and children – his third child, my brother Paul, was born on 10 June 1915 – the darkest fears that had haunted his boyhood now seemed likely to be realized.

The obvious solution of our financial problems was that we should sell our house; and in the end he found a purchaser. A grim spinsterish woman, widowed or unmarried, she did not trouble to respect our feelings. The garden, she announced, must be entirely replanned; and the decaying elm trees hewn down; the wide lawn cut up into a chequer-work pattern of neat Victorian flower-beds. My mother wept; my father, who had a more sardonic turn, was able to extract some sparks of comedy from a tragic situation. He laughed aloud when he learned that the two enormous cart-horses, brought into the garden to drag off the fallen trunks, were called 'Buttercup' and 'Daisy', and watched their vast hooves trampling our borders, and their huge mouths pulling down the leaves of our carefully-pruned rambler roses.

* In the minutes of the Council, which the present Secretary of the Institute has generously permitted me to examine, I can find no mention of the episode. My father did not attend meetings very regularly; but his name appears from time to time until July 1915, and then completely disappears. There is one possible clue. In October 1915 a fellow member of the Council, who, unlike my father, seems to have attended almost every meeting, and who had been accused of certain professional malpractices, was exonerated by thirteen votes to five. If my father – and this, of course, is mere guess-work – was among those who had cast dissentient votes, he may perhaps have decided to resign upon a point of principle; which would have been a highly characteristic gesture.

A single condition, however, he did succeed in imposing upon Four Beeches' new occupant. He was fond of the noisy colony of jackdaws that had long inhabited our elms; and he stipulated that, before the trees were finally destroyed, the young birds must have left their nests.

II

FROM FOUR BEECHES, BOTH LITERALLY AND FIGURATIVELY,
we descended to a lower level – to a small Victorian house
in the damp and gloomy hollow that lies between Chislehurst and
Bickley. High above it, beyond the rough garden, rose a tree-
covered embankment surmounted by a railway-line, where a
series of heavy trucks, filled, we were told, with ammunition
bound for France, clanked and rumbled all night long. It was a
cheerless house; but we were poor now – a circumstance of which
my father repeatedly reminded us. Not that we lacked servants;
we still employed a cook, a housemaid and an energetic char-
woman. But my mother had given up her nanny; and she herself
was obliged to take sole charge of my younger brother, luckily
a robust, good-humoured child who gave her very little trouble.
I loved my handsome brother as much as I had once disliked my
sister. Since Paul's birth, under the pressure of misfortune my
mother had rapidly regained her strength; and, although she had
lost her look of youthful elegance and showed traces of approaching middle age – her high-piled coiffure was often a little untidy;
and with an air of gentle despair she would push back a rebellious
wisp – she set us an example that I admired and, in my own way,
tried to follow. We must 'make the best of things' – that was the
lesson I learned; though the war-time food we ate was frequently
unpalatable, and various shortages, including a regular shortage
of money, now circumscribed our whole existence. I knew that
my parents worried; they had every reason to worry; and their
apprehensions proved infectious, until worrying, if the motive
were sufficiently sound, acquired the importance almost of a
moral duty, and became a habit I found it difficult to break after
I had left home.

They were anxious not only about their financial prospects,

but about their children's health. Paul, it is true, was notably blithe and stalwart; but my sister – whose problems, I fear, may have been partly due to the unbrotherly attitude that I adopted – seemed a somewhat odd and moody girl; and I was experiencing one of the mysterious crises that I have referred to in an earlier passage, when, despite my reputation for cleverness, I sank towards the bottom of my form at school. I had also developed a number of irritating nervous tricks. I sniffed incessantly; and so pronounced was my sniff – I recollect a barber begging me to restrain it, while he did his best to cut my hair – that my parents sought medical advice as to how it might be remedied. The physician, a benevolent-looking elderly man, spectacled and white-moustached, obviously reached the conclusion that I needed stern treatment. Having requested my mother to leave the room, he informed me that, unless I ceased sniffing, he would have my nostrils sewn up with surgical silk, and pointed out how the other boys I met would ridicule my strange appearance. By the time my mother was called back, I had been reduced to a state of hysterical despair, and was led home again, sobbing and violently sniffing, towards the house in Lower Camden.

The procedure eventually adopted was a good deal less drastic. I was dispatched to a farm in Devon, at Moreton Hampstead near the slopes of Dartmoor, where my parents hoped that, by living on the land and doing easy jobs around the farmyard, I should overcome my neurasthenic foibles. Their plan to some extent succeeded. But I soon advertised a keen distaste – though I made a few exceptions, such as tending bonfires and feeding the farm-cats – for any kind of manual labour, and spent my time strolling across the moors and examining prehistoric monoliths, or trying to 'tickle' trout in the pools of a shallow golden-brown stream that cascaded between high turfy banks over a sunlit granite-pebbled bed. The water was so cold that it made my wrists ache; but, as I groped among the boulders and thrust my arm deep into a dark crevice, with a passionate tremor of excitement my predatory fingers would sometimes graze against a hidden fish.

These rustic pastimes undoubtedly strengthened my nerves; and I imagine that I also benefited from the solid farmhouse food. It was an old-fashioned farm, ruled by a patriarchal personage named Henry Hutton, whom his descendants called 'the Maïster'. The tiled kitchen had a cavernous open hearth; and above a heap of perpetually glowing wood-ash hung massive soot-furred pots and kettles, attached to a system of antique cranks and chains that ran out of sight far up the chimney. The parlour was seldom used; a musty ancestral shrine, in addition to some family photographs and a forbidding aspidistra it accommodated large steel-engraved portraits of the Maïster's previous landlords, two successive Earls of Devon, heads of the ancient Courtenay family that so excited Uncle Philip. The elder, a grave and dignified peer, my hosts remembered as 'a fine old gentleman'; his son, a languid, weak-chinned youth, they preferred to leave unmentioned.

The most attractive part of the farm, however, was the slate-flagged dairy. There slate shelves supported the huge earthenware pans in which fresh milk was set to gather cream; and every morning a heavy crust of cream, placed on a slice of new bread, was brought to my room by one of the daughters of the house. While I ate it, if the day were dull and wet, I could watch rain-drops gather along the beetling eyebrow of thatch that projected just beyond my window. Many years later, as I turned the pages of *The Tempest*, I came to Ariel's description of 'the good old Lord, Gonzalo':

> His tears run down his beard, like winter's drops
> From eaves of reeds

– and found myself suddenly transported back to the farm at Moreton Hampstead and my bedroom underneath the thatch. Later still, in a drawer of my mother's desk, I discovered some letters I had written home. During the last year of her life, when she burned so many other papers, she had affectionately preserved them. Dated 'Christmas term 1916', with a note on the wrapping 'Please keep', they make a curious collection. Since our journey abroad, I had firmly decided that I must become a writer; and in these letters I lose no opportunity of giving my descriptions of Coombe Farm a decorative literary twist.

The result is frequently stilted. Very often I seem to be echoing some phrases I had read, and then stored away for future reference. Reading was, of course, my deepest pleasure. But my parents felt that prolonged reading was a habit they should do their best to check; and, when at my repeated request they sent me editions of *Barnaby Rudge* and *A Tale of Two Cities*, they insisted that I should absorb the text in extremely small doses, having first spent most of the day outdoors. I agreed, or perhaps pretended to agree, but still occasionally complained. I assured them that I did not read till evening. 'It does not worry or hurt me', I wrote; but if my father really pictured his son 'dying of brain fever on top of the volume comme ca, then he better tell me so, and I'll sit in the great tiled kitchen and do *nothing* except look at the very interesting callender on the wall'. Otherwise, once 'the quiet shadows that are cows have passed into the fields, and nothing but the noisy patches of white, geese, are left what *shall* I do? Watch Mr Henry slowly putting on his spectacles?'

My handwriting, at the age of eleven and a half, was almost as mannered as my use of language; and I was apt to embellish my envelopes with fanciful curlicues, even with small coloured sketches. Life on the farm might have improved my health; but it could not change my character, in which a passion to express, and thereby assert myself, was already strongly working. I had begun to love argument, particularly if the crux of the argument allowed me to exhibit my superior knowledge; and among my letters I find an odd account of how I had astounded and pained my hosts by discussing the Buddhist doctrine of the transmigration of souls. The Misses Hutton 'were wondering together what in future lives we should be'; and I had referred them to a favourite novel, *Kim,* and the wise sayings of Rudyard Kipling's lama; when 'Whoofff comes Mrs Henry ... she believes it's dangerous to think, to talk on these pagan subjects, "Buddhism is heathen", she says. Though I mayn't be a Buddhist myself ... by the last ripple made by the pebble I've thrown some one may turn Buddhist ... 'Tis true, and very silly also, n'est pas ...'

Simultaneously, I was becoming an aesthete, and a severe critic of my fellow men both from an aesthetic and from a moral point of view. 'Never did I think', I announced, 'that the world could have upon its face such inquisitive, cattish, gossiping, and *very* feminine beings as we have here.' And, with cold disdain, I observed a pair of local dealers, come to talk of sheep or ponies;

'Yesterday and the day before I have been burning rubbish, it was hot and horribly smoky, and when we had come back again to tea I was obliged to shake hands with the two most ghastly creatures that ever sat on a settle and drank whiskey and gin . . . One was pig faced and had exceedingly pointed ears (so that he looked quite diabolical) the other was thin and looked a sot . . . Never shall I forget the thin one's face as he toasted Mrs Hutton in whiskey. There's some nice china, prints etc. here.' Besides appraising the Huttons' china and prints and loitering around the moors and the trout-stream, I had many similar distractions. Now and then, a drove of wild Dartmoor ponies, long-tailed and shaggy-coated, would pour into the farmyard; and, if I visited Moreton Hampstead itself, a pleasant little old town, I could admire its ancient pillared almshouses, or walk through the churchyard, studying the modest tombstones, carved in coarse-grained local granite, of unknown French prisoners who had died on Dartmoor during the Napoleonic Wars.

Meanwhile, I resisted the temptation to sniff, and presently had conquered it. I announced that I was feeling 'vastly better', and returned home a saner and solider child; but my parents were of the opinion that I needed further strengthening, and that being a 'day-boy' at St Alfred's, which allowed me to lead a comfortable self-centred life among the objects I valued and the people whom I loved, might encourage my introspective tendencies. Henceforward, they said, I was to be a boarder. Their decision caused me desperate grief. When I had accepted the decree of exile, however, I found my new existence far less hideous than I had imagined. Thanks to my knack of inventing bizarre stories, and telling them in the dormitory after lights-out, I gained a reputation as an entertainer; and in the school at large I was regarded as a privileged eccentric, whom my companions had been instructed to refrain from bullying, and my masters, even the hot-tempered Mr Jonathan, had elected not to beat.

So sure did I feel of my own gifts that I was completely unembarrassed by the position I occupied towards the bottom of a form of younger boys. Time would tell; and, until the moment came, I was glad to keep my head down, and only raised it should I see a chance of annoying Mr John and Mr Jonathan, or some dim-witted war-time usher. Commanded to join a side at cricket, I promptly volunteered for long-stop, but, growing abstracted and omitting to notice a ball, was sometimes ordered off the field. Our headmasters, being short of groundsmen, would set a troop of boys to rolling the pitch or weeding near-by gravel paths; and I discovered that, if I approached Mr Jonathan and enquired in a loud innocent voice, 'Excuse me, sir; but is this work *compulsory*?' I almost always caught him unprepared. With a sharp 'We want no unwilling hands here!' he would bid me leave his presence.

Luckily perhaps, I was removed from St Alfred's some months before the War ended. My parents were now becoming anxious about their children's education; and they had heard that the Hertfordshire town of Berkhamsted had not only an excellent grammar school, which called itself a public school, but a well-reputed girls' school. We reached Berkhamsted in 1917, when I had celebrated my twelfth birthday; and it would remain my family's home until my father's death in 1935. Eventually, I came to loathe the place, and used to employ the adjective 'Berkhamstedian' to describe any scene or human character that I found particularly obnoxious. Today I see the background of my adolescence through much more sympathetic eyes. I was already in love with the past; and Berkhamsted, I soon discovered, had a long and memorable history. Here William Cowper had been born at the parsonage; and, during the fourteenth century, Geoffrey Chaucer, as a diligent civil servant, had kept his account-books at the Castle – now reduced to some craggy masses of flint, overhanging deep green ditches – that rose just behind the railway station. Even earlier, in the reign of Henry III, Berkhamsted Castle had been besieged and finally taken by an invading French army, who had left a series of massive earthworks, thrown up, no doubt, to support their siege-engines, across the grassy moat beneath the ramparts.

The broad High Street, Berkhamsted's central throughfare, retained many of its old houses, dignified Georgian red brick and half-timbered Tudor black-and-white; and on one corner, so close to the Grammar School that the headmaster's garden and the churchyard shook hands, stood the tall, large-windowed parish church. Like other churches, the building had suffered severely from nineteenth-century restorations. Besides destroying the ancient tiled floor, Victorian iconoclasts had scrubbed off every trace of its medieval wall-paintings: 'you might almost have said they were *Chinese*', an elderly stone-mason – as a boy he had helped restore the fabric – latterly informed my father. But near the chancel screen a massive arcaded tomb displayed a pair of noble recumbent effigies; and I became deeply attached to the brass memorial tablet that commemorated a fine Chaucerian knight, *Johannes Raven Armiger*, who had served under the Black Prince.* His mailed gauntlets raised in solemn prayer, and his pointed steel feet lightly at rest upon a small heraldic lion, he strengthened my already warm regard for the English Middle Ages.

Beyond the town itself I discovered no less scope for reflection and imagination. Berkhamsted sprawls down a wide valley, following the London road towards the Chilterns; but, to the north, high above the Castle, stretches a huge windy common, a splendid expanse of turf and bracken and gorse; with here and there a clump of pines, that rolls away as far as Ashridge Park, once the refuge, during her dangerous girlhood, of the future Queen Elizabeth. Beneath in the valley, a hamlet named North-church, also built on the straight London road, and now a rural suburb of Berkhamsted, recalled another English queen. Caroline of Anspach, the consort of George II, was a highly cultivated woman. Neither her husband nor her father-in-law approved of her unroyal tastes; but, in 1726, while Caroline was still Princess of Wales, George I, aware that she was a keen collector of every kind of 'curiosity', had presented her, when he returned from a visit to Hanover, with an interesting human freak. This pathetic creature had recently been captured living alone among the woods, running on all fours, scaling trees, and devouring twigs and moss.

Apparently some twelve or thirteen years old, 'The Wild Boy' was incapable of speaking. He was, therefore, entrusted to Pope's friend, the learned physician Dr Arbuthnot; and 'the ablest masters' were engaged to teach him how to talk and read.

* Berkhamsted Castle, a royal stronghold, had been the Prince's favourite residence.

Meanwhile, he appeared at the Princess's court, where Dr Swift himself examined him, and he was said to have looked 'extremely uneasy' in new red stockings and a smart blue coat. But Dr Arbuthnot and his other tutors failed; the Hanoverian Mowgli proved impossible to educate; and he was eventually farmed out with a family near Northchurch, where he 'continued to the end of his inoffensive life', and died in the year 1785, 'supposed to be aged 72'. His simple tombstone, inscribed PETER THE WILD BOY, stands opposite the church door; while, just inside the church, a metal plaque on the wall exhibits a brief commemorative notice, accompanied by a small engraved portrait of a bearded, wild-eyed old man.

Returning homewards to Berkhamsted, I would pass a modern market-garden. In the Middle Ages that humdrum tract of ground had enclosed a mysterious magic spring; and one day a posse of armed officials, perturbed by the rumours that had reached their ears, rode out and discovered a flower-wreathed company dancing around the pool and celebrating secret pagan rites. But these associations, much as I valued them, could not quite disguise the fact that twentieth-century Berkhamsted was a drab, prosaic town. There was a heavy dank smell about its lower-lying districts between the station and the school, which rose from the surface of the sluggish canal that ran beneath the railway-line, and from the woodyard and pestiferous tannery that had been built upon its margin. Outside the town, where it was bordered with watercress beds and flowed parallel to a rivulet named the Bulborne, it became a pleasant feature of the landscape. The barges that passed along it were still generally drawn by horses; while the barges themselves and all the equipment they carried were boldly decorated in cheerful primary colours. But, crossing Berkhamsted, it looked dark and cold and sad; and native Berk-hamstedians, as a rule, seemed somewhat grim and uncouth people. They had an odd accent, produced by slurring over consonants and hoarsely accentuating vowel sounds. Nor was their outward appearance attractive. Facially, they reminded my school-fellow Graham Greene of the crafty knaves on playing cards.*

* See *A Sort of Life*, 1971.

We settled, however, once we had arrived at Berkhamsted, some distance from the centre of the town, in a populous Victorian suburb that ascended the hill opposite the distant Common. Our first house, rented for a few months, was uncommonly depressing. A previous occupant was said to have committed suicide; and my mother claimed that, especially around the cellar, she could feel a strange unnerving influence, and that she was often haunted by vague, yet horrible visions of a smallish white-faced, red-haired man. Far worse, dry-rot had attacked the woodwork; the legs of our heavier pieces of furniture slowly sank into the floor; and large evil-smelling bulbs of fungus sprouted from the skirting-boards. We were much luckier in our next house, though it lacked any kind of architectural charm – a slab-sided semi-detached building, which had a narrow poplar-shaded back-garden and an even smaller front-garden, but gave us, as some houses do, a friendly, understanding welcome. There the fragments of our past life – the oak chests, the eighteenth-century chairs, the Italian walnut cabinet, the prints, the faded Persian carpets – were provisionally patched together; and we began a new existence. To assist my mother in her household duties, she had engaged a housemaid and an inexpert, though amiable cook. The cook, I remember, was called Puddiphatt, a local corruption of 'paddock-foot', or 'frog-foot'* – a name that certainly suited her waddling gait around the kitchen.

At this stage, my once-ebullient father must have seemed a tired and saddened man. Having lost his professional income, he had accepted a war-time post as almoner to a famous City company, whose funds he helped to distribute among its various charitable enterprises. He hated the work, and much resented being obliged to take orders and daily fill in stupid forms. He also loathed the War, and was revolted by unending newspaper reports of destruction and disintegration. My mother, with her taste for myth-making, used afterwards to declare that his heart had been

---

* Paddock, as a name for frog, is used by Robert Herrick in his *Noble Numbers*:
Here a little child I stand,
Heaving up my either hand;
Cold as Paddocks though they be,
Here I heave them up to Thee . . .
Another Grace for a Child

broken by what she romantically styled 'the Rape of Belgium', and by the stories he heard of German attacks on ancient Flemish churches he had once admired. That legend, like other legends she cherished, I assume today, was largely baseless. Though the War had shocked and appalled him, I am sure it did not change his character. Indeed, his experiences during the war-years gradually strengthened his sense of creative purpose and, because he could no longer plan and build, encouraged him to express his private credo – his belief in the moral qualities of honest craftsmanship – through an entirely different medium. He resolved to produce a book. In the past, as it happened, he had often thought of writing, and besides his *Modern Suburban Houses*, had published a short guidebook for visitors to Durham Cathedral; but, when his practice increased, he was always far too busy to realize his more ambitious schemes. Now he had both the time he needed and an urgent personal motive. Rather than succumb to despair, he again picked up his pen, and began covering numerous foolscap pages.

His subject was history, the history of the English people, seen, however, not in terms of sovereigns and statesmen, politics and wars and revolutions, but in the lives of ordinary human beings, the work they did, the buildings they inhabited, the tools and furniture they used, the clothes they wore, all the hundred-and-one absorbing details that compose the social background of a period. I doubt if my father had often studied Ruskin; but he possessed a copy of *The Stones of Venice*; and Ruskin's chief message, the prophet's 'Gospel of Work', he found extraordinarily appealing; for he, too, regarded strenuous creative work as a universal panacea, and was convinced that only the man who worked, and succeeded, moreover, in enjoying his work, could be accounted wise and happy. Elsewhere, I shall describe the development of his project. Meanwhile, I am puzzled to fix the date when he raised its earliest foundations. He had already started his researches, I know, by July 1916. That month, my mother, who was staying in Devon, received a letter jointly addressed to her by her husband and her elder son. My contribution is a typical piece of verbiage. 'My dear Mother [I write] This afternoon, all is rain, and mist and distant thunder ... Every-

thing seems sodden and wet outside. Dad is paddling about inspecting his peas and Gillian thrums upon our worn out spinet,
which . . . tinkles wearily away like an old man with a cracked
voice reciting an endless creed. We all send our love . . . P.S. I am
getting on satisfactorily with every thing.'

My father continues in a more informative strain:

> This sounds rather gloomy – but it is the weather which is all
> wrong. Peter is doing famously & so is Gillian & very much
> so is Paul. We had a thunderstorm yesterday (Tuesday) about
> 6 & today is a dull indeterminate sort of a day – I don't think
> it has been fine since you left. No Viollet-le-ducs – why not
> laze? Costume is very engrossing & if I send them down
> you will get interested and start work. Play is what you want.
> The usual practice I think is to cut down your timber – have it
> sawn up & stacked so that the air can get at it . . . I'm afraid
> your holiday is going very quickly – by the time you get this
> the week will have gone . . .

Employing his customary small crabbed hand, so oddly
illegible that it suggested Babylonian cuneiform, my father concludes with an additional reference to the bad weather – 'the rain
has brought up a legion of weeds' – and with an abrupt, yet tender
goodbye: 'Well dear one – very little news but lots of love from
your aff. husband Charles.' This is the only letter of my father's
I still possess; my mother appears to have destroyed all the written
records of her marriage; and the letters he wrote me I very seldom
preserved, since they usually dwelt on my financial troubles and
included many passages of patient scolding. I quote from it here
for the light that it throws on my father's literary plans. My mother
was to be his collaborator in the work that he had undertaken;
and, though I cannot tell why he should suddenly discuss the most
suitable method of seasoning timber – perhaps her host and
hostess may have appealed for his expert advice – the 'Viollet-le-
ducs' he mentions were a splendid series of volumes, *Dictionnaire
Raisonné du Mobilier Français*, published by the mid-nineteenth-
century architect and archaeologist, Eugène-Emmanuel Viollet-
Le-Duc, whence the authors derived some of the basic material
of *A History of Everyday Things*.

It follows that my mother's services had already been enlisted, and that she had joined him in the labours that were to last until his death. Designated 'the Books' – they required no other title – they came to form the pivot around which our lives revolved. Neither my sturdy brother nor my nervous and difficult sister was yet old enough to be particularly drawn towards my parents' occupations. But me they engrossed; my mind was full of hauberks and helms, capuchons and liripipes, and how the head-dress of a fifteenth-century gentleman had been evolved by thrusting his head into the aperture that had originally shown his face, and winding up the remainder of the hood, which should have covered his shoulders, to form a decorative coxcomb. I loved the Middle Ages, and pored delightedly over the various medieval relics that my father had collected, a fragment of a painted medieval screen or some of the old decorative tiles that had once paved Berkhamsted Church.

The word 'high-brow' was not then generally used; but I suppose that some of our more philistine neighbours must have considered us an 'arty' household. We were priggish, too, and apt to be highly critical of standards less exacting than our own. Though my father detested the War, he repeated with solemn relish a sentence that he had read in an article by J. L. Garvin, who announced that the conflict was forcibly purifying the national soul, and would continue to do so until 'the last fatty globule of degeneration' – a phrase he greatly admired – had been squeezed out of the British social system. A few globules, alas, were still in evidence. London, we were told, remained an alarmingly frivolous place; painted 'society women' had their photographs taken organizing canteens and concerts; and young officers, fresh from the horrors of the trenches, attended a musical comedy entitled *The Bing Boys*, or applauded a bold young actress named Gaby Delys, generally regarded among people of our kind as 'no better than she should be'. I remember loudly condemning *The Bing Boys* (which, of course, I had never seen) and the vicious tendencies it represented. But in our immediate circle, we were encouraged and impressed by the war-time transformation of my Uncle Claude. Him the War had definitely enlarged and ennobled. A pale, retiring young man, he had passed through the

Artists' Rifles to gain a commission in a dashing Highland regiment. With his kilt and sporran and close-clipped red moustache, he was indeed the type of Happy Warrior.

Though I admired him in his new guise, I could not follow his example. At Berkhamsted School, which I now attended daily, I had been obliged to join the ranks of the usual military training corps; but rolling my puttees was a knack that somehow I could never learn; and, after a first parade, where they very soon worked loose and drooped in folds around my ankles, I was quickly released from military duties. Having shown a similar ineptitude on the playing-fields, I was next excused from games. I had a remarkable school life. Yet the school itself was a humdrum institution, and could scarcely have been called 'progressive'. Founded in 1523 by the Brotherhood of St John and their chairman, Dean Incent, it had originally housed over a hundred and forty boys – an attendance that, during the middle years of the eighteenth century, had dwindled to some four or five. A fierce Victorian pedagogue, who must have slightly resembled the celebrated Dr Arnold, had presently revitalized it, improving its moral tone, building modern classrooms and generally giving it the status of a minor public school. Berkhamsted was not at all fashionable – my contemporaries pretended to regard the Etonians and Harrovians they met on field-days as a crowd of dissipated snobs; but it had acquired a rigid class-system. Below an aristocracy of boarders lay a middle-class, which included myself, of easy-going day-boys, and, yet lower, a despised proletariat, the 'train-boys', so called because they arrived by train from various adjacent towns. The product of elementary schools, they had won scholarships to Berkhamsted and were educated gratis. We derided both their rough accents and their old, unsightly clothes, and even credited them with a rank, distinctive odour, which enabled us to detect their recent presence in any classroom that we entered.

Architecturally, the focus of the school buildings was the venerable Tudor hall. Once it had stood alone. But now Victorian blocks, uniformly hideous, had been attached to enclose an oblong quadrangle, the worst addition being a repulsive red-brick chapel approached by a range of ill-proportioned cloisters.

64

The old hall was raised on a large terrace; and here, his hands clasped behind his back, invariably arrayed in gown and mortar-board, we often sighted a short but dominant personage, fixing us with sternly watchful eyes as we went about our business, and sometimes lifting his voice to deliver a sonorous reprimand, bidding us remove our hands from our pockets or objecting to the colour of a pair of socks. This was our headmaster, Charles Greene, father of the well-known novelist, who had governed the school since 1910, and had continued the reforming work of his late-Victorian predecessor.

In my youth I failed to recognize his virtues; what I noticed were the portentous mannerisms behind which he hid his true face. I suspect that he was really a shy man. Short himself and latterly a little stout, he had married a tall slender wife, and be-gotten a family of tall children; and perhaps it was his own comparative shortness that had encouraged him to develop at school so majestic a persona. We assembled every day in the new hall, recited prayers and sang hymns, before listening to Dr Greene, who occupied the centre of the dais amid a company of lower masters. Occasionally his observations became a speech, and his speech a fine specimen of Ciceronian invective. Someone, on the hoar-frost that covered an outdoor bench, had dared to write a filthy word. Or, far worse, a gang of adolescent libertines had been run to earth conducting their lewd amours after dark in a remote laboratory. He would rather, he cried, that the school should cease to exist than it should become – as might well happen unless the evil were promptly scotched – a hotbed of unmentionable vice; and, later, we would learn of the various expulsions that had resulted from the scandal.

Yet it was to Charles Greene that I owed my freedom at Berkhamsted; through his benevolence that I escaped the roughest forms of schoolboy servitude. My father, I assume, must first have intervened, and suggested that I needed special treatment, alleging that I was highly-strung, unduly sensitive and, like my mother, had a weak heart. Charles Greene proved a sympathetic listener, and made me so many generous concessions, of which I quickly took advantage, that, by the time I left school, the position I occupied was exceptionally agreeable. I played no games; and, while my friends trudged off to the muddy fields, I was free to walk or bicycle or ride a hired horse about the Common. Nor was I obliged to study any subject that I found particularly distasteful – for example, French, because I hated the French master; and algebra and trigonometry, because the insoluble problems they presented often made my head ache. Was my headmaster's generosity mistaken; and did his lenience do me lasting damage? Should I have grown up stronger and braver and steadier had I been forced to deal with the hardships of an ordinary schoolboy's life? I cannot tell. But Charles Greene's tolerant regimen certainly increased my happiness; and for any addition of happiness, deserved or undeserved, one is bound to feel grateful.

During afternoons when I was free from work or games, I pursued my own interests. Brass-rubbing was now a favourite pastime. Having bought a 'heel-ball' – a disc of solidified blacking – and a roll of white absorbent paper, I would bicycle around the country, and visit every neighbouring church. Ancient parish churches, the more remote and neglected the better, were among the sacred places of my youth; and even today, as I push open a church door and recognize the curiously compounded smell that meets me when I cross the threshold, the scent of damp plaster and old masonry, of worm-eaten wood and dusty coconut-matting, mummified hassocks and shrivelled prayer-books, I feel the same expectant pleasure. I was usually alone, unless some solitary devoted old woman should happen to be polishing a lamp or arranging Michaelmas daisies in a side-chapel; and I would begin by examining the fabric itself and its sepulchral inhabitants: the cross-legged crusader upon whose armoured flanks boys had been carving their names for the last five hundred years; the Elizabethan landowner and his wife between two close-packed rows of children; seventeenth-century grandees reclining chin-in-hand, as if they had 'died of the tooth-ache', to quote a Jacobean dramatist; and stylish Augustan effigies, with palms and lyres, armorial shields and broken columns. Next, I would pull up the mats and discover hidden brasses. Making an impression by clamping my paper to the brass, then rubbing my heel-ball regularly up and down, was an easy but delightful task, which I continued until a clear-cut image had slowly taken shape upon the surface; and the completed picture rolled up beneath my arm, I could ride home through the evening.

Although they would have preferred me to lead a more active life, my sedentary pursuits did not much disturb my parents. But now and then, a meddlesome uncle lectured them about my education; and from time to time my own eccentric behaviour caused them serious alarm. For example, I was apt to burst into tears at any unexpected crisis. Thus my father once contemplated buying a house some way along the London road – an old house with big panelled rooms, large ruinous stables and a venerable tulip tree. The idea of inhabiting so legendary a house, after the suburban residence we now occupied, made a strong appeal to my imagination; and, when my father suddenly abandoned the scheme, my disappointment brought on a flood of weeping. Meanwhile, my cult of antiquity had begun to pass all bounds. In Berkhamsted's dingiest quarter a clump of decrepit half-timbered buildings, crumbling, insanitary and rat-ridden, stood near the canal bank. Called 'The Wilderness', it had long been a source of scandal; but it was indubitably *old* and, as such, I revered the place. Reports that 'The Wilderness' was soon to be pulled down provoked yet another tearful outburst. My parents shook their heads; they decided that they must do something to check my excessive lachrymosity, and that I might develop a measure of self-control if I lived under a different roof. I was, therefore, temporarily exiled from my home and placed in the household of the local doctor, a worthy but dispirited man, whose eldest son had recently been killed at Passchendaele. Here I behaved well and broke the habit of crying, as, some twelve months earlier, I had given up sniffing. My tear-ducts have since become atrophied; however poignant the occasion, I find I can no longer weep.

These episodes may perhaps suggest that I led a perversely self-absorbed existence, and had very few associates. On the contrary, I made several good friends, chief among them being the numerous family of the celebrated story-teller, W. W. Jacobs. At this period, too, I once more fell in love, with a little girl aged nine or ten. She inhabited a distant neighbourhood; and the only place where I could be sure of seeing her was St Mary's, Northchurch, which her family attended every Sunday – and there, unless I craned my neck, not until the congregation had turned east-wards for the Creed during the middle of the service. Then her face came briefly into view – a small oval face, transparently pale beneath a bell-shaped cap of fair hair, her hair itself being so faintly golden that, like her skin, it had an almost greenish tinge. Just before my mother's death, I asked her if she still remembered Inez. My mother was apt to take a somewhat critical view of my various Dulcineas, past or present; and she replied that, yes, of course, she remembered her – as 'a rather *giggly* little girl'.

Well, if she giggled, we were never close enough for me to hear the slightest sound she uttered. But she certainly smiled – a delicate feline smile, secretive and perhaps derisive, as often as she became aware, across the church, of my open-mouthed, adoring presence. Other characters I have disguised with the help of a pseudonym. Let me give her full name. It was Inez Richardson; and today I find that it still possesses a romantic incantatory power. In those days it was a mysterious spell that I regularly repeated, as I struggled to evoke an image that haunted and yet constantly eluded me. No sooner had I fixed her features on my memory, where I expected they would never fade, than I found that they were growing indistinct; and only if I caught another glimpse of her, with her distant teasing smile, did they regain their earlier freshness.

Then the Richardsons vanished; I suppose Inez's parents moved away. My next passion was equally nympholeptic, and had as imaginative a colouring. I had first admired Inez because she re-minded me of a picture of Jeanne d'Arc in an illustrated volume by Boutet de Monvel; and her successor bore a fascinating re-semblance to a statue of the young Mithras that I had seen in one of the serial instalments of H. G. Wells's popular *Outline of History*. I cannot remember her name; but she had the statue's straight nose and sharp-cut line of chin and mouth. Though she inhabited the same street, and I caught sight of her almost every day, I never met or spoke to her; and various stratagems I devised – for example, hurrying ahead and dropping a penknife or a handkerchief that I intended her to pick up – proved entirely un-successful. My last schoolboy passion was similarly connected with the arts, its object being the graceful stepdaughter of the middle-aged pedagogue who taught me Greek history; and her I likened to a maiden on the Parthenon frieze. I recognized the Athenian girl in her upright virginal carriage, her straight slender limbs and smooth unsullied brow.

Though these passions were sensuous as well as aesthetic; they remained entirely innocent; my highest hopes would have been satisfied by a brief meeting, a few words or a single touch. Of the amorous appetites I had still learned very little. But, years earlier, staying at the seaside with my Uncle Basil's family, I had been stirred, yet also deeply disgusted, to see a group of little girls paddling in a rock-pool and shamelessly lifting their petticoats to reveal their naked stomachs. They were evidently 'common children', offspring of the ignorant poor; there was something squalid about their big hats and their heavy crumpled skirts. The spectacle, however repulsive, was also alarmingly attractive, as was their shrill laughter when they exhibited parts of their bodies that I knew they should have kept hidden. Otherwise I had had no experience of lust. Certain early playmates, it now occurs to me, probably played sexual games; but, suspecting my lack of knowledge, they had refused to initiate me into the clandestine practices they shared. Under the influence of art I had already fallen in love; and it was through art that I eventually entered a world of new and dangerous sensations.

My entrance was unexpected. I had been eating my midday meal alone at my parents' gate-legged Jacobean table; and beside my plate lay an edition of Marlowe's works, which I had recently ordered and brought home from the local bookshop. I have the copy today; it bears the Everyman imprint; and I was reading *Hero and Leander*:

> Albeit Leander, rude in love and raw,
> Long dallying with Hero, nothing saw
> That might delight him more, yet he suspected
> Some amorous rites or other were neglected.
> Therefore unto his body hers he clung:
> She, fearing on the rushes to be flung,
> Striv'd with redoubled strength; the more she striv'd

The more a gentle pleasing heat reviv'd,
Which taught him all that elder lovers know . . .

Swept away by the torrent of Marlowe's verse, I hastened on towards the consummation, read how the frightened virgin plunges between the sheets –

And, as her silver body downward went,
With both her hands she made the bed a tent.
And in her own mind thought herself secure,
O'ercast with dim and darksome coverture

– and how she eventually gives up the struggle. *Hero and Leander* is one of the finest amatory poems yet written in the English language; and on me, seated at the oak table before a plateful of cold beef and salad, it made the same vibrantly disturbing impression as a fierce electric storm.

Yet the visions that *Hero and Leander* provoked were still impossible to realize; and, although exquisite succubi occasionally troubled my dreams – and, indeed, my waking hours – my attitude towards less unreal loves was still platonic and romantic. I recollect the end of one winter afternoon. Snow had fallen; the evening was cold and clear; and the last streaks of sunset had already faded over a hilly field that lay beyond our house. Some friends and I had been trying out a toboggan; but, as the sky darkened and the air grew sharper, we began to walk home. When I looked back, the snow shone a faint blue amid dim surrounding trees and hedges; the voices of the crowd that covered the hill had a distant tinkling clarity; and each toboggan that glided down the slope released a fiery trail of sparks. Somewhere in the crowd was my young Mithras. I had not met her; I did not hope to meet her; but I knew that she existed; and the whole prospect, with all its tenebrous details, gave me a sense of keen unearthly joy.

On my last visit to Berkhamsted, after nearly half a century, I found that that part of the landscape of my youth had completely dematerialized. Not only had a thick encrustation of modern buildings buried the familiar field; but the lie of the ground had somehow changed; and I could no longer identify the steep slope down which toboggans had once bumped and slithered. Elsewhere much was unchanged, including our ugly little house; and as it was empty and in process of being repaired, I ventured down the narrow side-passage that ran under the branches of an old elder tree just beneath my former bedroom window. My bedroom was both my study and my carefully guarded private museum, where I hoarded a variety of sacred objects, from the books I had collected to the precious antiquities that I had bought or dug up. My books, treasured in a small quadrangular revolving bookcase, nobody else must be allowed to handle; servants were strictly forbidden to dust them; and one Christmas Day, our clumsy young housemaid having swept a pile of new books off a chair, I swore at her with a ferocity that shocked my parents, who ordered me to leave the room, and stay out of their sight until I had apologized.

They themselves were considerably less bookish; and although they borrowed numerous works of reference, they seldom added to their library. The books that had followed them from Four Beeches stood neatly arrayed behind the glass front of a solid eighteenth-century escritoire. Besides one or two volumes of verse, a Keats and a Browning, illustrated respectively by Anning Bell and Byam Shaw, a calf-bound Byron and a copy of *The Faerie Queene* (bought, my father said, in his youth when he was 'trying to be cultured'), it contained such solemn prose-works as *The Stones of Venice* and *The Seven Lamps of Architecture*, Giorgio Vasari's *Lives of the Painters*, the collected essays of Ralph Waldo Emerson and, far more inexplicably, Oliver Wendell Holmes's *Professor at the Breakfast-Table*, accompanied, on a lower shelf, by the cheap 'Nelson' series of reprinted modern novels. Many of the lady-novelists assembled here wrote under their husband's name – Mrs Humphrey Ward, Mrs R. S. Garnett, Mrs A. Sidgwick, Mrs F. H. Barnett and Mrs Henry de la Pasture; each text had a monochrome plate opposite the frontispiece; and each of them told a sound and straightforward, but not unduly puzzling or alarming tale. My mother often re-read them, because, she claimed, she found them 'restful'; and I myself sometimes turned their pages, though for very different motives. I was anxious to master the contemporary art of fiction, and learn how an experienced novelist managed to develop his original idea, starting with a scrap of dialogue or perhaps a brief descriptive passage, then gradually and subtly enlarging his scope to produce a picture of a situation and the detailed account of a group of human personages.

A second bookcase, more recently purchased, held my parents' reference books, which they consulted almost every day. Since 1916 my father had been steadily at work. His architectural practice now showed signs of reviving, and he had once again a London office; but, as soon as he returned home, he would take out his drawings and manuscripts, and, my mother patiently seated beside him, continue his affectionate survey of the English Middle Ages. He had already secured a publisher. Harry Batsford, who had previously specialized in large illustrated monographs on architecture and the associated arts and crafts, was a gifted and engaging man. Long serpentine tendrils of brownish hair were woven round his polished skull; he kept a damp cigarette permanently glued to his lip, and suffered from a convulsive smoker's cough that, at its most extreme stage, often seemed likely to end in an apoplectic seizure. 'Mr Harry', as he was always called by his staff, genuinely loved books. He was also shrewd enough to grasp the possibilities of the book my father offered him. The project must have been approaching completion towards the close of 1917; and the first volume of *A History of Everyday Things in England, 1066–1499*, appeared in October 1918, about a month before the War ended.

On this rare occasion, my father's undertaking was exceptionally well timed. Books were still few; there was a feeling abroad that we could begin to look forward to an age of peace and reconstruction; and my father's preface, modest and simply written, sounded just the right note. 'Boys and girls,' he declared, 'who are now growing up will be given opportunities that no other generation has ever had; and it is of the greatest importance that they should be trained to do useful work and learn to use their hands.' If they were to 'become actual constructors and craftsmen . . . they must obtain a good store of knowledge – lay hold of tradition, so that they can benefit by what has been done – know that in one direction progress can be made, and that in another it will be arrested. Thus the coming generation may combine the wonderful appreciation for the uses and beauty of material that the old craftsmen possessed, with the opportunities for production which the modern machine gives . . .' My parents' first book enjoyed an immediate success. The sale of the whole series, launched in October 1918, has since amounted to well over a million copies.

For us the World War had had a happy conclusion; but the scenes that accompanied the Armistice were somewhat squalid and unpleasing. Young officers-to-be, then stationed at Berkhamsted, broke out of camp and swept down the High Street arm-in-arm with local roisterers, driving everyone before them. A number of my school-fellows had meanwhile joined the demonstration; and, when the crowd passed the church, it turned leftwards down a side-street, invaded the precincts of the school itself and burst into the Tudor hall, shouting the headmaster's name; whereupon Dr Greene wisely took refuge behind the locked doors of his study. To make this disturbing scene still more offensive, among the mob were various 'women of the town', who then hung around the local camp. I do not know how the rioters were expelled – perhaps the police were called in; but next day, from the platform of the new hall, Dr Greene delivered one of his loudest and longest and most sternly condemnatory speeches.

Although I had watched with excited interest while the mob rushed down the High Street, I was far too cautious to play any part in these extraordinary proceedings. At home we celebrated the Armistice quietly. But, before long, the return of peaceful conditions had an enlivening effect upon my father; and we learned that, once he could purchase an appropriate plot of ground, he meant to build a new house. About the same time, he became acquainted with a generous neighbouring landowner. Ashridge had had many occupants since the days of Queen Elizabeth. In 1800 the ancient monastic building had been demolished by that famous early industrialist, the canal-building Duke of Bridgewater; but in 1808 his cousin and successor had commissioned James Wyatt to design him an enormous Gothic mansion; and there, in our days, still lived the septuagenarian Lord Brownlow. A childless widower, he shared my father's devotion to history and archaeology. Sometimes they met and talked at Ashridge; and my father would describe the nobly bearded grandee, a dignified and amiable survivor of the late-Victorian period, spending his old age all alone among his vast inherited possessions. He seems to have enjoyed my father's cheerful company; and, when my father spoke of his proposed house, and said that it was difficult nowadays to purchase land, he offered to sell him a large field near Berkhamsted, adding that, as the Ashridge oak woods, his agent had told him, needed thinning out, he would be delighted to throw in some timber.

Both suggestions my father gladly accepted; and very soon he set about the work. But, with his usual erratic sense of timing, he chose an unpropitious moment. No sooner had the foundations been laid than the cost of building-materials began to rise; and, as they rose, many of the more attractive features of his first plan had to be summarily written off. His original design had included, for instance, a bow-windowed extension of the sitting-room, a pair of dormer-windows that broke the line of the roof, and, I believe, a modest wing. One after another, all were swept away, until the fabric was finally reduced to a simple box-like structure, which bore a certain odd resemblance to an infant's drawing of a house, and stood solitary and aloof at the top of a big empty field. Though Lord Brownlow had kindly provided oak, it was green, unseasoned timber; and, since he could not afford to postpone his operations while the green wood slowly dried, my father used it as it reached him; with the result that the floor-boards rapidly warped, and – my father having decided that plaster ceilings were an expensive superfluity, and that there was no reason why the floors of the rooms above should not become the ceilings of the rooms below – dust was constantly filtering through the cracks and settling upon our chairs and tables. Few more uncomfortable houses have ever existed. Four Beeches itself had been a somewhat noisy place; and in Crabtrees – named after the straggling thicket of crab-apples that separated its site from the adjacent farm and Common – every stout oaken plank performed the office of a sounding-board, and loudly creaked beneath our tread. When we moved house, the building was still unfinished. But my father had arranged to move in at a fixed date. To transfer his whole family to an hotel would have been an unthinkable extravagance; and for some weeks what little space we had was overrun by busily hammering workmen.

Most houses, in my experience, have a strongly personal character; and Crabtrees, which had endured so many early mishaps, seemed permanently ill-disposed. Nor was its garden inclined to flourish. The soil was a heavy, stony clay; and, although my father continued to dig and delve, and to grub out massive flints, the fruit trees and flowering bushes he planted often obstinately refused to take root. His avenues remained rows of feeble saplings; his roses wilted in their clayey beds; and not until several years had passed did they manage to penetrate a richer stratum, when trees we had despaired of developed such jungle-like zest that they obscured our paths and nearly hid our walls. Meanwhile, if we left the house, we enjoyed a minimum of privacy. A tall hawthorn hedge, at right angles to the crab-apple thicket, divided our garden and the road; but my father had apparently failed to notice that just inside this hedge there ran a public right-of-way; and Sunday strollers, who had climbed the hill from Berkhamsted, could walk to and fro along the path and, leaning over some defensive strands of wire, comment both on our house's bleak appearance – 'I've heard say', they would observe, 'that it was built by an *architect*!' – and on our sad attempts at gardening. My father laughed; but these criticisms of his professional achievement must, I think, have hurt him deeply.

Indoors, our good, if shabby, furniture produced a more encouraging effect. But again my father's anxious economies were apt to inhibit my mother's decorative schemes. For example, there was the problem of the sitting-room curtains, originally a fine dark-blue, that had hung in Four Beeches and, though she had provided them with a new hand-stencilled border, were now miserably drab and faded. After much argument, my father agreed that we needed new curtains. But it was a largish window that they had to fill; and we could not afford enough material, he declared, to cover the entire expanse. My mother was therefore instructed that she might buy sufficient material – she chose an oatmeal-coloured hopsack – to hang in decorous folds on either side, but not to draw across the window; and thenceforward, every

night of my youth, at one end of our lighted sitting-room we confronted a solid square of darkness, and in wintry weather watched
the rain-drops splashing or dribbling down the panes.

The greatest charm of our new house was its admirable situation, overlooking a shallow pastoral valley, through which the
London road ran almost unseen as it approached the town; and
at the bottom of our garden – or the field that my father was
doing his best to transform into a garden – rose a pleasant grassy
slope surmounted by some barns and stables. Here every Satur-
day evening, when they had finished their week's labours, the
farm-horses were turned loose. Scenting freedom, the massive
docile animals would immediately stampede and come thunder-
ing towards us down the slope. We could hear their hoof-beats
before they made their appearance; and during their tremendous
headlong descent they literally shook the ground.* Then they
swerved aside and stood heavily sweating and blowing, or dropped
to their knees, inclined their splendid arched necks, and rolled and
kicked upon the turf.

It was a weekly event that I always awaited with pleasure. The
nearness of the farm and of the windy gorse-patched Common
helped to reconcile me to the prosaic discomforts of the house my
father built. I still enjoyed my life at home, where we seldom
lacked domestic dramas, and slowly enlarged my view of my
parents as individual human beings. Previously, I had seen my
mother in full and endearing relief; my father as an impressive,
yet somewhat two-dimensional personage. Now it was he who
absorbed my closest attention; and very curious and interestingly
detailed was the portrait that I built up. My father had a dogmatic
mind; his opinions were strongly held and seldom changed; and
on any aspect of life he could not fit into his scheme he did his
best to turn a blank unseeing eye. Ruskin's 'Gospel of Work' remained his credo; and 'doing a good job', and doing it really
well, was still the remedy he advocated for every kind of human
problem. He abhorred both intellectual artifice and emotional

* Later, in a treatise on Greek mythology, I read that Poseidon, god of horses and
the sea, was also called 'The Earth-Shaker', because the nomadic invaders of
Greece, who had descended on the Aegean from some northern steppe, compared
the reverberation of an earthquake shock to the sound of galloping wild horses.

over-subtlety – the elaborate heart-searchings they provoked were, he felt, a frivolous waste of spirit – and believed that he himself was above all else a plain, straightforward man. Here, I believe, he misjudged his own character. He was by no means simple; and his apparent strength may perhaps have concealed a secret vein of weakness.

During his boyhood, he had suffered an alarming collapse, that might nowadays have been called a nervous breakdown, but was then entitled 'brain-fever', and been sent off to recuperate in a quiet Kentish village, where he first acquired his love of craftmanship by working at a local carpenter's bench and learning how to use his hands. Although he presently recovered, he had had various later troubles. They included bouts of acute insomnia, which often obliged him, he told me, to leave his bed and wander through the London streets, from his family's house in Kennington as far afield as Covent Garden. He always possessed the gift of striking up acquaintances; and on one of these expeditions he had met a friendly market-porter, who offered to provide him with a free supply of stolen vegetables – a suggestion that my father characteristically, if somewhat ungraciously, rejected.

I assume, therefore, that the difficulties my father had had to contend against in his youth were not only practical but psychological, and that, as a vigorous young man, he had preserved his innocence at the cost of many painful efforts. Possibly it was because he secretly distrusted the flesh that, even after he had entered a happy marriage, he tended to prefer things to people. He loved his family; otherwise he found a shapely object far more inspiring and appealing that the most attractive man or woman; and finely constructed objects had the additional advantage of never intruding on his established life-pattern, since they neither talked nor argued. They were safer companions; and it was safety he always prized. From his rough and difficult upbringing he had inherited a multitude of deeply-rooted phobias. He dreaded poverty; but he also dreaded the sexual passions, of which, in the stories his friends related, he had sometimes caught a horrifying glimpse. It might be wrong to say that he 'feared life'; but he was certainly aware that such a terror could invade and undermine the soul. Though he rarely opened a novel, the title of a book by

Henri Bordeaux, *La Peur de Vivre*,* had somehow stuck in his imagination; and 'We don't want the poor little fellow to get the "Peur de Vivre", do we?' I have heard him remark, half-lugubrious, half-facetious, to my puzzled, apprehensive mother, with reference to the unreasonably morbid point of view that he thought I was developing.

'Poor little' or 'poor old', I must explain, were among his favourite epithets. They formed part of the complex defence-system he had raised around his peace of mind. He had few relations or old friends to whom they were not now and then attached; and he was particularly apt to use them should a friend have been guilty of contravening his late-Victorian moral code. For example, there was a brilliant fellow-architect whom my father much esteemed, and who, with his partner, had raised an enormous public edifice in a florid Viennese-Baroque style – one couldn't help admiring their cheek! – almost opposite West-minster Abbey. What a magnificently dashing draughtsman he was! Yet, at an earlier stage of life, he had shown a lamentable propensity for pursuing loose women; and such a woman he had captured. But then, after a week or two of 'so-called bliss', she had summarily discarded him. He could no longer gain ad-mittance; 'and there', said my father, 'was poor old R. in tears on the staircase, trying to kick the door down . . .' Poets, he added, might talk of the ecstasy of love; but they did not trouble to describe the squalid consequences of illicit passion. Among its lowlier addicts he mentioned was an amorous Scottish foreman – a red-haired brute with tightly waxed moustaches – whom he had once employed at Bickley, and whose abandoned mistress had given birth to their bastard child in a vacant third-class carriage. Finally, he spoke of a ghastly disease that filled the London Lock Hospital. Let me be warned! Apart from the dangers one ran, there was the foolish waste of time involved. If only poor old R. had stuck to his drawing-board and his superbly

---

* When eventually I read the book myself, I found that its title was misleading. Published in 1902, the work of a *bien-pensant* Academician, it describes at weari-some length the struggle between an actively virtuous Catholic family and some purse-proud bourgeois neighbours, shackled by the conventions of their class and age.

fluent B.B. pencil!

Thus, the ethos that governed our household was both practical and idealistic. My father was not a religious man in the deepest meaning of the word. 'To work was to pray,' he agreed; but I doubt if he wholeheartedly accepted the divine origins of Jesus Christ; while God Almighty, I think, he envisaged in the guise of the Celestial Architect, the supreme Planner and unequalled Master-Builder who had created Heaven and Earth. Obviously, we needed some type of religious faith; and he stated his conviction with such hurried yet determined emphasis, as though he were anxious to dispose of the subject and pass to more immediate issues, that his announcement came to form in my mind a pair of lengthy hyphenated words: 'There-must-be-Something-somewhere,' he would exclaim. 'Else-what's-it-all-about-anyhow?' At my mother's gentle request, he might now and then attend a church service; but it was not a practice that he much enjoyed; and on one unfortunate occasion the clergyman delivered a discourse in which he compared the Christian priest to a zealous Fisher of Souls, casting wide his holy net, and got the images he employed so fantastically mixed-up – the net, the holes through its mesh, and the unregenerate fishes who escaped – that my father's lively sense of the absurd defied his efforts to control it, and he left the porch already laughing, pulled out and promptly lighted his pipe, and continued laughing all the way home.

My mother had a vaguely devotional bent; but her religious moods were short-lived. She would decide that henceforward at meals her children must remember to say Grace; and for several days we would beg, as we sat down, that for 'What we were about to receive', the Lord might 'make us truly thankful'. Somehow my father always spoiled the effect – not by demurring or refusing to join our prayers, but by repeating them in an unenthusiastic and slightly absent-minded tone. Then my mother forgot her decision; and we sank back into a state of irreligious quietude, perfectly pleased with ourselves as we were, and making no demands upon divine assistance. While I was still at St Alfred's, I had myself passed through a brief devotional phase. I enjoyed Evensong, when physical tiredness promoted a feeling of spiritual exaltation, and above the altar, owing to some trick of light, appeared a leaf-green shadow that resembled outspread wings. My ideas changed once I had reached Berkhamsted. There I experienced religious doubts, which crystallized during the course of an argument that revolved around the Mona Lisa.

It was provoked by my sister's governess. Miss Taylor was a small and sparrow-like person, with decided moral views; and on my showing her a photograph of the portrait, whose supposedly mysterious smile still captivated my imagination, she remarked that she found Leonardo's sitter a thoroughly 'nasty-looking woman'. I was outraged, and rushed to my idol's defence. Simultaneously, I felt that I faced a moral and intellectual crisis, and must choose between the Mona Lisa and Miss Taylor, between the aesthetic paganism that the portrait represented and the Christian puritanism for which Miss Taylor stood. I chose the portrait; and soon afterwards I so far declared my apostasy as to refuse to be confirmed. My parents did not insist. They regretted my foolish notions, but let me have my own way.

Neither was a disciplinarian; they did not believe in severity, and seldom thought of administering corporal punishment. One of my uncles, if his sons committed an offence that obviously required correction, although they had offended at breakfast, would inform them that they might expect a caning at precisely six o'clock, just before they went to bed. This revolted my father; a parent might cuff his child on a sudden impulse of exasperation; to keep the offender in painful suspense was unnecessarily savage. True, he had a violent temper himself, and was the kind of man who would leap from the wheel of his motor-car, and threaten to knock a lorry driver down; while he would occasionally exclaim that 'a damned good hiding' was what So-and-So had long deserved; but as a rule he managed to control his fury. Only twice can I remember him beating me, each time because I had provoked him by some shrewdly-aimed impertinence. But then his anger was terrifying; and he laid about me fiercely. Both the blows he dealt and the craven terror I suffered – I must have been twelve or thirteen; and he seemed extraordinarily large and strong – left behind them an indelible impression. For years I could not quite forgive my assailant; and even after his death he still sometimes appeared in a nightmare as the parental Enemy personified, a huge intimidating apparition that loomed towards me through the shadows.

Against these horrid incidents I must balance his habitual sympathy and kindliness. Should I attempt to draw in the style of the younger Holbein – I was not sure at the time whether I meant to display my genius in draughtsmanship or in literary composition – and required some sticks of red chalk of the kind that Holbein used, my father would search the London shops until he found the right materials. Nor, when I began to fresco my room, thereby grossly disfiguring the walls and roof, did he raise the least objection. We were fellow workers; that was excuse enough. Every worker, young and old, deserved his separate creative outlet; and he was happy so long as every member of his household pursued some energetic occupation. My mother agreed. It was a perfect marriage, said all our acquaintances, observing their harmonious partnership, from which sprang the delightful books that they jointly wrote and illustrated. Such friendly acquaintances did not, of course, suspect that, while she portrayed the minutiae of the historic past, my mother's thoughts were often elsewhere. She nursed a completely different ambition – to become a serious modern artist.

Any attack on my mother's artistic talents would have disturbed my father's sense of fairness; and he always praised her pictures. But he considered, rightly it may be, that she was of more use to the world as an historical illustrator than as an original painter; and he dealt with her ambitions, where they hampered his own projects, by mutely disregarding them. To paint was a hobby; to study costume and armour, and illustrate 'the Books', her appointed task in life. My mother did not revolt; she had outlived her rebellious period; but my father's opposition bred a secret germ of resentment that, had he ever dreamed that it existed, would have passed his understanding. 'Dear old M.Q.' – my parents had developed a habit of employing their respective initials rather than their Christian names – was frequently a little tired; but there was nothing really wrong; she enjoyed their work as much as he did. With his usual aptitude for ignoring awkward problems, he took an over-simplified view of my mother's private character. She, on the other hand, tended to dramatize her difficulties, and to see herself in the role of a frustrated artist, largely cut off by a devoted but masterful husband from the imaginative exercise she needed.

The course of her life had seldom been untroubled – that was a point that my mother always liked to emphasize; and, during her old age, when she described her youth, she very often spoke of *fear*, and said that it was certainly the strongest emotion she had experienced since her early childhood. In this context she told two separate stories. Her brothers had taken her to pick blackberries, and for some minutes had left her alone just behind a field gate. A tramp had leaned across the gate, and had beckoned her with hideous grimaces. According to a different tale, while she was seated in Nanny's kitchen the town idiot had crept down the garden path and, again savagely grimacing, had pressed his nose against the window. She told a series of similar stories, slightly less coherent, but equally alarming and grotesque; and the conclusion I drew was that, as a child, she had indeed suffered some peculiarly unpleasant shock; and that, whatever the facts were, they had gradually sunk deep into her unconscious memory, whence they emerged from time to time under a symbolic and perhaps an expurgated guise.

Yet, despite my mother's fears and my father's anxieties, we remained a cheerful household. Our small living-space perpetually rang with voices – my sister's and my brother's as they trampled up and down the stairs, and my father's as he cracked some preposterous joke or assured his children, almost every day of their lives immediately after breakfast, that, unless they 'showed a leg' and stopped their idle dawdling, they would certainly be late for school. He retained his exuberant sense of humour, though the subjects that aroused it were frequently a little grim. Death and destitution were both of them favourite themes; he himself would soon start 'pushing up the daisies'; and meanwhile we were all making rapid progress towards our ultimate refuge in the workhouse. The gloomier the topic, the louder the laugh he gave. I must admit that I often found my father exasperating company; and I was doubly exasperated because I felt that many of his jokes were intended to annoy, to 'take us down a peg' and crush any pretensions, social, financial or intellectual, that he thought we might perhaps cherish.

Snobbery was not among his failings. He had become, however, an inverted snob, a particularly English type, and was fond of telling stories, and delivering pronouncements that illustrated our modest position in the world. 'Don't forget,' he enjoined me at a family meal, 'that *you* are a member of the *lower* middle class!' Here my mother produced a tentative protest: 'Couldn't we say, dear, that we belonged to the *middle* middle class?' But my father would have none of it, and proceeded to explain the mysterious complexities of the English social system, that placed us a cut above plumbers and carpenters, but definitely some way below judges, barristers and bankers. Not that he took the slightest genuine interest in questions of social rank and precedence; but he liked to tease his family. It also amused him to tease our neighbours. He was fond of playing a part; and a part he greatly enjoyed was that of the proletarian good fellow, whose speech and mannerisms he adopted. If he met one of his more pompous acquaintances upon the station platform, he would make loud cheerful enquiries about 'the missus and the kids'; and 'my *wife and children* are in excellent health, thank you', the acquaintance would rather frostily respond.

Only when he regained his drawing-board did he put aside his jokes and whimsies. There he was altogether in earnest, and his real work lay before him. He had accustomed himself, as I have explained on a previous page, to draw and write throughout the evening; and, though this time-table did not suit my mother, who had been busy all the day, she patiently accepted it. My father returned home about six o'clock. Entering like a storm-wind, scuffing off his shoes and kicking them away beneath the hall table, discarding his overcoat, which smelt of train-smoke, and dropping an equally soot-scented copy of a London evening paper, he greeted his household, demanded the day's news and briefly peered into the garden. Work started once we had finished the meal that he insisted should be called 'supper' – 'dinner' he thought an unprofitable euphemism; and it continued until my exhausted mother was at last allowed to go to bed.

I should add that, at this period of their joint career, my parents worked by gas-light. Either electric cables had not yet reached the Common, or electricity had been voted too expensive. Gas was therefore installed; and from a series of fragile pipe-clay cones it shed a spluttering yellow light. As a rule, whenever he passed a gas-jet, my father quickly, automatically turned it down, thus plunging staircase or passage into a penumbral shade. But he was obliged to turn up the jet in the ground-glass lamp above the twin desks that he and my mother used, sitting side by side between the fireplace and the large half-curtained garden window. They had comparatively little space; other pieces of furniture surrounded them; for their work-room was also our living-room; and three children and a couple of somnolent dogs were usually assembled round the hearth. Provided they played no riotous games, my father preferred to work with his offspring grouped about him. But he did not demand or expect a complete hush, and was apt to keep the radio (a fairly new invention) blaring out a sequence of noisy programmes – a popular concert, the report of a boxing-match, a political broadcast or a scientific talk. Though he seldom listened attentively, the sheer volume of sound they produced had a beneficent effect upon his nerves. Certainly, they did nothing to impair his extraordinary gift of concentration. He worked steadily, his gold-rimmed spectacles glinting and his long hand swiftly moving, while his picture of a seventeenth-century manor-house or an eighteenth-century wind-mill – he was now preparing Volume II of 'the Books' – took clear and energetic shape upon a sheet of Bristol-board.

Next, it was my mother's turn. Having inked in the architectural background with a devoted attention to perspective – my father was almost as enamoured of linear perspective as the Italian artist, Paolo Uccello,* said to have been its first successful exponent – he left a series of neat blank spaces in the foreground of his drawing. These spaces would hold my mother's figures; he had never learned himself to depict the human body; and, placing the sheet on my mother's desk, he briskly indicated the kind of personages that she should devise to fill them. A large square

* The artist's widow 'used to relate how Paolo would spend the whole night in his study . . . and, when she called him to bed, would reply "*Oh che dolce cosa è questa prospettiva.*" ' Giorgio Vasari: *The Lives of the most excellent Italian Architects, Painters & Sculptors*. 1550.

called for a man on horseback; an oblong gap, for a woman and a pretty, lively child. And here, slightly behind the woman, perhaps it would be amusing to insert 'a rather jolly little terrier'. My mother complied – but, since she would have preferred to be painting portraits or landscapes, at times, I think, with some reluctance. Now and then the division of loyalties she felt seems to have had a certain effect upon her style. Occasionally the figures she drew appear a trifle lackadaisical, and fall into the odd positions that, in affectionate fun, I named her 'Anglo-Saxon attitudes'. Her inability to represent horses always caused her deep vexation; and she solved the problem by taking hints from the work of earlier illustrators, even going so far as to borrow a whole horse if she were especially tired and hard-pressed. Once she had completed her task, my father brought up the background to join the outlines of the figures, and added the artists' joint initials, M. & C. H. B. Q. cunningly laced together in a decorative monogram. He designed it, as a symbol of their happy partnership, with particularly loving care.

My father was not, nor did he pretend to be, a regularly trained historian. There were several such historians, including the celebrated George Macaulay Trevelyan, established in or near Berkhamsted; and I noticed that, although they approved my father's efforts, they were apt to regard his treatment of historical subjects from a faintly condescending point of view. Since his education had been cut short as soon as he had left school, he was partly self-educated. Eager to learn and quick to absorb ideas, he lacked an academic sense of order; and, should a speculative theory have become fixed in his mind, it proved almost impossible to dislodge. The scholarly habit of first considering and annotating one's sources, and then recording one's conclusions, was entirely alien to his nature; he researched and wrote at the same time – a practice that, in my own writings, I regret I have too often followed – and greeted every accession of knowledge with enthusiastic pleasure. Thus, after he had covered English social history between 1066 and 1799, he turned to prehistoric ages; and, having plunged into a study of the glacial and inter-glacial periods, he was deeply fascinated by what he read concerning the progressions and regressions of the northern ice-cap and their allegedly astronomical causes; which led him to a fresh examination of the solar system as a whole. Driving a knitting-needle through a large orange to represent the axis of the globe, he would explain how the earth revolved around the sun, and the moon around the earth, the background of his demonstration being the dining-room table-cloth, where a series of glasses and forks and spoons were employed to stand in for the other planets.

He had a jackdaw-mind; but the literary nest he built and furnished has weathered the storms of over half a century. His books are still bought at the rate of some thousands a year, and have had innumerable imitators, not only perhaps because they are copiously illustrated and densely crammed with interesting facts, but because they reflect the vivid enjoyment that he derived from writing them. Later, when I was asked to revise the text, I eliminated various quirks and oddities. My father could seldom resist an anecdote, if it supplied, he felt, the necessary 'human touch'; and there were a number of domestic topics that he found disproportionately engrossing. One was sanitation. On his visits to medieval castles, he would immediately look out for the 'garderobes', the rude privies that drained into the moat, and that the builders usually constructed behind an angle of the stairs; and even his account of the English nineteenth century is accompanied by several full-page diagrams, showing different types of water-closet. These, I decided, had better be cut down. But there was nothing morbid about the attention my father paid to the garderobe and its progeny. The benefits of really sound drainage he had appreciated since his youth; and then, there was the value he attached to a certain kind of frankness; for, although sexual references shocked and disgusted him, regarding the body's humbler functions he was very far from squeamish, and would leave our own lavatory, just as he entered the house, with the greatest possible degree of noise.

During my adolescence his character changed little. He had aged, of course; the decorative forelock that crowned his high forehead was now becoming sparse and grey. His face was heavily lined; in the well-worn ready-made clothes he wore he no longer took the smallest interest; and, beneath a starched round-ended collar, surmounting a striped flannel shirt, his tie

86

had usually slipped down to disclose a solid metal stud. Yet he retained, at least in his public existence, some traces of the old panache; and, although he was subject to moods of dark depression, his spirits very often soared. He was still inspiring, demanding, frequently exasperating; and he still directed the course of my mother's life with his old high-handed gusto. Towards members of the outer world the attitude he adopted was generally amiable rather than particularly hospitable; he was a gregarious, good-natured man, to whom friendship, in the last resort, had never meant a great deal. As at Four Beeches, he was apt to discourage visitors; and I cannot recollect a single dinner-party being given at our new house. We were a secluded household, but sufficiently pleased with ourselves to find our isolation right and natural.

Of the visitors who did arrive, there was none I liked so much as my mother's old friend Nelly. Their association dated back to the art-school, where the slapdash brilliance of Nelly's drawings had delighted her contemporaries, though she was always too vague and hopelessly ill-organized to win the prizes she deserved. Her father, M. Forestier, a prolific French draughtsman, had come to London in the eighteen-nineties, and, having joined the staff of the *Illustrated London News* – it had once employed Constantin Guys – helped to fill its pages with the large monochrome plates that in those days took the place of photographs, sometimes depicting an important contemporary scene, sometimes providing illustrations for an historical or archaeological essay. He painted, too; and among the most stimulating events of my early school-days was my first visit to the Forestiers' house at Dulwich. A big Victorian villa called Lutetia – the name, I learned, of the Gallic fishing village that developed into modern Paris – it had bleak lofty rooms, a dark and cavernous basement, and a shaggy overgrown garden. On to this garden opened the artist's studio; and there hung a twenty-foot canvas, which represented the poet François Villon, in a picturesque medieval tavern, drinking deep and declaiming his verses to a crowd of ruffianly admirers. Never before had I heard Villon's name; and, when his story was explained to me, it captured my imagination, as did the apparatus of the studio itself – a lay-figure propped against the wall, the easels, the range of paint-clotted brushes, the palettes, palette-knives and mahlsticks.

In later years I often returned to Lutetia and, under Nelly's affectionate guidance, spent a day or two there. Although the Forestiers had lived so long in Dulwich, they had little real connection with suburban London; and, during the course of years, they appeared to have become still more distinctly and incorrigibly French. Their exotic habits enchanted me; and the fact that M. Forestier was both an artist and a Frenchman made him doubly impressive. If he fell short of genius, he unquestionably looked the part. Short and strong-limbed, he had a splendid curling beard; while a large aureole of thick grizzled hair stood up around his noble head. His children usually called him 'Papa'; but Nelly and I, both great lovers of ancient myth and legend, secretly nick-named him '*le père Zeus*'; and, besides possessing an air of Homeric majesty, he spoke in thunderous Olympian tones. Particularly dramatic were his occasional fits of rage. He hated stickiness; and finding the smallest trace of treacle or marmalade on a door-knob or a piece of cutlery was enough to infuriate him beyond endurance, and send him bellowing back towards his studio. His wife, however – a small, unsmiling, dark-clothed woman, whose face had the wizened texture of an old prune – was so patient and unobtrusive as to be practically invisible. They had three children – Nelly, the favourite, who alone could please and manage Papa; her elder sister, with whom Nelly perpetually bickered; and a gentle, retiring son, Marius, who, after Nelly and his father and mother had died, was to meet a tragic solitary end.

I enjoyed every aspect of the Forestiers' way of life, even their prodigious quarrels; and, when we dined at the house of some French neighbours, and an animated discussion began over the British treatment of certain German prisoners-of-war (which was regarded as unduly lax) it delighted me to watch the contestants almost bounding from their chairs, as they leaned forward across the shaken coffee-cups with wild declamatory gesticulations. During my first visits to Lutetia, I doubt if I was much more than ten; and we had not yet removed to Berkhamsted. But, after our move, Nelly would frequently join us there like some bright-feathered bird of passage, scattering her strange possessions around our humdrum premises and imposing her odd, extravagant habits upon our staid domestic routine; so that our bathroom began to smell of the powerful foreign scents she used, and the preparations she employed to soften the hard Berkhamstedian tap-water left an unsightly line (my father grumbled) about the inner surfaces of bath and basin. Myself I found her, and all her doings and sayings, irresistibly attractive. I adored my mother, and still worshipped the series of little girls of whom I have already written; but the feeling I entertained for my mother's friend had a very different quality. It involved both heart and mind, and had much of the strength, without any of the disruptive effects of a genuine adult passion.

How completely a human being vanishes! None of the Forestiers I knew is alive today. And, although her sister married, and she may have had nephews and nieces, since my mother's death who now remembers Nelly? The only portrait that time has spared is a faded cutting from a newspaper, which my mother must have snipped out, and which I discovered several months ago between the pages of an old book. There she is young – when I met her, of course, she was nearly middle-aged; and a bridesmaid's veil envelops her black hair and frames her keen romantic features. It is a seductive, almost a beautiful face, the mouth sensuous and finely drawn; while naturally dark circles, often seen in Frenchwomen of southern birth, surround the large and brilliant eyes. Above all else, it has a vivid, enquiring gleam; and there is something about it – *'quelque chose d'ardent et de triste'** – that immediately commands attention. The face of a young woman, one would have said, bound for great successes and for high adventures. Yet Nelly was destined to fail in life; she remained the reluctant prisoner of her obligations; and every effort she made to escape her domestic servitude ultimately came to grief. The fault was partly her own. She had ambitions and talents; but she could never carry through her plans. Having left her art-school, she had chosen to earn her living as an independent dress-designer. But the dress she had promised to produce for some special occasion was seldom completed at the time agreed;

* 'J'ai trouvé la définition du Beau, de mon Beau. C'est quelque chose d'ardent et de triste . . .' Charles Baudelaire: *Journaux Intimes*.

and she would reach her client's house, already behindhand, carrying a pile of unsewn tissues, and do her best to stitch them into shape upon the wearer's restive body.

Despite their joint regard, my mother and Nelly were somewhat ill-assorted friends. Nelly, I suspected, was in some ways the more experienced of the two; and many years had passed, and Nelly herself had died, before my mother, whose desultory conversation sometimes threw out unexpected sparks, told me a curious and pathetic tale. Nelly, she said, was thought at one time to have been passionately involved with an old acquaintance of her father's, like M. Forestier a foreign artist and a diligent contributor to English illustrated magazines. I knew his name well; I also knew his drawings – historical scenes that covered an extraordinary range of subjects, from prehistoric times and the Roman Empire to the Middle Ages and the present century. The background of every scene is depicted in painstaking detail; and the figures that occupy the foreground have all the solidity of a carefully posed and brightly illuminated waxwork-show. Silks gleam; a polished breast-plate flashes; the eyeballs glisten and the muscles bulge. Meanwhile, I happen to have acquired a photograph of the artist in his old age, his virile Italian features characterized by a piercing deep-set glance, a determined mouth and a handsome hooked nose. A few years older than Nelly, he must indeed have been a compulsive personage when she first encountered him; and, although, of course, there is no solid evidence to support my mother's story, it is not difficult to imagine a love-affair springing up between the adventurous artist and the restless home-bound girl, which, broken off in circumstances unexplained, may have done her lasting damage.

It seems clear that, at the time I knew her, she was a frustrated and unhappy woman, and that much of the love she had failed to place elsewhere, was now bestowed, luckily for myself, upon her old friend's elder son. She enlarged my view and quickened my love of life – that, of the many debts I owe her, was probably the most valuable. Yet, looking back, I cannot feel quite sure exactly what it was I learned. Her knowledge was limited; she was not deeply read; and, as the daughter of an old-fashioned academic artist, she had little use for modern painting. If she broadened my mind, it was through the affection she showed me and the constantly enlivening interest that she took in my development. What did we talk about while, my arm beneath hers, we wandered round the airy Common? Frequently, I suppose, about my own attempts to write. Nelly was an affectionate ally, but a stern unsparing critic. One effort, she said, was good; another, '*tirée par les cheveux*', unmistakably forced and artificial. She was anxious, however, that I should not neglect my health and become a mere etiolated *homme de lettres*. I must study the physique of Greek statues, and every morning, as soon as I got up, perform Dr Müller's 'Swedish exercises'. The pattern of physical perfection she wished me to emulate was the famous French boxer Georges Carpentier, who read poetry, consorted with literary men, yet had the solid, well-proportioned frame of a twentieth-century Apollo.

On other occasions she entered more dubious ground, and would branch off into such subjects as magic, astrology and demonology. She believed in magic, black and white, and informed me that every human being, or disembodied spirit, possessed an individual 'aura' – a large circumference of shimmering light that, at least to the trained eye, now and then revealed itself. Thus, she had glimpsed one day, she said, a commonplace middle-aged man, hurrying along a Dulwich street, clothed in the murky brown fog that indicated his secretly satanic nature, and had observed a heavenly presence, clad in delicate iridescent hues, hovering beside her bed. Though she did not cast spells or attempt to invoke spirits, she had learned to predict the future by the method known as 'geomancy', that necessitated drawing up an elaborate diagram of the various planetary houses and filling them in with the help of the random dashes I was inspired to make upon a separate sheet of paper. Excited by Nelly's example, I, too, became an amateur occultist, and eagerly awaited some dramatic revelation of the mysterious world surrounding us, peopled by spirits good and bad, fairies, demons, elementals. None was granted me; evidently I was rooted to the earth. Yet I retained my interest in the study of magic throughout the first two or three terms I spent at Oxford, where I purchased a folio copy of Cornelius Agrippa's *De Occulta Philosophia* from an antiquarian bookshop, and passed unprofitable hours attempting to translate the author's crabbed dog-Latin.

Nelly was also an excellent story-teller; and the memoirs of the eighteenth-century Marquise de Créqui (which I have since discovered to be a largely spurious work) and other volumes of the same kind provided a fund of anecdotes, grotesque, fantastic, even mildly erotic, with which she amused me on our expeditions. We made a remarkable pair – Nelly, no longer young and beautiful, but gay, flamboyant and expansive; her companion, a thin, pale, hollow-chested youth, wearing a coloured school-cap. Our association was frankly sentimental – I kissed Nelly and she readily returned my kisses; yet I never lost my innocence. Nor had I any desire to do so; and, later, when I noticed that embracing Nelly and reading *Hero and Leander* was apt to provoke a slightly similar reaction, I was prudish enough, or perhaps sufficiently cautious, to resolve that henceforward I must be somewhat less demonstrative.

My parents, however, were clearly a little worried by our peculiar relationship. 'Dear old Nelly', as one of my mother's closest friends, was obviously above suspicion; and they trusted her completely. But they could not help noticing the delight with which I greeted her appearance, and the profound dejection with which I saw her go. For several days I remained silent, abstracted, gloomy, while I awaited the promised letter from Dulwich, written in purple ink and a boldly sloping foreign scrawl. My emotions were those of a lover; and her attitude towards me bore some resemblance to that of a beloved mistress. Our relations were not unclouded; sharply and dreadfully I would be made to understand that I had fallen out of favour. She became remote, moody, unresponsive, yet refused to explain what I had done or said that could have merited such chilling treatment. Again and again I begged for elucidation; but 'Haven't you heard the old saying, "*Souvent femme varie*"?' was the only response I could evoke.

III

I WAS LUCKY, I THINK, TO INHABIT BERKHAMSTED, though, during the days I lived there, I often detested and despised the place. Not only did it provide some stimulating friends, among whom were one or two professional writers; but all about it opened the green perspectives of a beautifully various landscape. To the north, for instance, straight across the Common, I could ride or bicycle through Ashridge Park, with its broad oak-lined avenues and majestic colonnades of beech; and, leaving Ashridge, the road curved down to Aldbury, a pretty secluded old village built beside a large pond. Near the pond stood a worm-eaten pair of stocks; and, close to the village, the red-brick manor-house, apparently named after them, that until 1920 had been the home of Matthew Arnold's niece, Mrs Humphrey Ward.* Immediately behind her house, another steep road climbed the escarpment of the Chilterns, a lengthy wind-swept ridge surmounted by Ivinghoe Beacon and its commanding prehistoric barrow.

The Beacon looked out many miles across the placid Vale of Aylesbury; and one day, walking near the barrow and happening to disturb a mole-hill, I unearthed in the chalky soil a yellowed wolf's tooth, which an authority at the British Museum identified as originally part of a necklace manufactured by a Stone Age hunter, pointing out that the eye pierced through the end had been ingeniously 'counter-bored' – the maker had used his flint gimlet to grind two opposite convergent holes. Such expeditions formed the imaginative background of my life. I remember, for

---

* Henry James, who, perhaps rather disingenuously, professed to entertain the 'profoundest respect' for his fellow story-teller's 'cleverness', visited her at Stocks, accompanied by Edith Wharton, his 'Angel of Devastation', in June 1909. Later, the young Aldous Huxley often stayed there with his literary aunt.

example, a summer evening when a bonfire had been lighted on the Beacon – just why I can no longer recollect; and I and two or three friends bicycled from Berkhamsted to Ivinghoe past the row of limes that bordered Mrs Ward's garden, and I breathed in the heavy honeyed fragrance of the unseen lime-flowers far above. Later, trees were succeeded by hedges; and amid the tangled grass-verges that followed the course of the road shone innumerable glow-worms, each solitary mysterious insect tented in its own green-golden light. At that time, glow-worms were fairly plentiful. Today those delicate love-lamps have been almost all extinguished.

It was not difficult to feed my imagination; but simultaneously I sought for knowledge, outside the somewhat restricted ground that my father's studies covered; and here I made a series of valuable acquaintances. Among Berkhamstedian writers, George Macaulay Trevelyan was unquestionably the most distinguished. By birth and marriage alike – his wife was a daughter of Mrs Humphrey Ward – he belonged to the intellectual *haute bourgeoisie*, the renowned group of families that included the Arnolds, the Huxleys, the Stracheys, the Wedgwoods and the Darwins; and he had all the virtues, and some of the limitations, of that proudly self-sufficient clan. He offended my father, I recollect, by reading him a short lecture, which my father judged superfluous, on the meaning of the word 'humanism'. But to me, though often slightly stern, he proved a sympathetic mentor; and at times I was allowed to join him while he tramped at breakneck speed through woods and fields.

He had silver hair, a bristling silver moustache and narrow silver-rimmed spectacles; and his talk displayed a rare blend of puritan unworldliness and unobtrusive worldly shrewdness. Humour he certainly did not lack; and one curious anecdote he told me seems to merit preservation. His father, Sir George Otto Trevelyan, had been himself an historian and a well-known civil servant; and, as he lay dying (his son said) his children had become aware that there was a message, or important piece of information he was labouring desperately to impart. Years earlier, he had published a biographical portrait of his famous uncle, Thomas Babington Macaulay; and now, when they bent above his pillow, they caught a single faltering sentence. 'Uncle Tom,' Sir George Otto murmured indistinctly, 'wasn't *quite* – a gentleman . . .' At that point he lost the power of speech; and exactly what he meant – Macaulay, after all, had passed muster among the haughtiest Whig grandees – the historian admitted that he could not tell.

Less celebrated – and bravely conscious of the fact – was my old friend Esmé Wingfield-Stratford, a fine specimen, so long as he lived, of the eccentric English scholar, who had a high, light, whistling upper-class voice, cheeks as round and roseate as those of a plump schoolboy, and an enormously expansive frame. Once a Fellow of King's, he had settled down at Berkhamsted to write a long series of historical and controversial works that, except for a popular history of British Patriotism, had never received from reviewers the amount of attention that he felt they had deserved. He wrote poems, too, both serious and ribald, and passionately adored music, which he played himself – not on a piano, however, but on a decrepit pianola, first inserting a slotted parchment roll, then bending over the keyboard and, by manipulating various brass pedals, imparting the right degree of tone and volume, while he did so loudly puffing and snorting in bold imitation of a virtuoso pianist. Dear Esmé! he was the kindest of the fellow writers to whom I showed my verses; and he possessed a fund of literary knowledge – around the library chair he filled and overflowed books were piled up knee-deep – that he poured out for my benefit with unbounded generosity. Like Nelly, an even earlier critic, he seemed to throw wide an unending succession of intellectual doors and windows.

Near Berkhamsted, though some miles from its centre, three very different historians had set up house – Richard Henry Tawney, author of *The Acquisitive Society* and *Religion and the Rise of Capitalism*, and Barbara and J. L. Hammond, joint-authors of *The Village Labourer*, *The Town Labourer* and *The Skilled Labourer*, volumes that throw a painstaking, if distinctly partial light upon the history of the British working classes. Tawney I never knew; but the Hammonds I presently met and found an odd, endearing couple – old-fashioned Fabian Socialists, belonging to the same high-minded school as Beatrice and Sidney Webb. Several years earlier, each had developed symptoms of pulmonary tuberculosis; and they had therefore removed from London to a modest country house, where, besides spending their nights on a draughty open verandah, they had taken up riding. Their horsemanship was mediocre even by my own standards; and the two horses they had purchased were ageing, inoffensive beasts, which, since they were permanently put out to grass and can have very seldom seen an oat, grew increasingly lethargic. Nor were they often groomed. The Hammonds in the saddle, jogging along the skyline, made a strangely picturesque impression – Mr Hammond wearing a starched collar and a hispid knickerbocker suit; Barbara Hammond, who rode side-saddle and was roundish, small and pink-faced, a big flower-wreathed straw hat and a gauzy floating scarf; while their horses' manes and tails, lengthy and unkempt, drifted out against the breeze.

Very occasionally, they broke into a slow trot; for a moment or two, at the beginning of a ride, they might perhaps attempt a quiet canter. But, as a rule, they walked – the gait their mounts preferred; and, when I accompanied Mr Hammond, as I sometimes did if his wife were indisposed, I was promptly checked should I presume to quicken our pace by a single word or nudge. The Hammonds were ardent humanitarians; they were also vegetarians; and their house was decorated with signed photographs, pleasant Italian water-colour sketches and faded reproductions of the Old Masters. A devoted pair, lively and energetic, they radiated an air of bright untroubled innocence. They were splendid representations of the school of Socialist thought, based on a firm belief in the dignity of the individual human being, that Communism and fascism combined were very soon to sweep away.

Finally we had a successful imaginative writer living in the town itself. W. W. Jacobs had made his name with a collection of humorous stories entitled *Many Cargoes*, published a quarter of a century earlier; and, while I lived at Berkhamsted, his reputation as a popular humorist (who had also produced one excellent ghost-story, 'The Monkey's Paw') still attracted many readers on either side of the Atlantic Ocean. His favourite subjects were skippers and bargees; his tales had a breezily rollicking turn. Yet a man of gloomier aspect has rarely come my way. Short and meagre, his red-rimmed eyes set in a shrunken yellow face, he was never seen to smile, but moved silently, when he emerged from his study, which smelt of stale cigar-smoke, around the big Edwardian house he and his family inhabited on the road between Berkhamsted High Street and the hill-top playing-fields. Among his children and his children's friends, though we were aware of his taciturn disapproval, he attracted little notice; and it was evident that he and his handsome talkative wife – Mrs Jacobs was said to have been a close associate of H. G. Wells, and to have received her reward by having her portrait drawn in an un-distinguished *roman-à-clef* – pursued entirely separate courses. Mrs Jacobs, a former suffragette, held liberal and progressive views. Her clothes were made of rough hand-woven fabrics; and she wore the kind of 'peasant jewellry' that Socialist craftsmen, living in Sussex villages, then hammered out for local sale.

At the Jacobs' house I first met Evelyn Waugh. Their eldest daughter, Barbara, I learned, had just become engaged to his elder brother Alec, who, in 1917, at the age of nineteen, had pro-duced a novel called *The Loom of Youth*, a picture of public-school life that, because it suggested, discreetly and inoffensively, that homosexual relations were sometimes practised by English middle-class boys, had shocked and astounded the contemporary reading public. Presently the author himself arrived – as rubicund, un-pretentious and good-natured then as he would be in the 1970s. Accompanying him, on that occasion, was the adolescent Evelyn. Still at school, he was a lively, cheerful youth, fresh-cheeked and bright-eyed, with a gaily inquisitive expression, wearing a dandified pearl-grey suit and, I seem to recollect, a yellow waistcoat. I enjoyed our meeting; but we did not meet again until I had gone up to Oxford, whither he preceded me. About the same time, I acquired the friendship of another future novelist, Graham Greene, my austere headmaster's son.

If I had not encountered him as soon as I reached Berkhamsted, it may have been because he was a little older; and in 1920, his autobiography explains,* he had been temporarily released from school-work after suffering a nervous breakdown. On his return, however, we became friends, and he used to accompany me on

* *A Sort of Life*, 1971.

my rides across the Common, where (he writes) 'Quennell always rode a far more spirited horse than mine, galloped faster, jumped higher.' This is a tribute I was flattered to read; but Graham's memory has played him false. The hack I rode was by no means spirited; and I have seldom taken a jump if it could possibly be ridden round. Far less vaguely I remember our conversations and the books that we exchanged – for instance, *Madame Bovary*, not the kind of novel that either his father or mine would have encouraged us to open. His talk had an exuberantly sceptical and blithely pessimistic turn; and his contemplation of the horrors of human life appeared to cause him unaffected pleasure. His pessimism did nothing to sour his temperament; while Evelyn Waugh would change beyond all knowledge, the young and the old Greene have remained relatively consubstantial. At each fresh insight he obtained into human absurdity or wickedness, his pallid, faintly woebegone face would assume an air of solemn glee.

We both intended to write; and by 1920 I had made an unexpected leap forward. That year I submitted some pieces to a new anthology, entitled *Public School Verse*, which Richard Hughes and two of his Oxford associates were assembling for publication. The editors welcomed them; and, when the anthology emerged, it received sympathetic notices. My contribution, 'The Masque of the Three Beasts', a fantastic piece of *vers libre*, to which I had attached an introductory note, 'This is absolutely serious', was described by the critic of the *Daily Chronicle* as 'exquisite in its whimsicality and fanciful satire, a dream picture of grotesque charm and quaint dramatisation'. And, a year later, when a second volume appeared, certain journalists, sometimes under the entirely mistaken belief that I was parodying modern poetry, added further words of praise. Under the head-line 'Schoolboy's Weird Poem', the *Evening Standard* gave me several long paragraphs. 'All the new poets – Futurist, Imagist, and the rest – must look to their laurels', the reviewer wrote. 'They have been outdone by a schoolboy . . . It is difficult to decide whether Master Quennell is a new genius or an unusually clever and imaginative schoolboy bent on leg-pulling.' The *Morning Post* took me even more seriously. I was 'a budding Maeterlinck', I discovered, 'with a wayward sense of humour'.

I have transcribed these eulogies for various reasons. Not only did they give me, at the time, a much too encouraging idea of my own creative gifts, which may help to explain the somewhat hubristic state of mind in which I finally went up to Oxford; but they reveal a curious contrast between the present day and the far-off Georgian period. Poetry then was still 'news'; and that it existed, and might occasionally be worth discussing, was a fact reluctantly acknowledged by the toughest Fleet Street editors. How many modern journalists would devote a whole half-column to the 'weird' productions of an entirely unknown schoolboy-poet? And then, besides encouraging my natural conceit, my appearance in *Public School Verse* secured me many new friends – Richard Hughes, who introduced me to Edith Sitwell, and Edward Marsh, who civilly sought my acquaintance, and published some work of mine in the last of his famous collections, *Georgian Poetry 1920-1922*. But first he invited me to lunch with him at one of his less distinguished London clubs where, rather than at White's or Brooks's, he entertained his literary guests. I met a small, neat man, wearing an impressive eye-glass beneath a circumflex of tufted eyebrow and a quietly dandified demeanour. His friendly reception of me soon dispelled my alarm and eased my schoolboyish embarrassment; and he seemed doubly delighted to learn that, in addition to writing, I was also fond of drawing. Before long I had become an established protégé, a junior member of the assemblage of poets and artists that he liked to gather round him, and entertained at his comfortable picture-lined flat in Raymond Buildings, Gray's Inn. He would watch my career with deep attention, he wrote on 7 November 1922, 'praying on both knees that you make the best of yourself'.

As our friendship developed, he even expressed a wish to visit my family at Berkhamsted. His week-end visit, however, was not a conspicuous success; the hurly-burly of our family life evidently disconcerted him; and he was pained by being handed a cup of tea without an accompanying spoon. My mother apologized, but remarked that, since Mr Marsh had refused a lump of sugar, she had supposed no spoon was needed. 'It looks so *naked* somehow!' he plaintively replied, peering round his vacant saucer. We were a little relieved, I think, to see him go; nor, I suspect, was he particularly sorry to catch the London train that evening. In his lifetime he was often accused of snobbishness; but, although artists and writers frequently disturbed him by their odd bohemian ways, his social bent never impeded his friendships; and he felt just as privileged to enter an artist's studio, an actor's dressing-room or a poet's country cottage as to attend a fashionable party – during the Season he danced at every ball – or the latest 'brilliant' first night. His artistic protégés soon acquired the status of old and valued personal friends; at an early stage they were begged to call him 'Eddie'; and in certain instances, the warm affection they aroused was apt to militate against his better judgement. Rupert Brooke, the Golden Youth he had adored, was still his literary beau-ideal; and his attitude towards the art of the theatre was similarly prejudiced. Not long after Brooke's death, the young Ivor Novello had made the conquest of his heart; and Eddie would return again and again to any theatre he embellished, and, sitting at the front of the stalls, would now and then shed tears, wiping his eye-glass on a folded silk handkerchief, while the hero exhibited his faultless profile in some peculiarly vapid play.

Yet, as an editor, his tastes were remarkably catholic; and the twenty-one contributors to his closing *Georgian Book*, besides a series of minor versifiers nowadays not often read, included poems by W. H. Davies, Walter de la Mare, Robert Graves, Harold Monro and D. H. Lawrence. 'Snake', Lawrence's prose-poem, was probably the most memorable contribution; but Davies, de la Mare and Harold Monro all deserve an honoured place in early-twentieth-century literature; while Graves, then still working his way through the juvenile stage of his poetic evolution, was to develop into one of the most interesting and consistently creative poets of his day. There was a genuine poetic ferment abroad; poetry was written for its own sake; it had not yet acquired any of the political and ideological bias that would distinguish the brave young men who, between the publication of *The Orators* in 1932 and the outbreak of the Second World War, would follow Wystan Auden's lead.

My own contributions I need not list here. Since their appearance under Edward Marsh's editorship they have occasionally been reprinted and, every time they re-emerged, have earned me two or three guineas. In each I was endeavouring to record a moment of visionary exaltation. That, I thought, was a poem's main purpose; and I still assume that the proper function of poetry is to depict an experience, spiritual or intellectual, that a writer could not effectively express with the help of any other method. Should he succeed, he may be said to produce poetry; should he fail, as he very often does, he is merely versifying, however agreeable the frame of words that he weaves around his subject. Elsewhere I have described the process of crystallization to which, I believe, a poem owes its birth, when some sudden incident precipitates a series of ideas and emotions already vaguely assembled in the poet's mind. 'It was a genuine need that set me versifying as much as a youthful desire to make my mark; and the need was less to convey my sensations . . . than to release the tension that had been built up by the secret pressure of many different feelings, which might include both the pleasure I felt at the beauty of the world beneath my eyes and the emotions derived from a book first opened several days earlier. In combination they had engendered a state of excitement that could only be relieved if I attempted to write a poem; and, during the attempt, I sought to produce a pattern of rhythmic and evocative words, through which the tension that excited and troubled me might be accounted for and exorcized. Writing verse, then, was a semimagical manoeuvre; and the result I aimed at was not an exact description of something I had felt or seen, but its symbolic equivalent, realized by the powers of language.'* The verses I inscribed were primarily spells; and, while I composed them, I suffered a period of acute anxiety, lest a 'Person from Porlock' – there were many round about – might perhaps disturb my incantations.

Some, written between the ages of fifteen and twenty-one, possess, I like to think, a certain merit. At least, they have occasional good lines and images, here and there, that have not yet completely faded. All are in *vers libre*. Previously, I had tried my hand at rhyme, often imitating Walter de la Mare, whose fairytale poems then struck me as the quintessence of literary grace.

* *The Sign of the Fish*, 1950.

On a double sheet of foolscap, headed 'Written & sent to me by Peter while away at school', and dated from February to December 1917, my mother carefully copied out thirteen specimens of my juvenilia. My subjects are various; and, here and there, they embody recollections of our memorable stay at Rouen – of the old fountain and of the hats of long-dead cardinals hung beside a Gothic window. I seem to have been much concerned with the antique past, with the flight of time and with agreeably mournful ideas of human transience and evanescence. The effect is stilted and quaint and pretty; and not until I was about fourteen or fifteen did I acquire a more adventurous attitude towards a modern poet's business.

The next few years were full of intense excitement; through my nights and days, amid all the troubles and disturbances of my life at home and school, ran a tenuous thread of visionary emotion, which produced, now and then, the tense, ecstatic mood that compelled me to seek relief in writing. There were moments, however, when it dwindled and declined, and exaltation was suddenly succeeded by a bout of dark depression. My inability to sustain the creative mood often bewildered and enraged me; and once, on the walls of the British Museum, having seen a Graeco-Roman bas-relief* – a representation of Dionysus and his attendants visiting a friend beneath the trellis of a vineyard – that caused me deep, mysterious pleasure, I decided that, if I could hold the scene in my mind and constantly return to it, I should be able to infuse my prosaic daily existence with the same atmosphere of peace and joy. Naturally, I failed, and continued to alternate between euphoria and accidie; but writing verse and becoming 'a great poet' was still my only real ambition. At times I believed that I was well on the way to my goal; and my appearance in the list of Georgian poets gave me added hope and energy.

During the month that saw the publication of *Georgian Poetry*, November 1922, I had a further stroke of luck. Harold Taylor,

---

* Soon after describing this relief, which I had not seen for more than fifty years, I sighted it again among the photographs in the current issue of a London art journal, where it was identified as 'probably a Graeco-Roman copy of an original of the third century B C', that had once belonged to the great collector Charles Towneley.

the proprietor of a private printing-press, to whom I had been introduced by Richard Hughes, suggested that he should bring out a volume of my verses, illustrated with my own drawings. Issued on November 4, MCMXXII, in a nicely printed and handsomely bound edition of '375 numbered copies for sale in Britain & 175 numbered copies for sale in America', it must now be a very rare book; though it is not the kind of rarity, alas, that arouses much interest among contemporary bibliophiles. My own copy I long ago destroyed; but latterly I inherited the copy that I had presented to my mother. The drawings are vaguely Beardsleyesque, and have remarkably little relationship with the verses they surround, some of which came out simultaneously under Eddie Marsh's aegis. Still, I was proud of the volume, reflecting that not many poets, at the age of seventeen, had read their names upon a title-page, and felt more than ever determined to fulfil Eddie's sanguine expectations.

Producing a self-portrait is always a difficult task; and it becomes doubly difficult when the person to be represented stands over half a century away. The chief virtue this far-off self revealed was a determined single-mindedness – the 'undaunted courage of a virgin mind', to borrow a phrase from one of Blake's lyrics. I believed that I was a poet by vocation; and only when I wrote a poem, though I had many other pursuits – I practised a variety of delightful arts and crafts, painted, drew and even carved – did I feel that I was really living. As for my vices, they were those which disfigure every ambitious adolescent. I was conceited, irritable, self-pleased, an odd mixture of literary arrogance and disabling worldly ignorance. I had made few expeditions into the world that lay outside my parents' house; and neither my father nor my mother – my mother through no fault of her own – had had much experience of ordinary social life. My father feared the world, which constantly threatened to distract him from the occupations he preferred; my mother was haunted by the dark anxieties that had pursued her since her childhood; and, once they had to admit I was growing up, they alternately encouraged and discouraged me, with the result that, besides becoming slightly precocious, I remained extraordinarily backward.

I might have been less backward but for my father's theories.

Some curious idea he had long cherished frequently held up my education. On the intellectual plane, he attempted to censor my reading; on the physical, though he often wished that I were more athletic, he obstinately refused to teach me to swim, because he remembered that he had learned the art himself when 'a low gray mother-wave' – here he was quoting from Kipling's *Captains Courageous* – had 'tucked him under one arm' as he splashed on the edge of the water, and shown him how to make his first strokes. Such idiosyncratic theories he frequently supplemented by seeking the advice of any friend or acquaintance whom he happened to encounter. Should his son read *Tom Jones* or the memoirs of Benvenuto Cellini? A helpful assistant at the London Library thought that they were 'strong stuff' for a boy of fifteen; and my father readily agreed, suggesting that, as an alternative, I should try *The Stones of Venice*. I refused; but, luckily, my father's censorship was not consistently enforced; and many books that he had never troubled to open, including Chaucer's collected works, soon found their way into my private library. Though he admired Chaucer's 'Prologue', my father knew nothing of 'The Reeve's Tale' or 'The Miller's Tale'; and my introduction to those lubricious anecdotes proved exciting and disturbing. Thus, as a rule, I had a fairly free run; and today I still own two or three small volumes, each neatly inscribed and dated, that record some stages in my tentative progress through the world of European literature.

In 1918, for example, I acquired Swinburne's *Poems and Ballads I*, which both puzzled and delighted me. I could not understand the poet's preoccupation with the joys of suffering and what he calls 'the sanguine grapes of pain'; but I enjoyed the tumultuous sweep of his verse and, having consulted a classical dictionary, made minutely pencilled notes along the margin of the text – '*Priapus, god of procreation, hence of gardens and vineyards*'; '*Cottyotto, goddess of lewdness*'; and '*Lampsacus, city of Mysia, on the Hellespont*'. Another memorable discovery I made in 1919, when I was presented, perhaps by mistake, with Havelock Ellis's edition of Heine's selected prose-works. 'Florentine Nights' at once became my favourite romantic tale; and, reading the editor's preface, I was deeply moved to learn how Heine, suffering from the last stages of the disease that would soon condemn him to a 'mattress-grave', and already half-paralysed, had crept in May 1848 through the fire-swept streets of revolutionary Paris, until he reached the Louvre, where, sitting beneath the pedestal of his divine protectress, 'our dear lady of Milo', he had begged she would grant him her assistance; and the statue, he imagined, had sadly responded: 'Dost thou not see, then, that I have no arms, and that I cannot help thee'.

Meanwhile, at school, I had embarked on Latin and Greek; and, once I had begun to construe Homer – Butcher and Lang's version of the *Odyssey* was the main present I received for Christmas 1919 – I gradually enlarged my scope. The poems of Theocritus, Bion and Moschus, again translated by Andrew Lang, seem to have reached my private shelves in January 1921; and, during the same period, I purchased *The Greek Anthology*, under the mistaken impression that it covered the classic period of Greek verse, only to find that some of the writers included – for example, Agathias Scholasticus and Paulus Silentarius – were contemporaries of the Emperor Justinian. The first volume, devoted to Amatory Epigrams, though, here and there, the translator abandoned English and gave a modest Latin rendering, turned out to be the most enjoyable. Both Agathias and his friend Paulus celebrate a large variety of mistresses, Rhodope, Rhodanthe, Ariadne, Philinna, Galatea, Chariklo, Laïs, Cleophantis; but Plato, among the earlier poets anthologized, evidently preferred young men – 'kissing Agathon [he declares] I had my soul upon my lips'; and homosexuality, a subject of which, in all the years I spent at an English public school, I had heard comparatively little, became familiar to me through the Greek poets.

It was through books mainly that I extended my knowledge of life; but my sophistication left some odd lacunae. I had gained numerous insights into the nature of sexual love, and knew how children were begotten. As to how they were born I remained absurdly ignorant. When I arrived at Oxford, I still believed that an infant's route of exit must unquestionably be the navel, since that superfluous, if decorative feature seemed to serve no other purpose; until a pencil sketch by William Blake of a woman giving birth – I had undertaken to write a biography of Blake – finally enlightened me. Apart from my habit of relying largely on books, in my efforts to complete my education I had several other disadvantages. I was not courageous, but had inherited much of the timidity of my always apprehensive mother. And then, the old story, which had helped me so much at school – that, besides a weak heart, I had unusually weak nerves – possessed some genuine foundation. I was the victim of many fears and manias, which assumed a peculiarly exaggerated form if I were over-worked or over-tired. Once, for example, alarmed by the un-controllable turmoil of my thoughts, I suspected that I might be going mad; and, happening to open a volume of Shakespeare at Lear's dreadful 'That way madness lies', I felt that I had heard the voice of Fate, and that it confirmed my gloomiest premonitions.

Even worse was the general fear of life that would inexplicably descend on me. Such a fear I had known from early childhood; it was the dark reverse of 'the ecstasy of living' that I now and then experienced;* and occasionally it would assume the shape of a single terrifying or disgusting image. I remember, for example, that, while I was still at St Alfred's, I learned that the school cat – an animal I rarely saw, and of which I was not particularly fond – had tumbled out of an attic window and had been dashed into the basement. A friend happened to observe the cat's agony, and reported that he had found it, left by the servants to die, on a wretched scrap of half-scorched blanket. The fact that I imagined the blanket *charred around the edges* transfixed me with a sudden thrill of horror. That poignant detail, for reasons I could not explain, seemed to epitomize all the misery of physical suffering and all the unspeakable solitude of death. Even today the image will sometimes return; and I know that, so long as I retain the power of remembering, I shall never quite escape from it.

I came to *The Prelude* comparatively late in life – the Romantic poets I preferred were Keats and Shelley; but, when I read it, I learned that Wordsworth, during the wonderful boyhood that he spent at Hawkshead, had himself been divided between an exultant joy of living and the 'terrors, pains and early miseries'

* '*Tout enfant j'ai senti dans mon coeur deux sentiments contradictoires . . l'horreur de la vie et l'extase de la vie.*' Baudelaire: *Journaux Intimes.*

that had overcast his youth. On my own small scale, I experienced, now and then, the same haunting malaise and sense of 'visionary dreariness' that had once afflicted Wordsworth; and, in adolescence, my imaginative malaise began to assume an uncomfortably physical shape. I suffered from violent attacks of nervous nausea, which occurred most often, if I left home, in some odd and unfamiliar place. I loved museums; but, once in the Victoria and Albert Museum, looking down across an immense room that was crowded from wall to wall with musical instruments, virginals, harpsichords, spinets and early-nineteenth-century pianos, I felt dismayed, even deeply terrified, almost to the verge of fainting. Later, the fear of 'feeling sick', should I venture out among people I did not know, regularly tormented me. Nausea clutched my throat; a cold sweat beaded my forehead. Yet I did not disgrace myself; and the wave of apprehension would unexpectedly recede, as the peace of mind I thought I had lost for ever gradually flowed back again.

Later still, though this particular affliction had passed, I would suffer – at long intervals, but with painful acuteness – from a slightly different kind of panic, the 'dark feeling of mysterious dread' that both William James and George Borrow have described, and that Borrow, whom it sometimes reduced to a state of agonized distraction, called 'the Horrors' or 'the Fear'. I have already attempted to discuss its origins myself, and have suggested that there may be a hidden connection between neurotic anxiety and the imaginative, creative mood,* which results from a secret anxiety that has been resolved and subjugated. In my own case, I was the child of anxious parents; and I tended to follow their example. Every member of my family, except for my stalwart brother Paul – and even Paul had his disturbed moments – assumed that he or she was 'highly-strung', a condition we were apt to regard as the badge of our intellectual and moral superiority rather than a serious failing. Nor did it greatly impede our progress. My mother and father continued to produce 'the Books'; and, after one or two brief reverses at school – the hideous problem of the Greek irregular verbs had plunged me into deep despair – I climbed steadily from form to form. I gained a

* *The Sign of the Fish.*

succession of useful bursaries and scholarships; and then heard that sitting for a Balliol scholarship was to be my next move.

Thus, in 1922, beneath my father's protective wing – at that period I seldom travelled alone – I went up by train to Oxford, completed my examination-papers, which I found a fairly simple task, and was interviewed by an array of good-natured dons, assembled at dinner around the table of the Senior Common Room. My surroundings awed me; I did not expect to succeed; and I was astonished when a letter reached Berkhamsted informing me that I had gained the English Scholarship, and could embark on my undergraduate life once the autumn term began. It was considered, however, that, as I was not yet eighteen, I might be well advised to wait another year. My father and Dr Greene assented. But, during the interval, what was I to do? My parents, with greater boldness than usual, thought that, to broaden my knowledge of life, I should spend the intervening period at a foreign university. Soon afterwards, alas, they changed their minds; such a plan would be expensive; and at home I remained, restless and bored and unsettled, until October 1923.

Those months of waiting did me little good. Hitherto, for all the discomforts of Crabtrees and the many peculiar limitations of the life we lived there, I had readily accepted our domestic pattern. Now it became, if not unbearable, far more difficult to tolerate; and I dreamed of inhabiting a large, carpeted, curtained house where the floors would never creak, or the wastepipes be heard discharging their contents in a hoarse torrential flood. My mother, she freely admitted herself, was an ineffective manager. She detested housework; the cooks she employed were always sadly untrained; and, although as a young woman she had appreciated small luxuries, her taste had been gradually worn down by my father's quiet opposition. I longed to escape from Berkhamsted, and seized every opportunity that came my way of exploring the world that lay beyond its frontiers.

I have described elsewhere my first visit to Edith Sitwell,* and how Richard Hughes and I, having climbed three or four flights of forbidding stairs, confronted the famous woman in all her Gothic elegance, sheathed in a golden robe, and wearing a

* op. cit.

cap, or toque, of gilded feathers, with many encrusted rings on her long noble hands, and on her breast a large jewelled cross that had once belonged to Cagliostro. Besides providing this important introduction, Richard Hughes also welcomed me at his lonely Welsh cottage among the wild Snowdonian mountains. The whole neighbourhood was full of ghosts and spectres, including, he told me, a phantom dog that pattered up and down the mountain paths; and almost every farmhouse that he pointed out had some strange and dismal history – a tale of incest or murder or suicide – concealed behind its white-washed walls. In a sudden burst of sunshine, as one looked from Hughes's threshold, one saw a dark far-off figure wandering alone between the slate-roofed sheds, and caught the deep cadences of a melancholy Welsh hymn echoing across the valley.

My visit ended when I trod on a rusty scythe that nearly clove my foot in half. For some time I did not return to Wales; and the next expedition I undertook was a great deal more ambitious. A photograph of the theatre at Taormina had filled me with a passionate desire to visit Sicily, to spend an hour among those broken Greek columns, and follow the three-fold curve of Etna smoothly declining towards the Mediterranean. At any cost, I felt I must go there. It proved a difficult assignment. Richard Hughes had agreed that he would meet me en route, which greatly reassured my father; and at length I succeeded in collecting the money I needed by selling pen and ink drawings to the local editor of a scholastic magazine. Thus I accumulated thirty or forty pounds and, after considerable discussion and argument, set out during the spring holidays.

It was the second time that I had left England; and, until Richard Hughes could join me in Rome, I was a solitary traveller. I knew very little about foreign travel; nor had my unsophisticated father troubled to instruct me. Having never had to tip a porter myself, I had a vague notion that tipping was optional rather than obligatory; and, when I arrived in Paris and reached the Gare de Lyon, lacking any coin that seemed to be of the right size – my paper money had been stuffed into a secret pocket – I decided I would merely shake the porter's hand; whereat, as I mounted the steps of the carriage, he laid hold upon my coat-tails and vigorously dragged me down again. Other humiliations awaited me – but, at the same time, what a wealth of pleasures! Opening my eyes, for example, while dawn broke, and, through the steamy carriage-window, seeing an immense sub-Alpine landscape, terraced, bare and tawny-brown, lit up by the delicate pink explosions of the springtime almond trees.

In Rome I quickly found my bearings. At the hotel I occupied in the Piazza di Spagna, an old-fashioned German-Swiss establishment that has long ago vanished, the waiters would lean casually against the back of my chair, and use my table, when I lunched or dined, as a ledge for stacking unused crockery. But once I had emerged from the hotel and explored the city itself, I was perpetually enchanted – by a fountain-head, with a mossy grotto behind it, in the angle of a flight of ancient steps; Bernini's weathered elephant, supporting a miniature obelisk, in a piazza near the Pantheon; or the huge marble foot, the thongs of an antique sandal bound between its massive toes, still planted upon the pavement of a busy modern street,* among scraps of vegetable refuse, discarded lottery tickets and the crumpled sheets of old newspapers.

It was a warm spring; branches of purple-flowering Judas trees leaned over yellow garden-walls; and, 'buried in air, the deep blue sky of Rome',† the city seemed both vastly solid and divinely insubstantial, such was the miraculous quality of the light that suffused and transfigured every prospect. During the mid-1920s it was a relatively quiet place; and one heard the constant plash of water, a sound nowadays almost swallowed up by the hellish roar of traffic. Near my hotel gurgled Bernini's *Barcaccia*, the barque-shaped fountain spouting broad jets through the mouths of stone cannon on which Keats must so often have gazed from his cheerless rooms above the Spanish Steps, as he thought of Fanny Brawne and his own approaching extinction, and considered the miserable destiny of a poet who felt that he had lived and loved and worked in vain.

When Richard Hughes appeared, however, we very soon left Rome for Sicily, crossed the Straits of Messina and reached

* At the corner of the Via S. Stefano del Cacco and the Via Pie'di Marmo.
† Byron: *Childe Harold*, Canto IV.

Palermo. I was sensible enough to admire Monreale, where shafts of dusty sunshine slanted through Easter incense-smoke, the red Moorish domes and palm-shaded cloisters of S. Giovanni degli Eremeti, and the glimmering golden mosaics of the Capella Palatina. But at Girgenti, the ancient Akragas (renamed by Mussolini Agrigento), I gained my poetic destination. As we crossed the plateau of volcanic rock along which its ruined temples stand, we stumbled on a small orchard, sunk in a stony crevice, crowded with orange and lemon trees, simultaneously blossoming and bearing fruit; while amid the deep, lush grass below sprang the pale-green stalks and bright saffron-yellow petals of the flower called *Oxalis stricta*. Neither the orange nor the lemon was known by Europeans until the Middle Ages; but here, I thought, was a perfect realization of the Theocritean landscape; and I was afterwards glad to learn that the inhabitants of Akragas had been an especially carefree and pleasure-loving people, who, said Plato, designed their magnificent shrines and houses as if they had no idea of death, and dined as if they expected that today's feast might be the last they would enjoy.

I returned to Berkhamsted a hardened man of the world, at least in my own sanguine view, capable of confronting the surliest porter or the most intransigent head-waiter. But I was still avid for knowledge. While middle-life is a long delaying-action, one of the weaknesses of youth is a refusal to await experience; the clock's hands revolve so sluggishly that again and again we try to push them forward. Many of my notions, as I have already indicated, were principally derived from books; and not all the books I read were worth reading. I admired, for instance, the novels of Compton Mackenzie and the two volumes of Rupert Brooke's poems; and each suggested that a literary young man ought to be surrounded by attractive young women, like Brooke's inconstant nymphs and the exquisite Jennys and Sylvias who danced across Mackenzie's pages, and embark on a love-affair that, should it turn out unhappily, would do him all the more credit. I, therefore, became engaged; but in what circumstances, and after how long a courtship, I must confess I have forgotten. B. was a handsome, modest girl, the only child of a good-humoured middle-aged actress; and her link with the fabulous world of the theatre – her mother regularly toured the provinces in a play that had had a triumphant urban run – was not among her least attractions, and enabled me to weave a romantic garland about her unpretending brows.

I was in love with the idea of being in love; but at seventeen I could not give her the real affection she deserved. My parents accepted the situation quietly – they appreciated B.'s feminine gentleness and her unselfconscious virtue; and her uncle-by-marriage, who, after a long career as an army officer had recently, through the death of his remote kinsman Lord Brownlow, inherited Ashridge and its large estates, remarked in a grandiose Trollopian way, that, if I took Holy orders, he supposed he could present me to a respectable family living. Nelly, on the other hand, did not conceal her displeasure. As I grew up, we had slowly drifted apart; but she reappeared to show her poor opinion of this ridiculous relationship and of my foolish adolescent boastings. I was not sufficiently in love myself to support the role that I had chosen; I remembered that Oxford still lay ahead, and that, when I had gone down from Oxford, I should be entirely penniless. I then adopted the easiest means of escape – again I have forgotten all the details – and proceeded to break off my engagement. No doubt I provided some specious excuses; but it was considered – both by B.'s mother and by my own parents – that I had acted shabbily and selfishly.

The affair had begun before I left England, and ended soon after my return. I went up to Balliol, this time unescorted, on October 10th 1923, was ceremoniously received at the porter's lodge and taken off to my allotted rooms, painted a dark depressing brown, in the oldest quarter of the college. They occupied half a top floor. My sitting-room commanded St Giles's; my bedroom overlooked the Broad. Though meagrely furnished, they gave me a sense of space and, what was more, a glorious sense of privacy. I had a college servant to attend to my well-being, make my bed, and, if the weather demanded it, build me a huge coal-fire in my Victorian black-leaded grate. But I still needed friends, and therefore sought out the staircase on which my school friend Graham Greene lived. Our reunion, however, was disappointing. Having taken up residence a year earlier, he had already formed his own circle, which, rightly or wrongly, I considered rather tedious; and, after a week or two of sharing their honest fun, I wandered off into a different milieu. Why Graham at Oxford should have so carefully avoided notice is a question that I cannot answer. But perhaps he did well to avoid the showy, expensive world that I myself was soon frequenting.

Though much could be said in dispraise of the Oxford I knew, it proved a nursery of distinguished writers. Among my friends and friendly acquaintances between 1923 and 1925 were Graham Greene, Evelyn Waugh, Cyril Connolly, Anthony Powell, the brilliant ill-fated Henry Yorke (who wrote under the pseudonym Henry Green), David Cecil, Edward Sackville-West, Robert Byron, Kenneth Clark, Patrick Kinross, the renowned polemicist Claud Cockburn and the noteworthy historian Richard Pares. Each was destined to make his name in prose; while Harold Acton represented poetry, performing his part with a flamboyant verve that would have captivated Oscar Wilde, and with all Wilde's eloquent scorn for contemporary philistines and moralists. Him I met, I suppose, through Evelyn Waugh, who, remembering our Berkhamstedian links, had decided to visit me at Balliol. Since our early meeting Waugh had scarcely changed. An alert, slender, dandified youth, he found Oxford, he tells us in his autobiography, a modern Kingdom of Cokayne; and it was either he or Harold Acton who introduced me to the notorious Hypocrites Club, where for the first time I became extravagantly drunk, and whence I staggered homewards by long and difficult stages, reeling into Balliol just on the stroke of midnight beneath the porter's sharp but sympathetic eye.

The Hypocrites was then the chief citadel of bohemian life at Oxford, which at that time seemed to possess almost as many coteries as colleges. Oxford, indeed, was a microcosm of the adult universe, with its own snobberies and elaborate class-distinctions, its own social shibboleths and intellectual vogues. Thus, we had a *Côté de Guermantes*, made up of fashionable young men, who hunted and rode in Bullingdon Grinds, but were often by no means averse from the company of so-called 'aesthetes'; a High-Bohemian world of rich and pleasure-loving dilettanti; and, attached to them, a much more genuine bohemia – among its representatives were several wild eccentrics – that boisterously disregarded fashion. In one respect, however, we were all alike: we were extremely lavish spenders; and, except for the very rich, we most of us went down leaving many bills unpaid.

That was largely the fault of Oxford tradesmen. I had only, I discovered, to present myself at a shop, give my name and state my college; and the assistants would allow me to carry off any article that caught my fancy. At Adamson's I could order new suits; at Blackwell's, collect a pile of volumes; even at the college-stores I was free to choose whatever provisions that I thought I needed – boxes of Russian and Balkan cigarettes, a magnum of champagne or some exotic liqueur such as 'Danziger Gold-wasser', which I favoured not because I liked the taste, but because, if it were briskly shaken, delicate fragments of gold leaf floated to and fro inside the bottle.

During my first absence I had my rooms repainted; and meanwhile I hung up various pictures – Dürer's print of a rhinoceros and a portrait by my mother of her old nanny that, as a representation of old age, had, I thought, a fine Rembrandtian touch – and purchased decorative strips of coloured material which I draped across the chairs and sofa. At the same time, I had my card engraved. Georgian Oxford preserved many of the habits of Edwardian society; and undergraduates, when they visited a friend but found that he was not at home, were accustomed to drop their card upon his table, adding perhaps a few scribbled words and carefully turning down a corner. Since our rooms were not equipped with telephones, we communicated by means of visits; and the visitors who climbed my wooden staircase were far more numerous than I expected. As a poet whose works had already appeared in print, I enjoyed a small immediate success – at least a success of curiosity; and, had my temperament been a little better balanced, it would no doubt have lasted longer.

Meanwhile, I entered the section of Oxford society that Harold Acton dominated. When he first arrived, he had been obliged to 'sport his oak' against the attacks of furious Christ Church athletes, who had smashed his windows and threatened that, should he re-emerge, they would duck him in the fountain. By the time I appeared, however, he was already well on the way to becoming an Oxford institution; and, after I had gone down – he both preceded and survived me – he had grown so popular that the Bullingdon Club once invited him to dinner, where he delivered a blithe and witty speech for which he was rewarded with uproarious applause. The son of American and Anglo-Italian parents, he had an impenitently alien look – the air of a Renaissance Prince of the Church and of a youthful Chinese sage combined. His voice was strange – dulcet and elaborately mannered; and a suspicion of a stutter, or trick of momentarily hesitating before he brought out his most pointed phrases, gave his conversation added charm.

That voice, I presently learned, he had inherited from the veteran actor Robin de la Condamine; and Condamine, in his turn, had inherited it from Oscar Wilde. The scraps of information we collect on our way through life have a curious knack of fitting together in the jigsaw puzzle of our memories; and, hearing Condamine mentioned, I recollected that my mother had described a young man of that name, whose family lived near The Postern, and who had terrified her by the faces he made as she passed their garden gate. Her tormentor was evidently Harold's old friend at an early stage of his existence, while he was still rehearsing his mimetic gifts. They had been considerable; and Webster's *Duchess of Malfi* was a play that had afforded him the fullest scope. Harold would imitate him performing the part of the fiendish half-mad Ferdinand –

'I have this night digged up a mandrake . . . and I am grown mad with't'

– so loudly and expressively that, if he were walking a crowded street, he cleared the pavement all around.

Harold's method of reciting his own verses was just as stentorian and dramatic. He occupied rooms in the Victorian annexe of his college, overlooking Christ Church Meadows; and, having provided his guests with an opulent luncheon, accompanied by large quantities of the steaming mulled claret that he had brewed upon the hearth, from his balcony he would declaim his latest poems through a large megaphone to crocodiles of Oxford schoolchildren trotting back and forth among the trees. Though mulled claret often leaves behind it a somewhat sickly after-taste, these were memorable occasions. Harold possessed the gift of raising the spirits, and electrifying the atmosphere, of any occasion he attended. The art of life, said Jean Cocteau, was to know 'just how far to go *too* far'; and Harold went too far with remarkable gusto and unfailing intrepidity. By aesthetic circles much admired, elsewhere he was fiercely criticized; and a good deal of the criticism he provoked was transferred to his supporters. From Christopher Hollis's autobiography* I learn that a future Prime Minister, Sir Alec Douglas-Home, at that period Lord Dunglass, besides abominating Harold Acton, wondered if Peter Quennell were 'quite decent'. He moved on a different plane; the Oxford I have attempted to describe was, of course, a comparatively small clique. We were surrounded by an immense array of unknown rowing-men and footballers; and some highly intelligent undergraduates, like Kenneth Clark and David Cecil, led a far less Dionysiac life, and would never have considered setting foot amid the drunken, noisy Hypocrites.

I had got into 'the wrong set', my father afterwards told me; and, from his personal point of view, his judgement was not entirely misguided. It was wrong for my education, wrong for my peace of mind, and had a disastrous effect on my standards of sobriety and solvency. I abused my freedom; but to find myself free seemed a wonderfully stimulating experience. Oxford was rich in oddly contrasted characters; and the most gifted were sometimes apparently the least promising. Who could have foretold that the carefree Evelyn Waugh was destined to become one of the finest novelists of his literary generation? At Oxford he made no special mark. The member of an obscure college, he had a group of devoted friends, including his fatherly admirer Harold Acton; but he showed none of the conservative social bias that he would develop during early middle age. He belonged neither to the *Côté de Guermantes* nor to any High-Bohemian clique. His tastes were simple; 'my absurdities', he writes in *A Little Learning*, 'were those of exuberance and naivety, not of spurious sophistication'. He wished 'to do everything and know everyone, not with any ambition to insinuate myself into fashion-

* *The Seven Ages*, 1974.

able London or make influential friends . . .'

Wisely, he refrained from frequenting the rich; and his only patrician friends were the amiable Lord Clonmore, a lively but unusually well-conducted attendant at the Hypocrites, Hugh Lygon – the 'original', if his literary personages can be said to have had originals, of Sebastian Flyte, the sweet-tempered and sympathetic young man he drew in *Brideshead Revisited* – and Hugh's monumental brother Lord Elmley. As a rule, he preferred bohemian misfits; and among his closest associates was the eccentric vagrant Terence Greenidge, who, among his bizarre habits, had a passion for purloining other people's small possessions, ink-pots, nail-scissors and hair brushes, and accumulating scraps of dirty paper, which he stuffed into his coat-pockets, preparatory to scattering them on Evelyn's carpet – a whim his good-natured friend did not discourage.

Evelyn's rooms in Hertford were then pleasantly spacious and decoratively furnished, with Lovat Fraser prints and Nonesuch editions of the English classics. Later, a dramatic change occurred. Finding himself in severe financial straits, he sold off all his most valuable possessions at a boisterous luncheon-party (where I bought his Nonesuch *Donne*), abandoned his former lodgings and retreated to the smallest and dingiest rooms that the college bursar could provide. He thereupon exchanged his dandyism for a truculent bohemianism, took to drinking beer in dusky riverside pubs, and after dark roamed the streets and quadrangles, carrying a heavy stick and venting his personal likes or dislikes in Bacchic chants and objurgations. He especially disliked the Dean of my own college – 'Sligger' Urquhart, who kept a modest intellectual salon above the St Giles's college-gate. Curly-headed, wrinkled and rosy-cheeked, 'Sligger' was fond of entertaining handsome youths, particularly if they displayed some intellectual promise, and had thus acquired a popular reputation that, I believe, was largely undeserved. By night, should Evelyn pass through Balliol, poor Sligger's alleged vices often excited him to ribald gaiety; and '*The Dean of Balliol sleeps with men! – the Dean of Balliol sleeps with men!!*' he would assure the college in a voice of thunder.

As a rule, however, though from the window of my room he

once hurled an empty champagne bottle at an inoffensive passer-by – an exploit that cost me a heavy fine – he was an amiable and notably generous companion. Not until he had left Oxford did he begin to assume the mask that afterwards grew so forbidding; and then, while the outlines of his character hardened, his talents simultaneously materialized. When I knew him best, it did not strike me that he showed very much creative promise; his drawings and woodcuts were unremarkable; and he wrote nothing I can now remember. Cyril Connolly, on the other hand, one of the brightest lights of Balliol society, was already an intelligence to be reckoned with. From College at Eton, he had come up to Oxford surrounded by a group of fellow Scholars, in whose company he cultivated the art of friendship, and discussed its numerous emotional problems, on a high Platonic level.

His was a protean character; nobody had a livelier wit or, if annoyed, a sharper tongue. His cynical *bon mots* were apt to stick like burrs. Yet his pensive romanticism was just as conspicuous as his cynicism; and, besides his passionate devotion to Nature, he exhibited many of the other traits of an eighteenth-century Man of Feeling. Whatever the subject that confronted him, he had his own immediate response; and I frequently admired, not only the spirited quickness of his mind, but the readiness with which he managed to produce some startlingly original opinion. '*Idées reçues*' always aroused his contempt. He loved travel. The Mediterranean, he announced, was a place to visit during the hottest summer months alone; and he co-opted five of his close friends into a 'Cicada Club', designed to carry out his theory. Our attitude towards Greek sculpture was similarly revolutionized; he proclaimed that we must study archaic statues, rather than the insipid classical masterpieces we had been taught we should admire at school.

Oxford, too, seen through his sharp eyes, developed unexpected beauties. To row down the Thames or Isis was a ridiculously out-moded pastime; he preferred the city's gloomier waterways. 'I haunt the Oxford Canal,' he writes in a letter dated May 1925,* 'where the squat tower of the Castle looks more like Provence than anything, furnaces and railway engines . . . old houses,

* Quoted in an article, published by *Harper's Magazine*, June 1973.

flowering chestnut and lilac hang over the dirty water and music comes from ancient inns.' Then, having quoted some Chinese verses, translated by Arthur Waley, he makes a flattering reference to myself: 'I canoed with Peter Quennell, who writes the best poetry in Oxford.' It is a characteristic letter; and, during a previous paragraph, he complains that he is miserable, though 'not quite at the suicidal stage', and contemplates 'disappearing . . . before Schools* . . . on the Orient Express probably . . .' In fact, he remained to enter the grim Examination Halls, whence he addressed the last letter that he was to write before he bade the city goodbye: 'My ignorance is colossal. It is like a cat playing with a mouse – just as I feel secure and playful a great paw knocks me over with Constitutional History from 1307.'

Elsewhere, he writes of his life at Oxford as a 'three-year day-dream'. Very different was his Etonian contemporary, the ultra-fashionable Brian Howard, whom I met about the same time, and who, having made me some preliminary advances – he knew that I had published a book of poems; and he professed a deep regard for art and literature – had almost immediately dropped me as beneath his social notice. Thereafter I watched his career from a distance; and an extraordinary spectacle it was.† Although at school Brian had been an aesthete, and with Harold Acton had founded and edited a little magazine they called *The Eton Candle*, at Oxford he had joined the Guermantes set, among whom he performed the part of *elegantiae arbiter*. His attitude towards his aristocratic friends was that of Petronius towards the young Nero, or of Beau Brummell towards the future Prince Regent. If Brian dearly loved a lord, he also greatly enjoyed tormenting one. Confronting a good-natured young peer, he would put him smartly through his paces: 'Your waistcoat, my dear Harry! What *do* you mean by wearing it?' 'Oh, I say, Brian,' the victim would protest, 'I think it's a rather good waist-coat.' 'Good, indeed! It makes you look, my dear, like some *ridiculous old bumble-bee*. Go away and take it off at once!' Not only did he lecture his friends on the subject of their clothes, and

* The final examinations, for which he knew that he was ill-prepared.
† See *Brian Howard: Portrait of a Failure*, edited by Marie-Jacqueline Lancaster, 1968.

order them to follow his example and have their racing-colours designed by Charvet, but he generally supervised their education and, to complete the process, at times would fall in love with them – a tribute they accepted just as amiably as his frequent gibes and insults.

Evelyn loathed Brian, and afterwards took several hints from his character when he created the personage of 'Anthony Blanche'; but in his autobiographical narrative he concedes that his old enemy possessed a certain curious fascination – 'a kind of ferocity of elegance that belonged to the romantic era of a century before our own'. Besides resembling Brummell, whose insolent aplomb he matched, Brian had also many of the traits of the youthful Benjamin Disraeli. Through his father he had inherited Jewish blood; hence his acute profile, his pallid fine-drawn skin and his large long-lashed, heavy-lidded eyes. Brian's mask was superbly self-assured; yet everything about him was a trifle suspect, even his patrician English surname. His father, a successful art-dealer, was said to have been christened Francis Harrison Gassaway, but during his youth had apparently adopted a more impressive patronymic. Brian, asked to identify himself by an Oxford proctor or his 'bull-dog', always rolled it out triumphantly. 'My name', he would announce, 'is Brian – Christian – de Claiborne – Howard', in the tone of the Baron de Charlus informing M. Verdurin of the various titles that he bore. Did it perhaps afford him an odd amusement to sail so boldly under false colours?

It was his ambitious American mother who had encouraged his social progress; and, during her sad old age, she would watch him decline into bohemian obscurity. Unlike the Prince Regent, his aristocratic friends did not summarily discard their Brummell; but, once they had gone down and assumed their appointed stations in life, they tended to outgrow his charm; while, at house-parties, their more conventional parents found him an alarmingly exotic guest. I myself happened to witness the occasion when a decisive break occurred. Once we had both left Oxford, he lowered his social standards, and we had renewed our previous friendship. He had invited me to supper at the Eiffel Tower; and, by way of filling a gap in our conversation, I said that I noticed that a favourite Guermantes friend had just celebrated his twenty-first birthday with appropriate pomp and splendour. On Brian the effect was violent; and he scarcely troubled to conceal his feelings. 'But *I* was not asked! Are you perfectly *sure* you're right?' And waiters were sent hurrying around the streets until they had collected a whole sheaf of papers, which he settled down to pore through. At this moment, I think, he renounced the upper classes, and became an impassioned, though slightly unorthodox supporter of the anti-fascist Left Wing.

Brian had a genuinely demonic nature; during his restless later life, he seems to have been driven by a host of furies, and wandered in search of his own salvation to and fro across Europe, always accompanied by some solid bewildered youth whom he loved and spoiled and often ill-treated, and who (except for the last, killed by a disastrous mishap, which precipitated Brian's suicide) eventually eluded him. Much more peaceful were the last days of another Oxford dandy. Alfred Duggan lived on my staircase at Balliol, where he occupied the first floor. He was very rich, the son by her earlier marriage of the splendidly opulent Lady Curzon, and thus the stepson of the famous Lord Curzon, then the Chancellor of the University. Alfred enjoyed a privileged position; and he made the most of it. While Brian Howard suggested an early-nineteenth-century exquisite, Alfred was the Edwardian 'heavy swell'. At Oxford he kept a string of hunters; and every night, wearing full evening dress, he would journey in a hired motor-car to a London night-club, the nefarious 43, and spend the next few hours drinking and talking and 'having a woman' – an essential part of the ceremony – before he travelled back again. Once he returned, he was obliged to scale the façade of the college and struggle through his first-floor window. The bribes he paid his scout, he told me, ran into several hundred pounds a year; and Thompson, also my attendant, a small, weak-looking, white-faced drudge, grew increasingly demoralized, and produced – much against his will, he assured me – an enormous family of children, which made it entirely impossible for him to refuse a five-pound note.

Drunk or sober, Alfred was always polite and impassive; and his starched shirt-front, with its gleaming pearl studs, at the end of the most tumultuous evening seldom showed a dent or crease. On his thick neck he carried the fine head of a beak-nosed Roman emperor; and, despite our immense dissimilarity, I found his conversation entertaining. That he had an excellent mind he revealed in later life, when he lost his fortune, became a Catholic believer and made his name as a distinguished historical novelist. At Oxford, he said, he had found that there was no need to write a weekly essay for his tutor, but would hold up a blank sheet and rapidly improvise half a dozen learned paragraphs. Meanwhile, he did not regard his rakish behaviour as exceptionally adventurous; he merely did what might be expected of a self-respecting English gentleman. A gentleman regularly attended a night-club, had a woman, and drank a bottle of champagne, just as he rode to hounds and, if he attended a ball, wore a pair of white kid gloves. Long afterwards I saw him at a party given in honour of his niece's wedding. Time had altered him; he looked weary and stout and sober; but the hand he extended, I saw, was still beautifully gloved, and he had preserved his calm Edwardian dignity.

The portraits I have so far attempted to sketch are, I must admit, only partial reflections of a large and crowded scene. I have included none of the politicians then learning their business at the Union, none of the promising young actors who had begun to flourish at the OUDS. These I have omitted, because I did not know them well; and, more regrettably, I have failed to describe a number of important intellectual figures – for example, Maurice Bowra, the most brilliantly active of the younger dons, and Kenneth Clark, remembered by Cyril Connolly as 'a polished hawk-god in obsidian',* because, although I should have liked to know them better, we never progressed – no doubt they had voted me awkward and difficult – beyond an amicable acquaintanceship. There have been, moreover, a number of recent books about Oxford in the 1920s that have done full justice to the age; and the subject I am dealing with here is my individual education rather than the period itself.

We cannot, however, escape our period; and its climate certainly contributed to my private rise and fall. Ours was a

* op. cit.

womanless Oxford. The Guermantes would occasionally enliven their rooms by importing a small flurry of attractive débutantes; but few of us had women friends; and my affectionate, though innocent association with a group of lively girls at Somerville was considered both perverse and vulgar. The part of Oxford society I knew had strongly homosexual leanings; 'a romantic interest in our own sex', writes Cyril Connolly, 'not necessarily carried as far as physical experiments, was the intellectual fashion'. Many of my contemporaries, who followed the fashion at Oxford, soon discarded it on entering the adult world; but, meanwhile, they were inclined to adopt the *mores* of an Hellenic city-state. Unable to share their affections myself – I had received no previous indoctrination at an English public school, and all my daydreams were of women – I observed them from afar, while Plato paid his court to Agathon, and Socrates and Alcibiades strolled arm-in-arm. I felt excluded; and little by little a general sense of exclusion, of being an outsider, though not an ill-treated outsider, began to creep into my mind; and I took to assuming the rather silly pose of an inveterate malcontent. I decided that Oxford was not for me, and lost no opportunity of abusing the place and neglecting every chance it offered.

Another serious drawback in my Oxford career was my economic situation. I had a scholarship, increased by the small sum that my father had provided – to raise it, I afterwards learned, he had realized his life-insurance. But I was still poor – poorer than most of my friends; and the habit I contracted of spending my vacations abroad proved so expensive that I frequently started the new term with only five or six pounds to my credit. Had I regained Berkhamsted, and passed the time beneath my parents' roof, I might, of course, have saved money; but that I regarded as a form of spiritual suicide. Whatever the cost, and the vexations I knew it would cause me, I must shun Berkhamstedian imprisonment; and again and again I hastened across the Channel as soon as the Oxford term had ended. When I returned, I was obliged to fall back on the local credit-system. This provided me, however, with an abundance of luxuries and superfluities; and, although I resented being obliged to dine in Hall, while my less penurious friends assembled at a cheerful restaurant named The George, I did not disdain the comforts of the Balliol Junior Common Room, where I could sit through the late afternoons drinking china tea and eating *pâté de foie gras* sandwiches, while I idly scanned the magazines, from *The Times Literary Supplement* and the *New Statesman* to the *Tatler*, *Le Rire* and *La Vie Parisienne*.

A disadvantage just as embarrassing as my constant lack of money was my social inexperience. Beneath my apparent boldness, which, now and then, I fear, may have degenerated into bumptiousness, I hid an adolescent gaucherie, which made it difficult for me either to enter or to leave a room, and to begin or end a conversation. At The George, on one of the nights when I felt rich enough to go there, I remember watching 'Puffin' Asquith, the redoubtable Mrs Asquith's only son, tackle a minor social problem with a calm aplomb I deeply envied. Having sighted a London acquaintance whom it was clear, he both disliked and disapproved of, but to whom he did not wish to seem ill-mannered, he glided towards his table, spoke a few words, and, all in the same sinuous movement, quickly glided off again. I knew that myself I should have faltered and hesitated and found it almost impossible to extract myself from a long unwanted colloquy. Sometimes I was over-polite, sometimes unduly negligent; and my natural self-consciousness tended to magnify every *faux pas* that I felt I had committed.

Quarrels were numerous and explosive among the undergraduates I knew; and a particularly unpleasant fracas – stung by an insulting phrase, I hurled a glassful of beer at my adversary, but succeeded only in drenching a pacific onlooker – caused me to resign my membership of the Hypocrites Club several months before the University authorities at last decided that they must close it down. Meanwhile, at the Hypocrites I had learned to drink. Ours was a period of heavy drinking; and most parties were expected to end in a general bacchanalia. I attended a good many; but I also drank alone, experimenting both with Danziger Goldwasser and Orange Curaçao and with other equally poisonous liqueurs, as I lay on my sofa, a glass at my side, reading a book that I had just bought from Blackwell's. This habit and my sedentary way of life – I took very little exercise, and refused to practise any kind of sport; though I recollect once hiring a horse named 'Spider', which shied and threw me in Port Meadow – had a depressing effect upon my health and spirits. Nor did I find the Oxford climate salubrious; and I disliked the damp river-mists that crept along the streets and saturated the ancient stone-work of the colleges.

As for work, I was engaged in tasks of my own, and had begun to write a biography of Blake; but during my whole residence I attended only one lecture, which, besides being largely inaudible, seemed remarkably unenlightening; and my academic tasks were confined to the preparation of a weekly essay. My tutor was a kind, good-hearted clergyman, who specialized in the English Roman-tic Poets, and, when I arrived, would always open a bottle of stout and a box of oatmeal biscuits. He listened with courteous attention to my often slapdash essay; but, should I have failed to prepare it and arrive empty-handed, he merely smiled and shook his finger, suggesting that I substitute a few pages from my un-finished book on Blake. Such was my formal education. Since I had persisted in choosing the English School, rather than History or Greats, I found that I was expected to study Anglo-Saxon; but its problems soon defeated me; and I decided that I could afford to abandon the effort until I had reached my third, and closing year.

Yet I did not completely waste my time. True, my biography was never finished; and the manuscript has now been lost. But sometimes I recaptured the mood of high creative excitement that had irradiated my earlier days, and produced a number of the poems that would appear, not long after I had left Oxford, in my single adult book of verse. Simultaneously, I was composing an elaborate pseudo-epic, inspired by learned translations of the Babylonian *Tale of Gilgamesh*. But, having finished it and care-fully copied it out into the splendid manuscript-book with which Evelyn Waugh presented me, I put the misbegotten work aside. If I were not writing, I continued to read omnivorously and end-lessly – poets, novelists, essayists, critics, the English and the French alike, and, with especial enjoyment, Constance Garnett's translations of Gogol, Tchekov, Dostoievsky and Turgenev. Russian novels became a kind of drug. I loved their strange and melancholy backgrounds, and the enigmatic personages they introduced. My room was over-heated; I felt lonely and bored; rain was falling outside. But through the muddy streets of the little town of R . . . had just driven an odd old-fashioned carriage, with yellow wheels and dark-green panels, from which emerged a gaunt bewhiskered man of military appearance, a fat elderly woman wearing a striped pelisse and an unhappy-looking fair-haired girl. As they passed a grey board fence and halted near the iron-roofed police station, the girl seemed to be on the verge of tears . . .

I had no political interests; nor had the great majority of my 'aesthetic' friends. We belonged to the carefree 'Age before the Flood', cynical, pleasure-seeking, unattached; and the only pro-fessing Communist I knew was the sturdy Graham Pollard, future joint-author of *An Enquiry into the Nature of Certain Nineteenth Century Pamphlets** – the work that exposed the forgeries of T. J. Wise, who had long been fouling his own nest by producing and marketing spurious 'pre-first' editions. Even Pollard did not often proclaim his faith, though I remember a day when a railway-strike happened to coincide with an important London book-sale; and he was much exercised as to whether he should miss the sale, or run the risk of travelling on a train behind a black-leg engine-driver. Most of my friends preferred to look inwards; we took our pleasures seriously, and felt our personal failures keenly; but there our vision of existence ended. How different were our lives from those of the deeply earnest, if at times somewhat muddle-headed young men, destined a few years later to refuse to follow in our footsteps!

Our literary and artistic tastes, however, had a fairly wide range. We venerated *The Waste Land*, which had appeared in 1922 – Harold Acton once recited the whole poem at a Con-servative Oxford garden-party – read the novels of André Gide, particularly *L'Immoraliste*, and bought copies, and carefully cut the pages of *Du Côté de chez Swann* and the volumes that suc-ceeded it. Paul Valéry's poems I began to appreciate with the help of Cyril Connolly; and, on a lower level, we were much attracted by Jean Cocteau's sparkling modish talents. Among us we had one or two scholarly musicologists, such as Kenneth

* With John Carter, 1934.

Clark and Edward Sackville-West, who had acquired splendid gramophones and fine collections of records. But my musical education, I am obliged to confess, never properly got under way – my ear has always been deficient; and the tune that comes back to me most clearly is a popular piece of light music, George Gershwin's haunting *Rhapsody in Blue*. On summer days, its poignant nostalgic rhythm would float out through the open windows of many a sleepy Oxford college.

I have said enough, no doubt, to suggest that my life at Oxford was neither directly profitable nor obviously creditable; and a moment came when the college authorities declared that I was doing far too little to deserve my scholarship, and that, unless I passed a preliminary examination styled Responsions, I might very well be disciplined. I passed it by sitting up all night, construing and annotating Plato's *Republic* – a work I have never opened since – with a wet towel wrapped around my head. I was then restored to favour; but my general way of life did not improve; and, because I had failed to attend a sufficient number of the early-morning roll-calls, I was very often 'gated'; which meant that, once the college-gates had closed, I could not knock for re-admittance.

At such times, if I were still abroad between nine o'clock and midnight, I could only pretend that I wished to visit Sligger and, standing beneath his window over the St Giles's gate, shout his name and ask him to throw down a key. This he readily did, assuming that, as young men of honour, his guests would not exploit his friendship. On a few occasions, nevertheless, I was obliged to climb in. It was an alarming climb – especially alarming should one happen to be a little drunk. My objective was Alfred Duggan's window; and, having scaled the tall barred Georgian casement that lay immediately beneath, I had to raise myself inch by inch until my feet were on the cross-bar and grope for the window-sill above – the most perilous part of the operation: had my fingers slipped, I should have toppled backwards – and, at last, now thoroughly frightened and exhausted, scramble up across the ledge. Arrived, I found Alfred and a group of kindred swells, in black ties and double-breasted white waistcoats – a fashion the Prince of Wales had adopted – playing cards and drinking whisky. But then, there were evenings when both methods of re-entry proved to be infeasible – Alfred was pursuing his pleasures elsewhere; Sligger had eventually grown suspicious – and, after the gates had closed, I had to remain at home and embark on yet another Russian novel.

Just as my literary projects showed a curious lack of direction – particularly my Babylonian epic – so in my social life I continued to hesitate between the different roles I wished to play. My literary tastes and my desire for social excitement were always hard to reconcile; and now I was the melancholic recluse, sitting alone beside my fire and cursing damp and foggy Oxford; now the eager gadabout hurrying off to a party, or the strayed reveller wandering home again. On rare occasions I became a host myself, and held an expensive luncheon-party in my rooms – once for a beautiful nineteen-year-old actress then appearing at the Oxford Playhouse, whose dark eyes and Titian-red hair seemed to support the legend that she was descended from the Empress Elizabeth; once for Natalie, a seductive young Russian married woman I had met through London friends, who had raised my hopes by promising to visit me at Balliol, but inconsiderately brought her lover.

I was not an efficient host; the dishes I had ordered from the college kitchen were often singularly ill-assorted; and, since my scout had to carry them across the quadrangle, they usually arrived half-cold. The least unsuccessful, I think, was the luncheon that I planned for Natalie. It was a disordered meal; but over our brandy glasses Harold Acton consented to declaim all three hundred and twenty-six lines of Swinburne's lesbian threnody 'Anactoria',* giving tremendous emphasis to the more sadistic passages –

> Ah that my lips were tuneless lips, but pressed
> To the bruised blossom of thy scourged white breast!
> Ah that my mouth for Muses' milk were fed
> On the sweet blood thy sweet small wounds had bled!

– while the afternoon faded above St Giles's, and smoke-wreaths

* For a somewhat different account of this occasion, see Harold Acton's *Memoirs of an Aesthete*, 1948.

128

thickened around the table.

Compared with the terms I spent at Oxford my various journeys abroad were innocent and health-giving. Twice I visited Greece, and each time I followed much the same route – from Venice or Trieste down the white Dalmatian coast, on my earlier journey pausing at Durazzo, where I watched the dawn break behind a minaret and heard a muezzin make his morning call, before I drove up to Tirana, in those days a romantic Eastern city, whose streets were full of bandoliered tribesmen, wearing embroidered jackets and curly-toed shoes; thence to Athens through the Corinth Canal, and, by way of Mycenae and Tiryns, south towards the Peloponnese. At Nauplia I took a sailing-boat that carried me over the Gulf of Argolis to a village on its western shore, from which I could walk through the mountains to the Valley of Sparta. We sailed in the small hours, as soon as the breeze had risen. It was a smooth and silent journey. I felt the dew descend, listened to the rustle of the water, watched the caïque's obliquely slanted sail sweeping back and forth across the stars, and, stretched out with a bundle beneath my head, enjoyed a high degree of happiness.

Not all my expeditions were quite so peaceful and idyllic. Hiring an old horse, I traversed the breadth of the Peloponnese from Sparta to Olympia, and stayed at a solitary peasant's hut. There I returned to the Middle Ages; the hut was windowless, with a small chimney immediately above the central hearth; and around the hearth, squatting on the earthen floor, clustered its inhabitants, occasionally throwing a few twigs into the smoky fire and constantly driving away a miserable cat and dog, which obstinately crept back again. The peasants had an infant child, its cheek disfigured by a large sore; the woman's features were half-hidden by the heavy shawl that she wrapped about her face; and they insisted, despite my protests, that I should occupy their only bed, a pile of dirty rugs heaped on a broad divan underneath a glimmering icon. I slept uneasily until a horde of bed-bugs began to penetrate my shirt and trousers, and I had the sensation of being boiled in oil, such was the agony of scalding and itching discomfort that possessed me all night long.

By the time I had reached Olympia and forded the shallow

River Alpheus, home of innumerable noisy frogs, I had very nearly lost my taste for travel. But the ruins consoled me; and I remember the scent of the pines that grow among their porous yellow shafts, and, in the museum, the noble effigies of drunken Lapiths and infuriated centaurs, over whom rises the statue of Apollo himself, once their focal figure of the pediment, extending his arm like a divine policeman to subdue the savage hubbub. On these Greek journeys, though I was often alone, I sometimes had a travelling companion. Once it was the poet Robert Trevelyan, the historian's elder brother. We had joined forces because we had happened to have met at the British School in Athens; and the fact that he joined me shows the high-minded optimism and inveterate altruism that characterized him throughout his long existence. No poet has loved his art more dearly, and practised it more conscientiously; yet the critical rewards he gained were always meagre; and the lengthy poetic plays he published are seldom either read or acted. Still, he continued to hope and persevere; and no doubt he hoped that a nineteen-year-old undergraduate, supposed to have certain poetic gifts – he himself was already over fifty – might make a stimulating fellow-traveller.

He was disappointed. We argued from morning to night as we trudged across the mountains. Not only did I question the genius of Virgil, maintaining that an official poet, the favourite littérateur of the Emperor Augustus, could scarcely be a great one; but, while we journeyed by train down the radiant Gulf of Corinth, for some reason – perhaps it was merely to annoy him – I decided I would not admire the landscape, and reclined full-length on the carriage seat, turning the pages of Huysmans' *Là-bas*. He was a late-Victorian enthusiast; I, a loquacious Georgian cynic. In 1944, when I opened *Windfalls*, a modest collection of Trevelyan's 'Notes and Essays', which he had published that year, I found a brief reference to my own discordant conversation. Under the heading 'Solitariness', he described how Desmond MacCarthy had warned him 'to "go alone" as much as possible, to beware of picking up companions . . . for expeditions and walking-tours'. This was advice, he writes, that, during a Grecian tour, he had temporarily ignored; and the result had been unfortunate. His fellow sightseer was at first 'agreeable enough'; then, 'time after time, just at those moments that should have been most sacred to contemplation, at Mycenae, at Mystra ... some ill-timed intrusive conversation would spring up about modernist poetry, psycho-analysis, or what not, and the spell would be broken'.

He had, therefore, 'eloped alone to Delphi', while I, pre-sumably, returned to London. I revisited Greece the next spring; but my last Oxford vacation I spent in Northumberland and Derbyshire. Through Edith Sitwell I had become acquainted with her brothers, Osbert and Sacheverell, who invited me to stay at Renishaw; and thither I went, and passed a couple of weeks amid that strange Peacockian household. The novelist himself could not have invented a more memorable set of personages. Sir George rose early; a tall, noble-looking, neatly-bearded man, he wore a wide-brimmed grey hat and, though always ceremonious and gravely courteous, appeared to have become more or less detached from the other members of his family, and lived a solitary, self-sufficient life. At fixed hours, he would walk around the lake or inspect his park and gardens; his conversation was a measured monologue, of which even his irreverent son Osbert could not completely break the thread.

His wife, however, rose late; wearing a black silk dress and a black toque, she would then totter gently into view, supporting her steps upon a small cane; and it was difficult to associate her with the bizarre adventures and tragic misadventures that had once distracted her existence. Lady Ida now seemed very old; and she still used the kind of upper-class Cockney – substituting 'ain't' for 'isn't' and dropping every *g* – that must have been fashionable in her girlhood. 'Ain't it amusin', Henry' she would ask Henry Moat, Sir George's devoted body-servant, as she showed him at luncheon, during his employer's temporary absence, a caricature of Sir George in the costume of a scout-master; to which '*Very* amusing, I am sure, milady', he replied, with an unappreciative growl. She and her daughter were veteran antagonists; Edith could never forgive her parents the lonely sufferings of her youth. But Lady Ida adored her sons, and did her best to like and understand the curious friends they brought to stay.

That summer the Sitwells' guests included, besides William

Walton, Sacheverell's musical protégé, and Edith's one-time governess, the formidably earnest and loquacious Helen Rootham, a Georgian poet named Wilfred Childe, a timid, scatter-brained, elusive creature, and the charming old eccentric Ada Leverson. Nicknamed by Oscar Wilde 'the Sphinx', she had gallantly come to his rescue when he awaited his second trial in 1895; and as a middle-aged married woman she had written a series of entertaining light novels, and was said to have conducted a large number of bohemian love-affairs. Her last attachment, now that she had grown old and infirm and almost completely deaf, was reserved for Osbert Sitwell. He treated her crepuscular passion with a rare combination of sympathy and delicacy. All that she asked was to be allowed to follow and worship; and the Sitwell brothers frequently permitted her to accompany them upon their holidays abroad. Osbert was never unkind, except when she indulged her awkward habit of getting up about seven or eight o'clock, and, at Renishaw, dressed in a long black velvet robe, her golden Gorgonian wig surmounted by a velvet picture-hat, could be seen tiptoeing across the lawn immediately beneath his windows. Then he would send out Henry Moat's assistant, with a message that Mrs Leverson must please go back to bed again.*

Osbert Sitwell possessed a warm heart, though he was sometimes touchy and suspicious; towards his literary antagonists and his father alone did he display a downright animosity. Against them he waged a campaign of cruel teasing that might continue several months or years. Sir George he teased whenever they happened to meet. Naturally, I was on the side of youth; and Sir George's attitude towards me had been never more than quietly civil. Yet there were moments when Osbert's peculiar tactics offended my notions of decorum. He had recently learned how to imitate a popping champagne bottle with a finger in the corner of his mouth; and, while Sir George at the dinner-table discussed Italian garden-planning – an erudite man of taste, he had reconstructed an Italian garden midway between his house and park – Osbert would emit a succession of loud pops, which delighted his friends and Lady Ida, but entirely failed to disturb

* For another portrait sketch of this remarkable woman, see *The Sign of the Fish*.

or interrupt his father's nicely balanced periods. Supposed to have been the original of Meredith's character *The Egoist*, Sir George had all Sir Willoughy Patterne's self-centred strength of mind and majestic self-assurance.

Such an intense concentration of personalities, each vigorous and vocal in its different way, filled the house to overflowing. And then, Renishaw contained a good many ghosts, from the damp little boy, drowned, I believe, by his jealous sister about the middle of the eighteenth century, to the impertinent phantom reported to have slapped Sir George's face while he was coming down the stairs, and the bat-like horror a postman claimed to have seen, hideously stuck to an outer wall, as he was bicycling up the drive. There was no electricity; the house was lamp-lit; and at night the enormous curtained beds, crowned with tufts of faded dusty feathers, looked forbiddingly sepulchral. The landscape, too, part of the Derbyshire coal-fields, had a somewhat melancholy air. Beneath the big yellowish castellated house, guarded by a small regiment of handsome Italian statues, stretched a broad industrial valley. Although Sir George had planted screens of trees to conceal the pitheads and smoke-stacks, he had never quite succeeded; and after dark a host of fiery points winked or glowed among the branches. The venerable trees in the park were often lightly blackened; and, if I leant a hand against a rugged bole, it acquired, I found, a sooty coating. Yet there was a sad magnificence about Renishaw that is reflected by the Sitwells' prose and verse; few writers have owed so much to the surroundings of their childhood. I have forgotten how long I remained there; but no doubt I lingered too long; for Osbert told me that he had received a letter from Sir George, after the house-party had broken up, in which he observed that 'some of our guests', he felt, had possibly outstayed their welcome.

My last visit, during the course of that summer vacation, was to one of the Sitwells' chief bugbears, the châtelaine of Garsington, Lady Ottoline Morrell. When I originally appeared at Garsington, I had not been very well received. As her visitors left, she had bidden a flattering goodbye to the young man just ahead of me, and said she hoped that he would soon return; whereas my hand she had silently and coldly shaken. Hostesses change, however; and by the autumn of 1925 I had begun to rank among her friends. Since Lawrence and Huxley and most of the Bloomsbury circle had in rapid succession fled her house, and the two novelists had published savage descriptions of her appearance and her personal character, the company she kept was less distinguished. But Lytton Strachey still came now and then; and I sat beside him at her table – a long limp figure, with big spectacles and densely matted russet beard. I recollect questioning him about his essay on Blake, which I impertinently criticized; and that, begged to explain himself, he replied in his faint falsetto voice, that he supposed he must have thought that he was being *clever* . . .

The artificiality of Lady Ottoline's setting offended her Bloomsburian critics. Me it delighted; I loved the old gardens and the stone-walled Tudor house, the brightly panelled rooms and the proud, forlorn peacocks wandering beneath the ilex trees between the ancient yew hedges. Nor did a touch of absurdity in the image she presented to the world – the swansdown trimmings of her green full-skirted dress, her rope of baroque pearls and mahogany-red coiffure – strike me as at all displeasing. None of the stories so often told against her was substantiated by my own experience. Clearly, she was an inquisitive woman; and perhaps there had been a period in her life when her passionate inquisitiveness and emotional possessiveness had gone too far; Virginia Woolf's coterie even asserted that she had steamed open one of Clive Bell's letters. But, when we discussed my problems at Garsington, the advice she gave me was both wise and kind. Since evidently I needed a good degree, should I not drink less, work a great deal harder, and do my utmost to keep out of trouble? Her counsels were timely; I listened with proper respect. Yet no sooner had I returned to Oxford than I completely disregarded them.

IV

THE LOVE OF CHILDREN FOR THEIR PARENTS, WRITES
Anthony Trollope in the last of the 'Palliser' novels, is 'seldom
altogether perfect', and adds that perhaps it 'had better not be
quite perfect' with his usual weighty shrewdness. Remembering
my own behaviour towards my parents, I feel embarrassed and
ashamed. I showed them little gratitude, forgot to write them the
letters that I knew they anxiously expected, and hurt them again
and again by ignoring their mild suggestions that I should cut
short a foreign holiday and spend a week or two beneath their
roof. But, though my behaviour was certainly unkind, it was not,
I think, either wholly unreasonable or completely inexcusable.
Had I returned home, I should have been travelling backwards;
Berkhamsted was an aspect of the past that I had already half
forgotten. My parents were firmly fixed in their habits; their
conversation offered no surprises; their ideals and prejudices
alike I had long abandoned. As to their surroundings, Crabtrees
seemed smaller than ever, and yet more crowded and prosaic.
Even the pets I had loved were nowadays vanished or dead.
Blooey my parents had had 'put to sleep'; the tame brown owl
I used to feed with trapped mice, and which, blinking its pale
azure lids, would then suddenly disgorge the remains of its meal
in the form of glossy brownish pellets, had flown away across the
fields.

Meanwhile, Nelly had died. In early days, a trusted inter-
mediary between my parents and myself, she had succumbed to
cancer, the scourge of the disappointed; an operation had failed;
and my mother wrote that, if I wished to see her alive, I should
immediately revisit Dulwich. I found her stretched on a narrow
metal bed in Lutetia's former dining-room. Table and chairs, of
course, had been moved out; but pictures hung around the walls;

and among them I saw a large and impressive mezzotint that I remembered from my childhood. No doubt the artist's gift, it portrayed a pathetic group of eighteenth-century ladies, recently captured at sea by the savage Barbary Corsairs, and now being forced to expose their nakedness in a populous Algerian slave-market. Overlooking Nelly's death-bed, it produced an odd effect. A single lamp stood near her pillows; her face had a pallid earthy colour; yet she recognized me with a smile.

This was the first occasion I had attended a death-bed; and she appeared to be suffering, not so much from pain or terror, as from intense physical discomfort. Her hands moved constantly to and fro in quick exasperated gestures; and for a moment I could think of nothing to say, until she smiled again and broke the silence, using a familiar piece of Berkhamstedian slang. 'They've told you, haven't they, that I'm going to kick the bucket?' she asked calmly, almost cheerfully. Then, noticing I held back, 'Aren't you going to kiss me? You know, I'm not contagious'; and I bent towards her parching cheek. Later she said that she had been received into the Catholic Church, and that she remained a faithful believer in the after-life, promising that, if the rules of her new existence permitted, she would return and talk with me.

She failed to keep her promise. I was full of guilt and remorse when I bade her goodbye, and took my leave of the ancient lonely couple – *le père Zeus* had grown miserably shrunken and aged – whom I met behind the sickroom door. But so remote is the prospect of his own death from a young man's point of view that losing an old friend has a strictly limited effect on his heart or his imagination. Though Nelly's death had closed a chapter of my life, there were many chapters still unopened. I looked forward to new worlds; and I needed fresh experience. None of my previous adventures had quite fulfilled my early hopes; and the love-affairs I had engaged in at Oxford had usually been un-rewarding. Thus Natalie had dismissed me as far too young, explaining, however, that she might possibly accept my love once I had reached my twenty-first year – an intolerable time to wait. True, her friend H., a member of the Somerville *petite bande*, had afforded me some consolation, and we spent happy hours upon my sofa. Yet I respected her innocence – the girls of that distant period were considerably less generous than their daughters and their granddaughters; and my scruples were once sharply rebuked by Evelyn Waugh's favourite boon-companion, the arch-bohemian Terence Greenidge, who had heard, he announced, that I received a girl in my rooms, and that 'you embrace her, but you *do not lie with her*!' Surely, for a scion of the Romantic poets, this was unbecoming conduct?

Just as indefinite were most of the attachments that followed. I found it hard to lose my virtue; and, when I passed through Paris and ventured into a brothel, my resolution nearly broke down upon a problem of linguistics. Having been received by an effusive madame, an almost caricatural type of her trade whom Guys and Gavarni might have loved to draw, I was first conducted around the establishment and asked to admire its various decorative splendours – '*Voici notre alcove Chinoise; voici la chambrette pompéienne*' – which I examined with only moderate interest. Next, my guide politely enquired if I wished to see '*une petite dame*'. I hoarsely admitted I did. Then, what type of *petite dame*? She should be *svelte*, I said, imagining that '*svelte*' was the exact translation of the English word 'slender'. I adored slender women; my feminine ideal was the kind of modern girl, long-limbed, sleek and small-hipped, that Lewis Baumer drew for *Punch*. But my helpful guide clearly gave the adjective a very different connotation, as I soon discovered on seeing a girl, entitled among her fellows *La Belle Hollandaise*, stroll languidly across the threshold. Plump, short-legged, with dimpled flanks and stomach, she might well have been an uncorseted nymph in the riotous foreground of one of Rubens's pictures; and it needed all her professional legerdemain to rescue her dejected client from complete fiasco.

I left the establishment profoundly disillusioned, uncertain whether I had advanced or receded in my feverish search for worldly knowledge. When I returned to Oxford at the beginning of my last year, I was still uneasily balanced between experience and innocence; and I might have long remained there had a remarkable night-bird not descended on the city. She was a predatory bird; but both her origins and her immediate circumstances seemed equally mysterious. Nina, I assume, belonged to a species that my parents knew as 'kept-women'. Who was keeping her I never learned. She asserted that she had been married, at one time, to the son of a well-known American novelist; and either he or her current protector must have provided her with a substantial income; for she had a large motor-car, a Daimler or a Rolls-Royce, employed a solid, old-fashioned chauffeur, and inhabited an expensive Maidenhead hotel. Physically, she was slender and slightly simian, her painted monkey-face framed in the blue-black side-curls of a fashionable 'Eton crop'. Michael Arlen might have made her the subject of a story, and described her brief, low-waisted skirts, the lengthy polished cigarette-holder that she flourished while she talked, and the pair of beautiful, half-witted Borzois* she was always struggling to control. Once she had alighted in bohemian Oxford, she caused a notable disturbance, and struck an unexpectedly feminine note at the kind of parties I attended.

After such a party, held by a friend of hers early in October, 1925, I found myself crammed into her motor-car, travelling through the suburbs of Oxford towards some now-forgotten destination. As her guests were numerous, I had to sit on the floor, near her high-heeled shoes and sharp-boned ankles; and their proximity not only aroused my senses, but brought back vivid memories of a book, Victor Margueritte's erotic novel *La Garçonne*,† that had recently achieved a popular success. Among other inflammatory episodes, Margueritte depicts a rakish young man making secret advances to a complaisant young woman, under the cover of darkness, in a crowded box at the theatre. Always ready to take my cue from a book, I chose to follow his example; and, since I was neither repulsed nor reproved, and Nina continued laughing and chattering, I grew more and more adventurous. That night I was carried off to Maidenhead. On the way I remember the long succession of illuminated details – the pink-washed flank of an old house, a stretch of tiled roof, the

* For these dogs, and my association with them, see A. L. Rowse: *A Cornishman at Oxford*, 1965.
† Cavalry officer turned novelist, Margueritte had published the book in 1922, when it created an enormous scandal.

skeleton branches of a roadside tree – that leapt up in the glare of the headlamps and went smoothly wheeling past the windows.

It is odd how little I can recollect about the next few nights and days. Physical pleasures, if they are sufficiently intense, often fail to leave a lasting mark – our pains and miseries, as we look back, are far less easily forgotten; and all I can now recover of that momentous episode is a rudimentary outline. I passed a number of feverish nights at Maidenhead. Nina was an expert guide; and the dreams that had first been inspired by *Hero and Leander* assumed a dazzlingly concrete shape. Though her motives were clearly not unselfish, I feel that I owe her a considerable debt. At the time, I often disliked her behaviour; she was cruel, *mesquine* and unscrupulous. 'I'm a mental sadist,' she once informed me, explaining, for example, that, while I shared her bed, she had had a disappointed lover – perhaps he paid her hotel bills – lurking in a near-by room. Yet I profited immensely from our brief attachment; and it was with a sense of Byronic wickedness that I spent the night at Maidenhead or accompanied her to London. I had also an exhilarating sense of danger. Unless I had obtained a permit, I was strictly forbidden to cross the boundaries of Oxford.

So, every night, a friendly accomplice promised that he would climb my stairs, and disarrange my sheets and pillows. The stratagem worked well; my absence went unremarked. Then one night he entirely forgot his promise; and Thompson reported I had slept out. His wife, he announced with his usual lugubrious air, was expecting yet another child; and, much as he disliked having to tell tales, he could not now afford to risk his job. Once the scandal broke, the Fellows of my own college might have merely fined and gated me; but meanwhile Nina's demoralizing presence had attracted the attention of the University authorities; and their henchmen had watched me get into her car and impudently drive away. I was thereupon summoned to the classic Clarendon Building where I faced the old Vice-Chancellor himself, a small, pursy, soft-spoken man, and a certain Dr Stallibrass, the far more unattractive Senior Proctor. I could scarcely have played my cards worse; for, instead of affecting submission and regret, I adopted an attitude that was described by the authorities as 'contumacious', referred to the rights of the citizen like a modern John Wilkes, and – still more absurdly and inappropriately – defended Nina's good name. 'I hope, Mr Quennell, you do not know as much about Mrs X as *we* do,' remarked the Vice-Chancellor with a gently dismissive sigh.

I believe that nowadays the University's standards have undergone a drastic change; and that girls, at least in one college, are permitted to stay overnight, the sole objectors being the college-servants, who sometimes complain of the unnecessary trouble that visiting young ladies cause. The Oxford I knew was still a semi-monastic institution; some of the dons clearly detested women; and the only kind of moral offence they condoned were discreetly managed homosexual passions, for which they often felt a secret sympathy. I myself had committed a number of crimes; I had fornicated, broken bounds and told the Vice-Chancellor outrageous lies. My sentence was quickly pronounced; I was condemned to rustication – sent down for a single term – and would then be gated, as soon as I reappeared, for the remainder of my Oxford life. I must leave immediately. And so I did, on a cold and cheerless autumn evening. None of my friends was available to see me off; but a good-hearted acquaintance, noticing my forlorn condition, kindly took me out to dinner; and later that night I caught the London train. Just over two years had passed since I first walked into Balliol. I had arrived, I learn from the college records, on 10 October 1923; it was on 18 October 1925 that I dismantled my familiar rooms and went down.

In London I sought refuge with Eddie Marsh at Gray's Inn; and, although he gave me his usual warm welcome, he was evidently flustered and perturbed. The following day, before I had left my bed – Eddie himself was already fully appointed – he brought me the news that we had both been dreading. My father was below; Eddie's expression, as he begged me to get up, registered intense alarm; and his eye-glass, dropping to the extent of its cord, tinkled nervously against a waistcoat button. I, too, felt a horrid stab of fear. But, during a crisis, my father's behaviour was almost always unexpected; and I found him darting around the library and inspecting Eddie's modern pictures. When he turned, he greeted me amiably. 'Well, well,' he opened in his loudest and heartiest voice, 'so Oxford seems to have been a failure, doesn't it? And I dare say you'd better not go back. The question is, poor old fellow, what you're going to do now.' At which he embarked on the practical side of the problem, and began discussing ways and means.

His proposals were generous. Though he admitted that he would prefer me to occupy a room at a University Settlement somewhere in the East End, and undertake some charitable work, he heard out my objections quietly; and only once did he reveal a glint of rage. I must give him my solemn word, he said, that never, never would I attempt to meet 'that woman. She's *filth* – debauching a boy!' he exclaimed; and there his indignation left him speechless. When I gave him the promise he asked for, his moral fury soon subsided; and, later, having agreed to visit the Settlement and found it singularly cold and drab, I persuaded him to let me go abroad. He would allow me the sum with which he had meant to increase my scholarship if I had remained at Oxford. Osbert and Sacheverell Sitwell, I knew, were spending a literary vacation at Amalfi, on the Neapolitan coast; and they had invited me to join them there. My father approved the plan; he understood that the Sitwell brothers led commendably hard-working lives; and, having bidden my mother goodbye – her grief, since she heard of my expulsion from Oxford, had been much more poignant than my father's – I travelled south by way of Paris.

The Sitwells loved Amalfi, and no doubt I should have enjoyed it myself had the winter skies occasionally cleared. But, alas, storm after storm pursued one another across the Gulf of Naples, blotting out the horizon and drenching the narrow ledge on which our hotel stood with incessant sheets of rain. The mountains that rose behind were seldom completely visible; below us muddy waves churned; and the streets of the little town of Amalfi, huddled about the ruined castle that had once belonged to Webster's Duchess, had a peculiarly damp and dispiriting smell. My companions were five – Osbert and Sachie and Sachie's newly-married wife Georgia, a blithe and elegant young Canadian girl, Willie Walton and the handsome Adrian Stokes. Osbert, a devoted champion of the young, had recently persuaded Adrian's father to grant him the small allowance that would enable him to cultivate his literary gifts. He was a striking personage, bronzed and bright-eyed, whose hawk-like profile and thatch of untidy locks – asked by the passport-office to describe its colour, he had answered 'old gold' – gave him somewhat the appearance of a youthful Afghan chief. We were each engaged, apart from Georgia Sitwell, on some arduous creative project and, the hotel having been built as a Capuchin monastery, each of us occupied a separate cell, and only emerged just before luncheon and dinner, when we met in Osbert's sitting-room for conversation and one or two of the anodyne cocktails that were then called 'White Ladies'.

Osbert was writing a novel; Sachie, weaving the rich auto-biographical tapestry of *All Summer in a Day*; Adrian, launching an imaginative expedition into modern art-criticism; William Walton, at work on his latest score, or hammering away at a decrepit upright piano. So much creative zeal excited and impressed, yet from time to time disheartened me. My own project – an ambitious historical romance, constructed around Alexander the Great and his tragic relationship with Cleitus, the friend and aide-de-camp whom he murdered during a fit of drunken rage – refused obstinately to come to life. Why I had chosen this subject I cannot tell. But I had decided that, as I unfolded the story, I would dispense with archaeological trappings, and would incorporate any modern details that I thought might be effective. It was a personal relationship I wished to describe rather than the events of a far-off historical period; and the result was an ill-combined mixture of vague 'psychology' and elaborate 'fine writing', which, as I laboured on from sentence to sentence, began gradually to seem more and more unreal. Since I had first opened *Southern Baroque Art*, Sachie was the modern stylist whom I most admired. But I had neither his incessant rush of ideas nor his continuous flow of imagery.

Once again I felt that I was on the wrong track; and my doubts increased as dark clouds continued to surge above Amalfi. My friends, behind their cloistral doors, were evidently faring better; yet hints of tension, of malaise and ennui, soon crept into our daily life. Osbert's Hanoverian features now grew particularly autocratic, and he gave free rein to his love of teasing; Sachie's visionary remoteness increased; while Adrian's high-flown speeches and romantic attitudes grated on my irritable nerves. There were rows at dinner, often provoked by me, when I heard a voice – I knew it could only be mine – making a remark I repented of even before I had completed it. I was not the sole cause of our general malaise; but I was unquestionably the chief offender. I felt that I had lost, if I could ever have claimed to possess, the precious art of making and keeping friends; and I was glad, early in the New Year, to be asked to spend some days on Anacapri.

There my hosts were Francis and Jessica Brett-Young; Francis, a successful popular novelist, yet a highly sensitive and sympathetic man; his wife, an exemplary specimen of the professional writer's consort, who sang his praises, abused his literary critics and managed his private affairs with unwearying solicitude. Their house was a quiet, delightful place; and beyond the wide valley, full of silvery olive-yards, that divided their garden-terrace from the sea, rose on the opposite rim the tower and battlements of an isolated villa. This they said was the home of the mysterious Dr Axel Munthe. Long the medical adviser, and perhaps the lover of the ageing Queen of Sweden, he was reputed to have strange magnetic gifts, that he exercised on women and the larger apes alike; the savagest chimpanzee would allow him to enter its cage, and the maddest, most hysterical *grande dame*, as soon as he approached her bedside, immediately regained her calm. I had nearly forgotten his name when, in 1929, at the offices of the *New Statesman*, I was asked to produce a review of his best-selling volume *The Story of San Michele*, which several other reviewers had already turned down, and which, after scanning two or three pages, and noting the touch of mythomaniac fantasy that appeared to colour every episode, I thought it wiser to refuse myself. But I then remembered the tales the Brett-Youngs had told me about their secretive Swedish neighbour, and my glimpse of his lonely towered refuge far away across the valley.

Munthe happened to be abroad at the time; and we never visited his house. I had an agreeable holiday on Anacapri; but a letter I presently received from the Sitwells, suggesting that, although they looked forward to seeing me in London, I should not rejoin them in Amalfi, hurt me more than I admitted. The Brett-Youngs, both of them kindly people, then proposed a brief Sicilian tour. They had previously explored the island, accompanied by D. H. Lawrence; and their memories of Lawrence as a travelling-companion were particularly strange and vivid. He could not avoid, they declared, attracting violent disturbances, and regularly touched off unexpected storms. He was alone – Frieda Lawrence had deserted him while he sought for a Sicilian haven; and, during a recent expedition to Germany, he had purchased a curious piece of native head-gear, small and round and bright green, which had inexplicably offended a passing group of sulphur-miners, who, wildly vociferating *Tedesco! Tedesco!*, put him to flight beneath a hail of stones. On a second occasion, when the day was calm and cloudless, and Lawrence was enjoying a solitary walk, a miniature whirlwind had suddenly sprung up, lifted him off his feet, rolled him along the ground and swept him through a cactus-hedge. Lawrence accepted these bizarre misfortunes calmly; they appealed both to his love of drama and to a quirkish vein of humour that in his literary works he seldom showed.

Having left the Brett-Youngs, I travelled north through Italy, sleeping at cheap hotels or sober family pensions, and making few friends on the way. It was not an unhappy period; as a rule I enjoyed my solitude and became an enthusiastic sightseer. At a previous stage of my life I had affected to have little use for sightseeing; one should *happen* to discover splendid landscapes or buildings, but never go in search of them. While I lived near Naples, I had deliberately shunned Pompeii, and, when I reached Capri, refused to investigate the legendary attractions of the island's Blue Grotto. On this journey, however, I bought a guidebook, and spent my days exploring churches, museums and galleries, wandering up and down precipitous stony streets, and in and out of sunlit courtyards. After dark, I entered the nearest café, and sat for a quiet hour among the local businessmen who had assembled to enjoy their nightly feast of small talk, watching them illustrate every point they made with those expansive, stylized gestures which lend even the dullest Italian conversation

144

so dramatic and intense an air.

Thus I saw something of the Tuscan and Umbrian cities, spent a romantic holiday at Venice (where I embarked upon a mild flirtation) and had a brief, but deeply moving glimpse of Ravenna's mournful splendours. Meanwhile, as my parents had been invited to stay at Rapallo, I felt that I should arrange a meeting; and our reunion, though their welcome was somewhat cautious, proved not completely unsuccessful. But the experience I remember best is my afternoon visit to a distinguished English man of letters. Max Beerbohm occupied a modest house above the noisy modern seaside town; and I discovered him pacing the black-and-white pavement of his pretty roof-top terrace that, with pots of camellias spaced along its edges, surrounded his lilliputian white-washed study. The old essayist wore a trim, tight-waisted suit – evidently the great-great-grandson of a fashionable Edwardian suit, copied and recopied by a succession of foreign tailors – a hard-brimmed Spanish hat slanted across his brows, and a red carnation in his button-hole. His reception was courteous; he offered me a glass of wine and, as he strolled to and fro, often returned himself to the flask of Chianti that stood upon the terrace-wall. His discourse – he discoursed rather than simply talked – had a kind of mannered ease; and he seemed glad to exhibit the various amusing trifles he had accumulated in his study – not only unpublished caricatures, but photographs of prominent personages he had painstakingly altered and improved, adding a squint, blacking out a tooth or lending the official mask a fiendish scowl.

He gave me revelatory descriptions, too, of some of his more celebrated fellow writers; and a memorable afternoon was under way, and I had drunk several glasses of Chianti, when I made a characteristic misstep. Which Italian city, he asked, did I find especially appealing? Determined at any cost to avoid an obvious reply, I answered – which was not entirely untrue – that I was rather fond of Milan; I liked the bustling *Galleria*, and the stout Milanese ladies, bunches of Parma violets pinned to their fur coats, greeting their acquaintances, gobbling ices and climbing into motor-cars. 'If you like Milan,' he responded indignantly, 'you had better stick to Brighton !' And then launched a ferocious attack against the horrors of the twentieth-century world. Even as he spoke, the thunder of modern traffic and dense clouds of dust and petrol-fumes were rising from the road below; but he obstinately disregarded them. The cult of the internal combustion engine, he exclaimed, was fast destroying the Italian soul; and young men, with the faces of angels and heroes, had only to peer beneath an engine's bonnet for a hideous change to take place. As a procession of heavy lorries rumbled beneath his walls, he grew angrier and angrier; and I felt much relieved by the appearance of the veteran artist William Rothenstein, one of 'Max's' oldest and dearest friends, smiling in his wheel-chair, which enabled us to forget the present day and take shelter among their memories of the past.

It was at Ravenna, when my funds were running low, and I was preparing sadly to return home, that I caught sight of D. H. Lawrence. Wedged between two massive middle-aged English women in the hotel dining-room, he looked extraordinarily slight and frail, with a keen mischievous glance above the thick-growing reddish beard into which his smile again and again retreated. His voice was toneless, faintly proletarian; and he did not very often speak; but, as I strained my ears to catch some fragment of conversation that I could memorize and carry off, I heard that he was giving his views on the Byzantine mosaics he had seen in a basilica. He had been unimpressed, he said, by all those female saints who reminded him of flatfish; like soles, they appeared to have both eyes on the same side of their faces.

During the next few days I was back again at Berkhamsted; and the period that immediately followed my return was among the darkest in my whole existence. I needed a job; and for most of the jobs I considered I was obviously disqualified since I had taken no degree. In retrospect, I feel that my lack of a degree was perhaps a heavily disguised blessing; had I graduated, I might have slipped into a museum or a public library, and there remained a life-long prisoner. Publishing then? But jobs at publishers' offices seemed to be reserved for those happy young men who had friends or relations on the board; while literary magazines, though the editors I met often encouraged me to write reviews, were customarily over-staffed. My efforts, which lasted several weeks, involved some curious experiences. Thus, I heard that a certain London savant, the author of learned books dealing with such diverse subjects as magic, witchcraft, demonology, the Restoration dramatists and the early-nineteenth-century novelists, needed secretarial help; and, having offered my services, I was invited to dine at his house in a remote and gloomy suburb.

My prospective employer, I found, was a stout, elderly person, wearing an ancient soutane, faded purple socks and square-toed, silver-buckled shoes. He had pendant jowls – lightly powdered, I think – false teeth, rapidly flickering eyes and a meagre crown of greyish hair. Evidently scholarship had brought him few rewards; and our dinner consisted of the kind of boiled fish, its gelatinous substance threaded with morsels of string, that only English cooks produce. We drank water; and, as I confronted my host, he came more and more to resemble a *mauvais prêtre* in Huysmans' novel *Là-bas*. Possibly I did him wrong; but the impression he made was unmistakably disquieting. He threw me secretive sidelong glances, and appeared oddly insistent that the services he required were both professional and personal. His previous assistant – who, alas, had just died! – had been a valued member of the household. There was nothing one could not ask him to do, whether it were deciphering seventeenth-century manuscripts or taking the dog out for its run! And somehow I suspected that his brief and vague description failed to cover the entire range of his late assistant's duties. So I said goodbye and walked off disappointed through the wet and empty streets.

After suffering a series of similar reverses, I grew particularly impatient with the life I lived at home; and my father, when he returned to the house each night, and saw me supinely stretched upon the sofa, reading a French book entitled *Sodome et Gomorrhe*, was apt to groan and raise his eyebrows. My choice of literature showed the sort of company I kept! Yet, so far as his moral prejudices allowed, he was a sympathetic and fair-minded man; and he admitted that, in my own way, I was a steady, careful worker. Not that my latest occupation promised to be very lucrative. I was translating Jules Laforgue's *Moralités Legendaires*, to which I had been introduced by Sachie Sitwell; and the delicate preciosity of the poet's prose-style, much as I admired its point and elegance, proved hard to render into English. At school I had been excused from French lessons; and what I knew of the language I had laboriously taught myself by trudging, a dictionary beside me, through Anatole France's *L'Ile des Pingouins* – a book that would have been easier to understand had I suspected that it was a complex political satire, founded on the Dreyfus Case.

Though I enjoyed my self-imposed task, I succeeded in translating only two of the *Moralités*; for by that time I had staged a sudden revolt and, at last, escaped to London. I announced dramatically that, with or without permission, I must lead an independent life, even if this meant sleeping on a park-bench or underneath a railway-arch. My father then agreed to renew my allowance. But he refused to pay it monthly; and it arrived every week inside an envelope that also enclosed a brief admonitory letter. He hoped that I should soon have learned to 'stand on my own feet', 'paddle my own canoe', or 'cut my coat to suit my cloth'. The amount varied; so far as I can remember, unless I told him that I faced a grave emergency, it was usually about three pounds ten shillings, and never more than five pounds, which I had usually spent to the last sixpence before another envelope appeared.

Yet, compared with the struggles of many young writers, mine were annoying and embarrassing rather than permanently disheartening. Soon after my return to England I had regained the Sitwells' friendship; and one evening, when I dined at Osbert's house, I met Leonard Woolf, who took a kindly interest in my fortunes and asked me what my prospects were. I said that I had various plans on foot, adding, however, that if they failed, I supposed that I should starve. His keen rabbinical face contracted. 'Well, you're not starving *now*, are you? People of your kind *don't* starve,' he responded rather sharply. I deserved the snub. I shared my mother's weakness for over-dramatizing a situation; and, although since my youth I have rarely been out of debt, and have passed through some exquisitely anxious moments, so far at least I have escaped the worst sufferings of a bankrupt modern author.

My original London lodging was a smallish basement room in Chelsea, only a few steps from the King's Road, part of a house that belonged to an amiable woman artist whose widowed mother lived near Berkhamsted. My fellow lodgers were an interesting collection – a short, square, crop-headed, double-breasted, bow-tied lady, the editress of a famous fashion-magazine, and her more decoratively apparelled friend and colleague; the deserted wife of a celebrated modern sculptor, who talked at length of 'Dobbie's' matrimonial misdeeds; and Freddie Ashton, now Sir Frederick, the doyen of British Ballet, then a gay and energetic young dancer. Our landlady, though she enjoyed bohemian company, was somewhat suspicious of her inmates' morals, and would now and then arrest a brush-stroke, as she stood before her canvas, and gaze up apprehensively towards the ceiling, since she had learned that the inhabitants of the first floor formed a slightly unconventional ménage.

She also employed a Communist housemaid from Battersea, to whom the goings-on of the dissolute middle classes were a constant source of indignation. Once, for example, while making my bed, she noticed that the sheets were scattered with a drift of tiny golden beads, and concluded – rightly, of course – that I must have had a female visitor. The visitor was a new arrival in my life. While I was still at Oxford, I had met a very young girl to whom a close friend had proposed marriage; and, at Ravenna, near the end of my long Italian tour, I received a letter she had written me, in which she explained that her engagement to my friend had suddenly been called off. I opened this letter as I was driving home from one of the churches upon the city's outskirts; and I remember tearing it up – not unkindly or dismissively, but because I seldom keep letters – and scattering its coloured fragments down the surface of the muddy yellow road that stretched away behind my cab. Its message I did not forget; and, as soon as I had returned home, I immediately responded. Whereupon S. and I promised to meet again; she was living, she said, in a lonely and romantic cottage with a single feminine companion.

It was a Dorset fisherman's cottage; and at the end of the garden stood a separate building named the Lobster House. S.'s companion, being several years older than herself, gave me some suspicious looks; but she made a habit of going to bed early. They had arranged I should sleep in the Lobster House; and S., having safely disposed of her friend, one night agreed to join me there. A huge wood-fire burned on the open hearth; firelight makes a beautiful covering for the naked human body; and the old timbered room seemed as remote from real life as Hero's tower above the Hellespont. Next day we walked out to the cliffs; a heavy summer mist obscured the sea; and dew-drops diamonded the hairy-leaved clumps of the bright-blue-flowering borage among which we lay and talked and pondered, while below us the fog-horns of distant invisible ships boomed or wailed along the Channel. Those warning voices perfectly suited our mood, a mood of exhilaration mixed with apprehension, with that 'certain sense of doubt and sorrow – a fear of what is to come – a doubt of what *is*' – which, Byron declared, accompanies the fulfilment of any form of mortal pleasure.* Soon afterwards a telegram reached the cottage; S.'s mother had somehow heard of my visit; and its opening words sounded an ominous note: '*Am unspeakably annoyed*', they ran.

S. and I were of about the same age. A small, slender girl, she had a charmingly cat-like head poised upon a graceful neck; and at our first encounter I noted the decorative contrast between her dark eyes and her ash-blonde hair. She was the prettiest girl he had yet seen, declared a worldly-wise acquaintance, the young man Natalie had brought to Oxford, for whose opinions I had then a deep regard; and, besides being pretty and intensely feminine, she was also exquisitely neat, 'as neat as a Brèguet watch', said a subsequent admirer, referring to the wafer-thin timepieces of the famous eighteenth-century craftsman.† She, too, was a literary aspirant; and some of her verses had recently been published in an intellectual magazine. She loved poetry, and had read a great deal, though her tastes, I thought, were sometimes faintly prudish; and I discovered, when I happened to look into her copy of Mallarmé's verses, that a couple of pages, enclosing a rather improper poem – '*Une négresse par le démon secouée*' – had been elaborately glued together.

Perhaps she had done so to spare her mother's feelings. A massive elderly personage, Mrs T. watched over her beloved

* *Extracts from a Diary*, 28 January 1821.
† Abraham-Louis Brèguet, 1747–1823.

only child with inexhaustible devotion. S.'s father, a retired engineer, occupied the same flat. But evidently his wife had little use for men; all her emotional interests were reserved for her own sex – for her daughter, her countrified married sister and S.'s rich, imposing godmother, a 'country lady' whose red-faced husband, a Gloucestershire hunting-man, would eventually drop dead from the saddle and be carried home upon a gate. That dominant and closely allied trio had overshadowed S.'s youth; her silent, retiring father played a minimal part in her existence. During their honeymoon, he had decided to transport his wife, at that time almost middle-aged, to the upper reaches of the Amazon, where he was laying an electric cable; and the sight of the insects and vampire bats that every evening swarmed around her bed had so strongly and painfully affected her nerves that their union never quite recovered. Once S. was born, he had retired to a separate room. He decorated it with the miniature female dolls – if they wore skirts, he promptly snipped them away – that he had developed a habit of collecting.

S. and I nicknamed her mother 'Chang', after the heroine of an early nature film, the story of a courageous mother-elephant, who, her calf having been stolen by Eastern hunters, crashes through the stockade that surrounds their village and, fiercely stamping and loudly trumpeting, hurries off the young captive. We could not have expected that Chang would approve of our relationship. She had had high hopes for her daughter's future life; S. was to marry a decently rich young man with a solid county background, and establish the kind of household – preferably not far from her aunt's – at which her lonely mother would be made welcome. As it was, she had somehow become attached to an impecunious and disreputable nobody. But S. had a romantic view of life; and, though she could not entirely discard her mother's influence, she stood up bravely against Chang's threats and pleas. The ensuing conflict lasted for two years. We were obliged to meet in secret; and secrecy, a great preservative of passion, merely heightened our attachment. Having worked all day, I awaited the sound of the bell; and, when it rang at last and I opened the door, there was my expected visitor, often cloaked and concealing beneath her cloak the bottle of chablis and the basket of fruit and cold chicken on which we were to dine that night. They were happy encounters; we shared the radiant conviction that at last we had really begun to live; and that ours was now the legendary *vie de bohème* we had so far only glimpsed through books.

Meanwhile, my second volume of poems, a thin but elegantly laid-out volume published by Chatto & Windus, had appeared in 1926, and had received from my staunch friend Edith Sitwell an almost embarrassingly generous tribute. It included three pieces of *vers libre*, written in 1921 or earlier; and, except for a single poem issued as a separate pamphlet, which emerged in 1929,* it was my last poetic product. I have often been asked why I gave up writing verse; and the only answer I can provide is a very simple one. The need to write verse, described on an earlier page, became gradually less and less imperative, and I ceased to experience the moods of visionary excitement that I felt obliged to translate into a rhythmic verbal pattern. Should I begin a poem, I now became aware that I was making a self-conscious literary effort, merely assembling images and manufacturing lines; and I had read enough to believe that manufactured verse, however clever, competent and smooth, was among the dullest types of literature.

At the same period, I embarked on a long struggle to master the art of writing English prose. At Oxford my undergraduate essays had been diffuse and ill-constructed; and, though the good-natured tutor whom I have already mentioned rarely criticized my work, his predecessor, as I read a paragraph aloud, would frequently complain that it was either too 'adverbial' or – didn't I agree? – unnecessarily 'adjectival'. If my style has since improved, much of the improvement is due to the daily grind of book-reviewing. Desmond MacCarthy, in those days, was the literary editor of the *New Statesman*; the contributors he enlisted were customarily young men; and, because he valued and sympathized with youth, he allowed them a remarkable degree of licence.

His personal qualities matched his professional virtues. Disappointment had dogged him throughout his life; he was never

* 'Inscription on a Fountain-head'; Ariel Series.

to produce the masterpiece, a definitive biography of Byron, that his hopeful friends expected; and even his quotidian tasks, noticing a book or a play, he seemed still to find unconscionably difficult. There can have been few occasions when he delivered his copy on time; and he appeared always to be a single jump ahead of the literary creditors pursuing him. Yet he retained a singularly unembittered spirit. 'I think we'd better *not* wait for Desmond,' the hostess who had invited him to a luncheon-party would remark soon after half past one; but in the next quarter of an hour or so he would invariably reach the house, carrying the small black bag that held a partly finished manuscript, and looking blithe though dishevelled and vaguely harassed, and plunge into the midst of an absorbing conversation. Thus engaged, he forgot his distant office, and revealed a facility and spontaneity that, as a journalist, he seldom quite achieved.

Both Cyril Connolly and I were among the youthful reviewers whose work he published in the *New Statesman*, despite the protests occasionally raised by Clifford Sharp, the chief editor, a very different and much less appealing man. Sharp was an alcoholic; he had a nobly handsome face, swollen and ravaged by his dissipations, a fierce eye and a brazen voice. Compared with his earnest successor Kingsley Martin, he was a giant in his trade; but he had acquired an awkward habit, when he got particularly drunk, of driving down late at night to the East End, invading the printers' establishment where they were making ready to set up an issue, and heavily rewriting articles. His additions some-times provoked a law-suit – he had even questioned the integrity of Lord Hewart, the draconian Lord Chief Justice; and Sharp was at length removed from the *Statesman*'s editorial chair, to be replaced by the sober, ingenuous Martin, a dedicated Man of Good Will. Whatever his vices, Sharp commanded respect; and, besides possessing a hard-earned knowledge of the world, he understood the English language; having summoned me once, he sternly pointed out that to use 'infer' in the sense of 'imply' was a vulgar modern solecism. I accepted the reproof; and, since that far-off day, I have done my best to avoid a similar offence.

On the whole, Desmond MacCarthy's recruits suffered from

very little censorship. While Cyril was gaily disembowelling Galsworthy, Walpole, Arnold Bennett and other celebrated twentieth-century novelists, I lashed around at the contemporary poets. Sacheverell Sitwell and Robert Graves were writers I always enjoyed discussing; but a brace of popular versifiers, Gerald Gould and the literary civil servant Humbert Wolfe, became my favourite Aunt-Sallys. Reviewing verse is not an easy task; for, whereas even a bad novel unfolds some kind of human story, and may contain a few interesting records of personal experience, bad verse, being largely negative, is almost impossible to describe or analyse; and there were times when I hated the pile of 'slim volumes' that mounted week after week upon my table. Neither Cyril nor I was overpaid. In his *Enemies of Promise* he suggests that the promising young writer he calls Shelleyblake should set his financial objective at about four hundred pounds a year, which he can only achieve by 'reading two books a day' and contributing to three different papers. I doubt if I ever reached that target; but the work provided useful training; and, although I often felt that my laboriously corrected typescript was bound to be sent back by the editor, again and again I had the agreeable surprise of seeing a review appear in print. Thus I acquired the literary self-confidence I needed, and began to rub off some of the rougher edges of my erratic prose style.

Reviewing verse, luckily, was not my sole employment; and, now and then, I received a literary biography, a critical essay or a current work of fiction. At that period stimulating new books were particularly numerous. *The Great Gatsby*, *Mrs Dalloway* and Eliot's *Poems* had already come out in 1925; in 1926 we had *The Plumed Serpent* and *The Sun Also Rises* (for the English edition renamed *Fiesta*); in 1927 *Men Without Women* and two remarkable works by Wyndham Lewis, a critic of near-genius, *Time and Western Man* and *The Lion and the Fox*; in 1928, *The Childermas*, *Point Counter Point*, Evelyn Waugh's first novel, *Decline and Fall* and Lytton Strachey's *Elizabeth and Essex*; in 1929, Henry Green's *Living*, Ivy Compton-Burnett's *Brothers and Sisters* and Hemingway's *Farewell to Arms*. Among these I am glad to remember that I reviewed and applauded Hemingway's earlier novel, which, I think, remains his masterpiece, and that I managed to see through the flimsy fabric of Strachey's Elizabethan opus. One is apt to forget how rich the period was; and much of its activity revolved around Virginia Woolf and her group of life-long friends. Hanging on the fringe of the literary world, I was not myself attached to Bloomsbury, either by birth or by election. But a pair of distinguished Bloomsburian figures, the art critic Clive Bell and the translator Arthur Waley, occupied an important place in my existence.

Clive was a resolute lover of life – always an endearing trait. He adored art, was passionately devoted to women, enjoyed parties and travel, wine and good food, and an occasional day's shooting. Though he had a bohemian family circle, and shared his Sussex house with his wife Vanessa Bell and her fellow artist Duncan Grant, from his own point of view at least he was, above all else, an *homme du monde*, who moved easily and cheerfully between half a dozen different milieus. The author of a book entitled *Civilization*, he employed the adjective '*civilized*', – stridently hissing out the first syllable – as the highest praise he could bestow. The civilization he tended to prefer was that of eighteenth-century France. He was an ardent Francophile, closely and affectionately acquainted with every distinguished modern French artist; and, should a *nouvelle vague* sweep through the art-world, he was certain to have taken its measure, and might soon be boldly riding it.

Clive's physical appearance was agreeably odd. He had a fresh pink face, a brightly roving eye, a somewhat ill-adjusted *râtelier* – here the French word seems obligatory – and, concealing his incipient baldness, a wreath of blond hair arranged around his dome-shaped head, and held in place, unkind observers asserted, by a multitude of microscopic hairpins which occasionally became detached. My father's publisher affected a similar wreath; but Clive's was considerably more extensive – so long that, on a Mediterranean cruise, when Clive was swimming off the ship and his hair had floated free, a little girl, who watched from the rail, was said to have uttered a sudden shriek of fear, noticing, as she thought, a golden sea-serpent which followed him across the water.

None of his vanities impaired Clive's natural charm. He was a magnificent host, who possessed the invaluable gift of communicating his enthusiasm for a party to the guests he had assembled. Such a collection of clever and attractive people could seldom have been gathered together in the same room! Horace Walpole, Madame du Deffand, Benjamin Constant, Madame de Staël, even Voltaire and Diderot, would surely have considered it a privilege to join us at his flat this evening. And, under his inspiriting influence, one was encouraged to talk with an energy and volubility that fulfilled his expectations. As to beauty, the party almost always included some young woman Clive was energetically besieging; and, though his opinion of her looks was often higher than mine – she might be a mousy little woman novelist, wearing a low fringe and a string of amber beads – her, too, he managed to encircle with a halo of romantic elegance. Clive was a life-enhancer in the literal meaning of the term – a hedonist who could only enjoy himself if he were conscious that he shared his pleasures.

In character and training Arthur Waley seemed Clive's exact antithesis. A devoted scholar-poet, he had inherited a strain of personal puritanism from his hard-working Jewish forbears, and was as quiet and reserved as my other old friend was exuberantly communicative. He despised any form of luxury or fashion; and his Bloomsbury flat was dark and low-ceilinged and plainly furnished. It contained few beautiful or interesting objects. Where I had expected one or two precious artifacts of earthenware, or jade, or bronze, I saw English crockery, text-books and notebooks, schoolroom pens and homely pots of ink. His domestic surroundings at first appeared so bleak that a visiting Japanese scholar had suggested that a fund should be set up to relieve the great man's poverty. But Arthur was not poor; he had a modest private income, which he carefully administered; and he was never interested in collecting works of art, no doubt because all the aesthetic masterpieces he required were carried round inside his own head. Similarly, despite many flattering invitations, he refused to visit China and Japan, since he was reluctant to destroy the visionary images of the T'ang and Heian periods he had already built up. He was perfectly content to spend his days at the

British Museum discharging his official duties, and his leisure-hours construing some difficult text above the trees of Gordon Square.

Our friendship had begun before we met. It was in 1919 that, excited by a review I had seen, I acquired his *More Translations from the Chinese*; and, having read them through, I felt almost as much attached to Li Po and his successor Po Chü-i, as to Words-worth, Shelley, Keats and Coleridge. The extraordinary range of Chinese classic verse astonished and delighted me; and Arthur Waley himself, I discovered, was a gifted literary craftsman, a master of *vers libre*, which he handled with far more ease and skill, and with a much keener appreciation of the value of words, than the average modern poet. His exacting taste I found particularly impressive when I came to know him well. Sometimes he would criticize the manuscript of the book that I was then engaged on; and no one was better at disentangling a confused and overwritten paragraph. 'Don't you think you should say . . . ?' he would en-quire, after silently examining it, in that gentle, unemphatic voice of his. Or 'Wouldn't it be wise perhaps to remove that image and cut out the last four lines?' And reluctantly I would agree to sacrifice the superfluous trope I had thought so apt and vivid.

Arthur had a fine, austere mask, the features of a sage or saintly hermit, for whom the world most of his contemporaries in-habited was an alien and mysterious place. He did not pretend that he could understand their interests, or that he shared their physical and social needs. His own needs were always extremely modest. Arthur was a born ascetic; and, having met Cyril Connolly on a Mediterranean island and been invited to luncheon at an expensive new hotel, he appeared, like Beatrix Potter's Alderman Ptolemy Tortoise, carrying a separate meal – a rustic salad, bought in the local market – stuffed into a large string bag. Arthur's asceticism was the only aspect of his character that occasionally I thought annoying. But I was also disconcerted by his stubborn refusal to talk unless he had something he really wished to say. Thus, our conversations were interrupted by long, curiously unnerving pauses, while, through narrowed eyes, he seemed to set out in pursuit of some remote and memorable vision, and allowed the pageant of vulgar everyday life to sweep unnoticed past his head. If he did talk, he spoke quickly and precisely, often accompanying his words with a brilliant disarming smile. The quality of his voice I have mentioned elsewhere. It was faint and high, and, should he be bored or irritated, might reach an almost supersonic level. By comparison Strachey's voice was loud; Arthur's, dismissing a tedious subject or annihilating a stupid opponent, recalled the sound of a faraway autumn wind as it travels through a bed of reeds.

Though not a conceited man, he took his talents for granted. Clearly, it had never occurred to him there was anything in the least odd about reading a Chinese poem before breakfast, and then going off to spend the day on skis, or, at the age of nearly seventy, deciding to explore the intricacies of an obscure Far Eastern dialect. He neither concealed nor paraded his erudition; and I remember hearing a collector of Chinese porcelain, who had recently acquired a graceful little wine-bowl, ask him to translate the scrap of poetry that had been painted round the bottom. Arthur glanced at the characters, and handed back the bowl. 'What it says,' he answered quietly, 'is "We scoop the glittering moonlight in our cups".' He must have enjoyed the romantic beauty of the phrase; but he scarcely raised his reedy, whispering voice and added no effusive comment.

Arthur was a frequenter, but not a conspicuous member of the great Bloomsburian hierarchy; and Virginia Woolf's notebooks contain a characteristically acid reference to the pair of ancient white-flannel trousers that he often wore on summer days. He and his autumnal Egeria, Beryl de Zoete, led a separate domestic life, cooking their own meals, which were usually vegetarian, reading, writing, making music together – Arthur played a Japanese flute – and, at times, dancing. Beryl, a devotee of Eastern dances, was the older of the two, but considerably the more gregarious. Travelling alone, she would visit Egypt, North Africa or the dance-schools of the Dutch East Indies; and she had an awkward habit of sending home to Arthur some outlandish local genius – once her protégé was a deserter from the Foreign Legion – whom she happened to have picked up. Arthur loved her devotedly, and bore with her enthusiasms patiently. He had a warm heart, as I soon became aware, and, despite his reserved and even alarming manner, an indomitable sense of fun. I have already described his effect on my education. At that time I was making a third attempt to construct a work in prose; and, though *Baudelaire and the Symbolists* is by no means a well-written book, it might, I am sure, have been a good deal worse, had Arthur's keen, yet friendly eye never glanced across its pages.

The completed book, under Chatto & Windus's imprint, finally appeared in 1929. It is a pretty volume, bound between waxed grey boards, with admirable typography, generous margins and a splendid choice of illustrations. As to the contents – essays on Charles Baudelaire, Gérard de Nerval, Villiers de l'Isle-Adam, Jules Laforgue, Tristan Corbière, Arthur Rimbaud and Stéphane Mallarmé – when, in 1954, an optimistic publisher suggested I should prepare a new edition, having seldom for the last twenty-five years ventured to look into the text, I could scarcely recognize the author. His book, I felt, was a serious labour of love; and, besides portraying his characters and defining their individual talents, he had done his best to evoke the atmosphere of a far-off literary period. I was dismayed, however, by his lack of coherence, his vagueness and his cocksureness. Clearly, at Oxford, he had read too much Pater, and was anxious to confer on every passage a vivid Pateresque colouring. Image was extravagantly added to image; and often these images were introduced merely for the sake of their supposed poetic value. From simple statements he was apt to shrink away; and, while his opening sections were obscure and dimly allusive, again and again he invested his closing lines with what Byron, in one of his letters, calls an air of 'rather rich confusion . . .' I found it difficult to edit the text; so many sentences had to be drastically simplified; and a number of overblown paragraphs I could only strike out. Despite my strenuous efforts, *Baudelaire and the Symbolists* remained an unmistakably juvenile production.

The idea was better than the author's prose; and the basic plan I owed to T. S. Eliot. After years of grim commercial servitude, he had now emerged from his underground office in the City, where a banking firm had employed him to translate their foreign correspondence, and occupied the editorial chair at the *Criterion,**

*Eliot's editorship lasted from 1922 to 1939.

the high-principled literary magazine that an affluent well-wisher had founded. To meet the poet of *The Waste Land* was an historic privilege. He still wore the short black coat and pin-striped trousers of an old-fashioned City gentleman, had a long sallow face, sympathetic brown eyes and a slightly twisted smile. His manner of speaking was quiet and precise, and his whole appearance '*un peu clergyman et correct*', as Gustave Kahn said of Jules Laforgue, when he first encountered him. Under my arm I had my translations of Laforgue's *Moralités Legendaries*; and Eliot shrewdly suggested that, instead of trying to translate these almost untranslatable tales, I should endeavour to write a book on the Symbolist Movement and its adventurous protagonists. No such book, he remarked, had been published in English since Arthur Symons's famous study,* which had come out over a quarter of a century earlier, and was written very much from the point of view of a late-Victorian 'decadent'. His authoritative advice encouraged me; and I immediately adopted it. Eliot revered Baudelaire; but with Jules Laforgue he had particularly close links. As a young man, for example, in 'The Love Song of Alfred J. Prufrock' and other verses of the same years, he had been much beholden to the Symbolist poet's influence, even borrowing a phrase here and there;† and Laforgue's close friend, the novelist Alain Fournier, had once taught the young Harvard graduate French.**

Villiers de l'Isle-Adam was my own choice. Eliot would not agree that the author of *Contes Cruels* deserved much critical consideration; but, during my Oxford period, I had read and enjoyed Villiers's exquisite tale 'Les Demoiselles de Bienfilatre'; and his wit and ironic grace and contemptuous opposition to bourgeois standards irresistibly attracted me. But Baudelaire, of course, was my chief hero. Had not Rimbaud, who dismissed Victor Hugo as a colossal vulgarian, acclaimed him as the greatest of *voyants*, or visionary poets? In Baudelaire's works, Marcel

* *The Symbolist Movement in Literature*, 1899.
† In the poem entitled '*La Figlia che Piange*', Eliot's line 'simple and faithless as a smile and shake of the hand' is an almost direct translation of Laforgue's '*simple et sans foi comme un bonjour*'.
** By a strange coincidence Laforgue had been married to his English wife in the London church where Eliot was later to serve as churchwarden.

Proust declared, each separate poem was a fragment that, once we have read it, links up with the fragments we already know to produce a huge imaginative landscape; and among the aspects of his genius I most admired was his feeling for the life of an enormous modern city, which he evokes at every hour of day and night, from dawn when the calls of military bugles ring out distantly across its roofs and Aurora creeps along the Seine,* until darkness has fallen, and an army of prostitutes descend upon the gas-lit boulevards.

Baudelaire, essentially a modern poet, was both fascinated and horrified by the age through which he lived, detesting the squalor and corruption of commercialized nineteenth-century Paris, yet finding in the immensely various spectacle a strange and unexpected beauty, 'le beau multiforme et versicolore qui se meut dans les spirales infinies de la vie'. He had introduced, moreover, into French literature an entirely new note – 'le miaulement [wrote Jules Laforgue], le miaulement nocturne, singulier, langoureux, désesperé . . . solitaire' of a lost soul or a vagrant cat. And it was Baudelaire, too – again I quote Laforgue – who, after all the airy flights of the Romantic poets, had been the first to employ some matter-of-fact image that, amid the harmonious cadences of a period, suddenly brings his reader down to earth.

From his Fleurs du Mal and Petits Poèmes on Prose I moved on to his magnificent critical essays and his posthumous Journaux Intimes, the preliminary draft of the 'terrible book' in which he meant to lay his heart bare, and which would have raised against him, he thought, the whole of middle-class society. Baudelaire's complex character seemed no less absorbing than his literary achievement; and I grew as much involved in his tormented private life as, subsequently, in that of Byron. Thus, I became a biographer; and, despite one or two excursions into allied fields, a biographer I have ever since remained. Biography is a rewarding branch of literature, at least for those who practise it. One re-lives the past, moves through the crowded scenes of an unfamiliar social period, makes odd friends, is told fantastic stories and, above all else, plunges into the mysterious existence of a true

* L'aurore grélottante en robe rose et verte
  S'avancait lentement sur la Seine déserte

creative artist, who very often creates upon one plane, but destroys himself upon another. In Baudelaire's life I was struck by the close connection between his weakness and his strength, between his failures and his triumphs. Had the poet not failed as a man – and his personal catastrophe could scarcely have been more atrocious – he might well have lived and died a cultivated amateur beneath his family's protective wing.

It must have been about the time I embarked on *Baudelaire and the Symbolists* that I exchanged my Chelsea lodgings for a couple of top-floor rooms above a bookshop near High Holborn. Below me were slightly larger rooms that the young composer Constant Lambert occupied. In 1926, his ballet *Romeo and Juliet*, commissioned by Diaghilev, had already brought him fame. But it had not brought him fortune. Neither his creative gifts nor his literary and critical intelligence were ever fully recognized; and, so long as I knew him, with his shapeless overcoat, his rough scarf and his heavy stick – he had a slightly lame leg – Constant remained a hard-working, hard-living and almost invariably hard-up bohemian, whose powerful voice, whether he discussed the arts, sang a favourite folk-song or recited a lubricious limerick, penetrated to the farthest recesses, and startled the drowsiest *habitués* of a London bar-parlour. He would have been perfectly at home in Paris during the Romantic 1830s. Gérard de Nerval had developed an idealized passion for a minor comédienne named Jenny Colon; and Constant's *princesse lointaine* was the Chinese film-actress Anna May Wong. To do her honour, he often drank Chinese wine; and squat earthenware flasks of that singularly unpleasant fluid stood ranged along the top of his piano. Its intestinal effects, he once admitted, were no less disturbing than its taste and smell.

Our landlady, the owner of the shop, inhabited the first and ground floors. A tall, elegant, fair-haired young woman, not long before billed as 'The Beautiful Miranda' in one of C. B. Cochrane's popular revues, for some reason never explained to me she had given up the stage and had adopted, with moderate success, the unlikely trade of book-selling. Below Edward Wadsworth's decorative signboard, *The Miranda Bookshop*, she moved casually about her business, assisted by any acquaintance who, seeking conversation and a free drink, might happen to have dropped in; but, when the day ended and she closed the shop door, a Comus-rout of fresh acquaintances arrived. The party that followed, with occasional expeditions to lively Soho pubs, often lasted till the small hours; and a homeless guest – I remember particularly a sixteen-stone translator of erotic Eastern verse forming a colossal mound – could sometimes be discovered next morning fast asleep among the book-shelves. In Chelsea I had been considered mildly rakish; in my new lodging I was regarded as an effeminate and squeamish prig, who avoided pub-crawls, and had neither the stomach nor the nerves for the kind of strenuous fun the Miranda Bookshop offered. 'There you sit', a woman familiar complained, 'in your *tidy* little room, scribbling away at a *tidy* manuscript, waiting to see a *tidy* little girl'; and a moment came when the Beautiful Miranda herself suggested we should go our separate ways.

Not that, on principle, I was at all averse from party-going. The mid-1920s was an age of extravagant parties, held in ball-rooms, night-clubs, studios, or even in the Westminster Public Baths; and I attended a number of these bizarre occasions. Fancy dress was almost always worn; and Cecil Beaton has described a period of his life when, for eight or nine days at a stretch, he never once assumed his ordinary clothes, but would discard a fancy dress on going to bed and assume a new travesty before he again left home. There were fashionable parties, too; and such a party, under the Sitwells' auspices, I remember observing at a Georgian house in Chelsea. Our hostess was Mrs Somerset Maugham; her guest of honour was a Royal Duke, whose high sloping forehead and long straight nose, which formed a single backward line, recalled portraits of his great-great-great-great-great-grandfather, the unlucky Frederick, Prince of Wales. Around him circled some seductive young women, curtseying to him with an agreeable mixture of gay familiarity and loyal deference, just as his women friends must surely have curtseyed to the future George IV. The scene was Hanoverian; and so was the Duke's behaviour; for, after he had taken his leave and pre-pared to drive off, a caterer's van happened to reach the door bearing fresh supplies of champagne; and he ordered his detective to appropriate a case and have it stowed away inside the boot. Another remarkable personage was the small dark man, with an eye-glass and a thin moustache, whom I noticed when I left the house. He stood alone amid a crowd of departing guests; and 'Where's that bloody bitch my wife?' he kept demanding fiercely of the world at large.

I cannot date the occasion; but if, as I think it must have done, it took place in 1928, this was the last festivity of the kind I should attend for some while. In the May or June of that year, I retreated to a country cottage which I had leased from William Rothenstein, where I spent several dull and solitary weeks struggling to complete my book. Before I had quite succeeded, S. arrived on my threshold, the bearer of dramatic news. Chang's resistance had suddenly collapsed; since her daughter was now thoroughly compromised, and she had abandoned any hope of separating us, she supposed that we had better marry. What was more, she had decided that the untoward event should be hurried through as soon as possible. She had therefore taken all the necessary steps and, indeed, had even fixed the day.

During the brief interval that still remained, I thought it right to see my parents. My mother was surprised, though, on the whole, relieved; my father regretted that he could not attend my wedding, as he was bound for the United States. A local capitalist who had developed *folies de grandeur* (which eventually brought about his downfall) had decided to rebuild his works, and had commissioned my father to execute a rapid survey of American industrial systems. This wild plan my father, despite his lack of any previous experience, had enthusiastically accepted; and, when I appeared, he was already packing his bags and considering the details of his expedition. Meanwhile, he had little time to spare. But first he delivered a brisk lecture on the blessing of a happy marriage – the greatest blessing in a man's life – such as he himself had long enjoyed; next, produced a pen, rushed towards his desk and wrote out a cheque which he handed me with a congratulatory flourish. I thanked him, and wished him a good journey. Once we had parted, I glanced at the figure he had written, and saw that it was fifteen pounds.

Our marriage, early in July 1928, proved a rather doleful

ceremony, overcast by the sorrowing presence of S.'s mother and her mother's friends. S. herself, moreover, was wearing a hat that I instantly deplored, a white cloche hat on which a large blue swallow – could it be Maeterlinck's Blue Bird? – had unfortunately come to rest. Chang remained calm. But she had not expected to marry off her only child at a vulgar Registry Office; and, as soon as we had been pronounced man and wife, she and her solicitous attendants made a swift and gloomy exit. All three fled to the big old-fashioned limousine that had been drawn up outside; and, even before the vehicle had rolled away, we saw them, like a trio of melting snowwomen, dissolve tearfully into one another's arms.

That afternoon we crossed the Channel and spent a memorable night in Paris, dining at a celebrated restaurant beneath the trees of the Bois de Boulogne, and returning home to bed down the summery Champs-Elysées, full of champagne and romantic fire. Our eventual destination was the Forest of Fontainebleau, where we meant to stay at Barbizon. Yet again I had been ridiculously misguided by the excessive reliance I always placed on books. Among George Moore's stories I had read a charming description of Barbizon as a quiet little village, lost amid pinewoods far from modern traffic. We found a colony of stucco chalets, clustered along a noisy street; and a brief glimpse was enough to send us back to Fontainebleau. We chose a sober family hotel near the splendid stone and red-brick Palace; but in that pleasant town the mood of romantic exhilaration unaccountably deserted us. The weather was torrid; our rooms were small and dark; S. suffered a series of agonizing headaches; and often she was obliged to lie abed, while I explored the Forest's labyrinthine sandy paths and climbed the gigantic lichenous boulders that raise their saurian shapes between the trees. I also sought refuge in the magnificent formal gardens – a vast pattern of walks and clipped avenues, of gaudy parterres and smooth dark sheets of water – stretched immediately behind the Palace buildings. Whenever I revisit Fontainebleau, I return to the right-hand corner of a certain shallow stone-rimmed pool; for there, on the hottest and stillest days, now almost fifty years ago, I would sit and listen to the melancholy twangling and strumming of a distant piano in the Palace music-rooms, and watch a shoal of minnows that occupied the angular shade cast by an old anchored punt. With marvellous precision, the shoal had condensed itself into the shadow's geometric outline, beyond which not a minnow stirred.

Having completed our honeymoon, we took up the duties of marriage in a top-floor flat above the King's Road. It had a fine view of Chelsea's roofs and chimneys looking south towards the river. But these were not the kind of surroundings that S.'s relations expected that she would inhabit; and, although her godmother and her godmother's husband were persuaded to ascend our stairs – a feat that they accomplished with much stumbling and puffing – once they had arrived they did not conceal their dismay and could scarcely be prevailed upon to sit down. Soon afterwards, however, we deserted Chelsea, and took a larger flat in Kensington. The neighbourhood was more respectable; but the stairs again were long and steep; and again we occupied the top floor, over the offices of a busy firm that taught the art of writing for the popular press by means of correspondence-courses. Our rooms were irregularly shaped, yet neither cramped nor ugly; and S., who had a natural sense of style, quickly set about improving them.

Here we stayed from the latter months of 1928 until the spring of 1930; and, when *Baudelaire and the Symbolists* at length appeared, it elicited some satisfactory reviews. I cannot pretend that I have been unkindly treated by critics; the most unpleasant review I have ever had to stomach was a venomous diatribe by Evelyn Waugh; and the only rebuke I now received was delivered by my good friend Francis Birrell, son of the statesman and essayist Augustine Birrell, and himself among the gayest and best-hearted members of Bloomsburian society, a small gnome-like man with a deep and penetrating laugh and enormous horn-rimmed spectacles. Though he admitted that the book had some merits, he hastened to point out its grammatical and syntactical deficiencies; and, as I felt that his criticisms were well-deserved, I was neither vexed nor deeply pained. Otherwise, my essays enjoyed a modest *succès d'estime*, a kind of success, agreeable rather than remunerative, to which I afterwards became accustomed. I doubt if the volume had a very wide sale; certainly it did not earn me large royalties; and our joint income at the time was so small that, when the Commissioners of Inland Revenue sent me an alarming letter, and I begged S. to visit the Collector's office and personally plead my cause, she found him ready to accept the sum of five pounds in full settlement of all his claims.

Meanwhile, I continued journalizing, both for the *New Statesman*, where Desmond MacCarthy had at length resigned his editorship, and for *Life & Letters*, the recently founded periodical over which he now presided. It was an anxious life. True, S. possessed a diminutive private income, and my father kept up his allowance; but we were seldom quite sure, if a promised cheque failed to arrive, how we were to pay the next month's bills. Such anxieties had a disquieting effect on my nerves; and old photographs, taken about this time, show me gaunt and hollow-eyed, with bent shoulders and a haunted, hag-ridden air. I was absurdly thin; until I had reached the threshold of middle age, my weight never exceeded ten stone; and the fact that, at six feet, I am fairly tall gave me an almost skeletonic look. We led a quiet existence at Palace Gate. Neither of us was very sociable; S.'s friends did not invariably like me; mine had scattered since I left Oxford. Robert Graves, my trusted literary mentor whose Oxfordshire cottage I had so often visited, had set out for Cairo in 1926; and, although he soon returned, he brought with him Laura Riding (originally Laura Riding Gottschalk), a belligerent transatlantic Muse; and Laura hastened to make a clean sweep of most of his previous acquaintances.

Another old friend had suddenly developed into a fierce antagonist. While I still lived above the Miranda Bookshop, I had been aroused by a violent knock upon the door, and, looking down, saw a perplexed postman, holding out a single letter. 'Got a person here called Judas P. Quennell?' he demanded loudly from the street. I agreed that that was my own surname, if not the Christian name to which I answered; and, once I had descended, he handed me an envelope that contained two or three pages of virulent abuse. The writer was Harold Acton. I was not accused, I learned, of any personal misdeeds. My offence consisted in having published a review of a biography of William

Beckford that included some derogatory references to the great man's private character. It revealed, I was assured by my correspondent, a thoroughly craven, mean and snobbish spirit.

Cyril Connolly remained a good friend; but he was constantly travelling abroad. When he went down from Oxford, he had been obliged to adopt, for the first and almost the last time in his life, a wholly uncongenial occupation, as tutor to a rich Jamaican youth. But it had not detained him very long; and he had now secured the post of secretary and amanuensis to the fastidious Anglo-American littérateur Logan Pearsall-Smith (brother-in-law of Bernard Berenson), who paid him a small but adequate salary, and granted him all the independence he required. My way of life, compared with Cyril's, was severely circumscribed. If I travelled, my holidays were bound to be brief; and at home I lived in a restricted circle, busy, of course, and usually placid enough, but sometimes troubled by a sense of solitude – of 'missing something' – as rich and carefree friends gathered fresh experiences and rushed ahead through new adventures.

Kensington Gardens lay a minute's walk from our flat; and I would go there many afternoons. My usual companion was a Bedlington terrier – the gift of a good-natured lady, the mother of my Oxford friend, John Sutro, who said she thought I needed more exercise; and Bedlingtons, though not very clever dogs, since over-breeding has diminished the size of their skulls and systematically squeezed out their brains, possess a cursive streamlined elegance, and will clear the lowest shin-rail in a wonderfully high-arched leap. I enjoyed these walks; the breeze-fretted surface of the Round-Pond was alive with butterfly-winged craft; longtailed kites went veering across the sky; and before the rose-red seventeenth-century palace perched the wedding-cake statue of the young Queen. Only as I returned home, and crossed the motor-road, did melancholy now and then swoop down. I envied the girls and young men I saw driving past towards an evening of unknown pleasures, and felt cut-off – miserably 'left behind' – as I stood and watched them from the kerb.

S. herself may often have suffered a similar disquietude. For neither of us was marriage turning out precisely as we had expected; and this was no fault of hers or mine, but of the situation in which we found ourselves. I cannot always have been good company. Towards the end of 1929 I regularly felt ill and qualmish; and an old trouble – the attacks of nervous nausea that had plagued my childhood – reappeared to overcloud my adult life. When we spent Christmas with my mother and father at Berkhamsted, they therefore suggested I should consult their local doctor, a lively and strong-minded Scotsman whom they both of them admired and liked. Unluckily, Dr Macpherson was a born experimentalist, with a bad habit of picking up new theories, and proceeding to try them out upon his patients. After a cursory examination, during which I protested that in none of the areas he prodded did I feel the slightest pain, he announced that the cause of my trouble was a 'grumbling appendix'. He then hastened to recommend an immediate appendectomy; and, as his favourite theory at the time concerned the use of spinal, rather than of general anaesthetics, he persuaded me to have the offensive organ removed without completely losing consciousness.

The 'insult to tissue', he said, would be 'less severe'; but my own recalcitrant organism disagreed. My tongue thickened and furred by a sedative drug, I was wheeled into the operating theatre's hard white blaze, and lifted on to the table where a savage stab in the spine rapidly paralysed me from the armpits down. I thought of the prince in the *Arabian Nights*, who, as the result of some evil enchantment, becomes half marble and half living flesh; and, when I noticed that my iodine-painted abdomen was clearly reflected on the glass of a large lamp suspended just above the table, I begged that the apparatus might be shifted. Then, behind a narrow canvas barrier erected across my body, a coven of masked shapes, muttering beneath their masks, and exchanging scalpels and forceps and swabs, set about their horrid business. Occasionally I caught a sentence: 'Here, take a look at *this*, Sister!' My feelings are hard to describe. Below the arms my whole torso had congealed into a solid icy mass; and, although I suffered no definite physical pain, I had an atrocious sense of dislocation. It was as if I were an immobilized human clock from which the mainspring or some intimate cog-wheel was being brutally extracted.

I returned to the public ward – the private room I had hoped for was already occupied – in time to witness an appalling drama. Almost opposite me lay a very old man, once a gardener by trade, whose nightly wails disturbed his fellow patients. There was nothing really wrong with the poor old chap, the cheerful matron reassured me; yet his complaints grew more and more piteous. Finally, he ejaculated that he knew he was going to die; his wails became a poignant shriek; there was a sudden rush of nurses, carrying screens which they hoisted all around his bed; and from behind the screens we heard his last words. They resembled the victim's farewell speech in an Elizabethan tragedy: 'I die! I die!' immediately succeeded by the stage-direction '(dies)'. During the hush that followed, the hospital wiseacre, a talkative and self-important clerk, solemnly approached my pillow, and quoted from Edward FitzGerald's popular translation of the *Rubaiyat*: ' "The moving finger writes, and having writ . . ." Remember what the poet said?' As a rule, I enjoy a poetic reference, but then it did me little good. For the next two or three days I could scarcely eat or drink; even a sip of orange-juice proved completely indigestible; and, on their first visit, my parents reproached me with my cowardly behaviour. No sooner could I manage my wavering legs than I hastened to discharge myself; and I regained our flat so peevish and weak and gloomy, and provoked such ridiculous household scenes, that S., usually a sympathetic young woman, declared she thought my mind was failing.

At this point, however, an angel of deliverance, neatly disguised as an itinerant Japanese professor, had already reached London. The university he represented, the Tokyo Bunrika Daigaku, had commissioned him to seek a candidate for its newly founded Chair of English Literature and Language, preferably a modern poet; and he had decided that the well-known Poetry Bookshop, which Harold Monro managed opposite the British Museum, might be the proper place to start his quest. In another volume* I have attempted Monro's portrait, and described a gaily convivial and pleasantly confused evening I spent with him and T. S. Eliot. Though he had a somewhat irascible character, aggravated by a chaotic private life, he was an affectionate and

* *The Sign of the Fish.*

loyal friend; and, on hearing his Japanese visitor's story, he remembered the account I had given him of my recent misadventures, and at once arranged a meeting. It went off surprisingly well. For a Japanese, Professor T. was an impetuous and incautious man. When I objected that I had neither an Oxford degree nor any kind of pedagogic training, he cheerfully brushed aside my doubts; and, after a second or third encounter, I accepted the appointment. That spring we gave away our dog, bade our parents goodbye and, having travelled overland to Marseilles, boarded a vessel of the *Messageries Maritimes* line that was to transport us to the Far East.

No air-link then existed with Japan; by modern standards it was a leisurely and lengthy voyage. I had never left Europe before; and, now that energy and peace of mind were returning, I had the convalescent's eager eye.* First, Egypt emerged as a hedge of lateen sails, tiny slanting strokes that pricked the far horizon; then as the scattered cubes of luminous masonry that represented Port Said. Down the Suez Canal we steamed through a swarm of locusts, big greenish, brittle, helpless insects with fine gauzy wings and long extended shanks, blowing from Asia, where they carpeted the bleak grey dunes, across the water into Africa. Once we had entered the Gulf of Aden, our earliest landfall was at the French port of Djibouti. Fragrant oleanders shadowed the main square; salt pans glittered on the beaches; and close to the outskirts of the modern town stretched the native camel-market, a dense forest of proudly arched necks supporting long-lipped supercilious heads, among which tall thin black Somali warriors stalked in snow-white cotton robes. My next memories concern the flying-fish – showers of silver arrow-heads, darting distractedly above the waves as they followed us towards Colombo; and, at Colombo, our expedition to a local jewellers' shop, whither we accompanied a shipboard acquaintance, a stout North-country businessman, who had decided, he said, to buy a little present for his girl-friend. Opals, moonstones, rubies, sapphires were then poured out over a dark velvet cloth; and

* In *Un Peintre de la Vie Moderne*, Baudelaire likens the artist to a 'perpetual convalescent', looking out from the window of his sickroom with 'a profound and mirthful curiosity'.

although such splendid objects were beyond our own means, we particularly coveted the star-sapphires, if only for the sake of the mysterious central star itself and its pointed glimmering rays that, however one turned or tilted the stone, swung in the opposite direction.

Meanwhile, the everyday life of the ship regularly provided some fresh human drama. A squad of French conscripts were journeying out steerage; and a homesick young private climbed the rail and leapt down into our widespread wake, where, though life-belts were thrown and a lifeboat was lowered, and passengers shouted their encouragement, before the vessel could manage to change its course we had left him far behind us, to disappear amid the hills and valleys of the sea. On a less tragic scale, we observed a poignant love-affair. The protagonists were a handsome Frenchwoman, travelling with her English husband and their child, and a small French naval officer, unmistakably an experienced *homme à femmes*, grey-haired, and very alert and dandified in his well-pressed white-and-gold uniform. He seemed to have appointed himself the whole family's devoted escort. He and the woman, at least, had become inseparable companions. But her husband, though he joined them for aperitifs and meals, often wandered round the decks alone; and sometimes, when they sat together in the bar, he would pass the open doorway and glance through at their quiet preoccupied figures, then move off looking dumbly anguished. On shipboard, one notes the development of an affair as one watches the growth and flowering of an orchid; and, if the child or other passengers were about, the lovers frequently expressed their feelings by means of a curious symbolic rite; he would polish her nails – her hands were large but shapely; and she would undertake to polish his. The rapid, insistent strokes of the pad no doubt recalled their more substantial pleasures.

They parted at Singapore. A crowd, which naturally included the lover, hung like a frieze of gargoyles from the ship's side; while on the quay below, among their luggage, stood the trio who were leaving us. Mrs J. had a statuesque grace; a breeze drove her skirts against her legs, moulding the sensuous outline of her body. She continued to gaze upwards; her husband, heavy and awkward, with his pouched eyes and bitter burnt-out mask, stared blankly straight in front of him. Then chains rattled and a whistle blew, signalling our immediate departure; and an abrupt and dreadful metamorphosis overtook the woman on the quay. One bare arm flew up towards her breast; her lips worked and her bosom heaved; tears began to blur her lids; her head drooped till it lay along her shoulder. Only the man she was losing retained his fixed smile, and, after a last nod and a last wave, soon took refuge in his cabin. Two nights later, we heard from an informative gossip, he had descended to the steerage; whence he emerged leading a rather bedraggled young woman, a French prostitute bound for Indo-China, with whom he dined alone in the first-class saloon.

It was not a dull journey; but we reached our highest point of enjoyment during the two or three hot and exhausting days we spent on Indo-Chinese soil. Saigon, at that happy period of history, was still a quiet provincial town.* Flame-of-the-Forest trees, bearing broad flat roofs of scarlet blossom, overhung its placid streets, where beautiful slender Annamite women, their tight black skirts slit up to show the knee, slipped soundlessly along the pavements, and stout French ladies, with gloves and hats and veils, bobbed past in rickshaws on their social errands. I had always hoped to visit Angkor; indeed, the discovery that *Messageries Maritimes* boats spent a considerable time at Saigon had been one of my chief motives for accepting a Japanese professorship. Now we hired a taxi and drove north across an arid plain, slept at Phnom Penh – all I can remember of that ill-fated city is the noise made by beetles or crickets scuttering and scuffling over stone-paved floors – and, about midday, sighted Angkor Wat. Opposite the bungalow-hotel stretched a wide brown moat; beneath the lengthy rampart that bordered the moat a single elephant stood knee-deep as it sluiced its wrinkled flanks and shoulders; and beyond the rampart a group of phallic towers rose flickering against a heat-pale sky.

* While these pages were being written, both Saigon and Phnom Penh fell to the Khmer Rouge.

V

ALTHOUGH WE HAD BEEN WARNED THAT WE SHOULD ON no account visit the ruins before the sun had passed its zenith and the day was growing cooler, after a restless hour spent in my shuttered room I decided I must venture out. In the hotel court-yard, the chorus of hidden insects, whirring, rasping, stridulating, produced a kind of muted roar; and the fierce sunshine, which dimmed every colour it touched, lent a brazen burnish to the smallest leaf or twig. Ahead, a broad flagged causeway marched straight towards the far-off pinnacles, traversing the moat and bisecting a huge grassy precinct scattered with a few dishevelled forest-trees. I entered the temple by a dark and narrow door; and there a long ascent began, through arcaded cloisters between deep-sunken courts, up flights of steps, each of them steeper and blacker than the flight that had preceded it, until I emerged upon an open platform immediately beneath the towers themselves, four prodigious cones stationed like guardian giants about the lofty central shaft. The innermost sanctuary of Angkor Wat, it is also the building's geometric focus; and the stairs that approach it climb at as sharp an angle as those of a Maya or an Aztec pyramid. A covered passage mounted to the Holy of Holies; within was emptiness and stifling darkness. What I had expected to find I do not know – perhaps an image of the god. But the darkness had a voice, or rather a multitude of voices which seethed and gibbered from the concave roof; and a peculiar animal reek, sweetish and acrid, hung upon the stagnant air.

The shrine was full of bats, thousands of fruit-eating bats hung upside down in leathery clusters; and when one wide-winged beast suddenly shot past, and its wing-tip nearly brushed my head, I soon retired across the threshold. My homeward journey was a good deal less exhausting. Readers of *A la recherche du* *temps perdu* will remember how Proust describes his hero's earliest visit to the church at Old Balbec, which Swann had warmly recommended, but finds it squeezed in among insignificant neighbours, near a café, an omnibus office and a modern bank. Only on a second and third view does it gradually unfold its beauty; and a similar disappointment often awaits the visitor to some famous long-imagined building. The temples of Angkor had just the opposite effect; they were larger, more splendid and more fantastic than any imaginative picture that I could have drawn. Angkor Wat owes much of its splendour to its look of classic symmetry,* the whole structure being built up stage by quadrangular stage around the towers that form its apex. As I descended, however, I noticed that every stretch of stonework was deeply incised with vegetable and human shapes; with multi-foliate patterns, sometimes admirably, sometimes repetitiously and crudely carved, and with rows of *apsaras*, the heavenly *corps de ballet*, nymphs who haunted this celestial mountain, and whose seductive features and polished shoulders and arms – they wore tall pointed head-dresses, and between their breasts lay jewelled pendants – gleamed delightfully in sun or shadow. A young Frenchman had accompanied us from Saigon; and it was this wealth of sculptured ornament he considered most impressive. '*Quelle richesse de décor! On dirait une cathédrale gothique!*' he continued to exclaim at regular intervals when he joined us on our wanderings.

The chronology of the monuments has been much discussed and revised. During our visit, we heard that the baroque edifices of Angkor Thom were far earlier than the classic Angkor Wat; but I am now told that they belong to a considerably later period. We drove there next day, soon after the sun had risen, along a dusty jungle-track, over a bridge bordered with a majestic balustrade of contending gods and giants engaged in their legendary tug-of-war,† and through a gateway topped by a

* This impression, however, proves to be somewhat deceptive. The Khmer architect had little knowledge of geometry and, building on so immense a scale, found it difficult to achieve a perfect quadrangle or square.
† In the legend of Vishnu, the gods and giants, using the serpent Naga as their rope, which they have wrapped around a sacred mountain, churn the celestial Sea of Milk.

quartet of sculptured masks. The city has vanished – it was built of wood and thatch; but, although the jungle has filled the enormous walled expanse where its palaces and thatched houses stood, archaeologists have cleared an open space around the sanctuary named the Bayon. At first sight it resembles a disordered heap of broken stone, of sagging terraces and dislocated spires. Then a beatific vision slowly emerges from chaos – one smiling face succeeds another. The Bayon has fifty different turrets; each is composed of four gently smiling heads; and each symbolizes the same member of the Hindu pantheon, Lokesvara, or Avalokileśvara, God of Mercy, the so-called 'Looking-down Lord'.* Some have been cruelly damaged; the square sandstone blocks have split apart, leaving a deep vertical fissure that cuts through nose or chin; while greenish damp-stains and tawny lichenous growths dapple the surface of the masonry. Yet their collective smile irradiates the Bayon as it wreathes and spreads among the ruined towers. Like the 'archaic smile' of early Greek statues, it has a grave, mysterious sweetness.

Close to the Bayon rose the gilded roofs of the wooden royal palace, above a street that led to the Gate of Victory; and here, in the year 1296, a Chinese envoy, Chou-Ta-Kuan, watched the Khmer sovereign pass on his sacred elephant, standing upright and holding the sword of state, preceded by a host of flower-decked girls and a regiment of amazons, who carried shields and lances.† All these glories vanished in 1432, when, after a three months' siege, a Siamese army took and pillaged Angkor, and destroyed both the palace and the city. Angkor Wat was preserved as a Buddhist temple; we saw incense-sticks smoking before gilded effigies of the Enlightened One, and met saffron-robed monks drifting to and fro along the cloisters. But Angkor Thom soon vanished beneath the forest; from which a French archaeologist** pertinaciously disengaged it early in the present century, and into which it may again be sinking.

Nearly three hundred monuments, some of them almost un-

* They were originally supposed to represent either Brahma or Siva.
† See M. Krasa: *The Temples of Angkor*, 1963.
** Jean Commaille, who was murdered by bandits in 1916. Three of his fellow archaeologists have also come to violent ends.

explored, are scattered round the royal city; and, of those we saw, only a few have been completely *débroussaillé*, or stripped of invading forest growth. A particularly vigorous and aggressive tree is entitled the *figuier des ruines*. It crushes a building to death; and among its oddest victims is a graceful little edifice encircled by a small round pool. On the summit a wind-blown or bird-dropped seed has given birth to a gigantic tree that has made the shrine its pedestal, its sinuous roots, smooth and ashen-grey, smothering the walls in a massive tentacular web, through which only some fragments of carved detail, and portions of a door and windows, can be distinguished here and there. The forest that surrounds the Bayon is a colourless and silent place, where the faintest noise – even the rustling of a snake amid the dead leaves – sounds extraordinarily clear and loud. Now and then, a bird would utter a cry that suggested the sharp note of a tiny gong; and, looking up, we caught sight of sapphire-blue wings and a sweeping lyre-shaped tail.

After our visit to Angkor, both Hong Kong and Shanghai left a rather vague impression; though at Shanghai we seem to have found our way into an attractive Chinese night-club. At Kobe, the head of the University's English Department, a small, neat, taciturn, swarthy man, came aboard while we were eating breakfast. In a travel-book, which has long gone out of print, I have given an admittedly superficial and, I fear, a somewhat unsympathetic account of our Japanese adventures.* I do not propose here to retrace the whole story. Professor H.'s expression, in so far as he ever thought it prudent to register his real feelings, suggested that our joint appearance surprised and disconcerted him; and that he found me much too young for the important post his over-sanguine subordinate had decided to bestow on me. Conversation proved difficult; but he gallantly did his best, transported us to Nara (where we fed the tame deer and inspected the fifty-foot statue of the Great Buddha, seated in its twilit shrine) and, next day, through the carriage-window, pointed out the distant peak of Mount Fuji. He was clearly exhausted, and had almost lost his voice, before the train ran into Tokyo.

Our earliest resting-place was the busy Imperial Hotel, the

* *A Superficial Journey*, 1932.

eccentric structure raised by the American architect Frank Lloyd Wright opposite the steep green glacis that surround the Emperor's hidden palace. It was expensive, however; and we soon moved to a homely students' hotel in a crowded district near the University, which we did not leave until the early summer, when we took possession of a neighbouring house. Meanwhile, I had been introduced to my colleagues, and presented to my future students. I had a warm welcome; every face beamed; I was asked innumerable questions; and, during our move to the new house, a host of good-natured young men regularly attended us, sitting on the floor, smoking cigarettes, talking among themselves with occasional private jokes, or translating our outlandish wishes. Our house, though elsewhere Japanese, contained one ugly 'Western-style' room; and we had decided we would have it repainted. Japanese women seldom issue orders; and our friends were astonished to hear S. transmit her commands to the painter in a distinctly authoritarian tone. If he shook his head over the colour she had chosen, she might even show annoyance; and, being great gossips, they described the episode to an inquisitive professor, who, after some hesitation and muffled giggling, reported their comments back to me. In such crises, he said he had asked them, what line did Professor Quennell take? He merely exclaimed 'Oh, God!' they answered, then retreated to his study, and began to read a book. Besides helping us, they also watched us closely; for the Japanese, Western habits and tastes are a perpetual source of surprise; and both at home and at the University I was under constant observation. The results of this intensive scrutiny were not, I think, entirely favourable. Though the dark, brass-buttoned uniforms my students wore often made it hard to tell their ages, several were married; a few were older than myself; and I had neither the academic weight they expected, nor the look of professorial dignity. Serious questions I sometimes dealt with in a mildly flippant style; and now and then I threw off a tentative joke, which, far from easing our relationship, merely accentuated my air of general strangeness. I am not a born teacher. As soon as I mount a platform and unroll my lecture notes, any belief that I have knowledge to impart or a message to deliver almost immediately deserts me, and is replaced by a surge of commiseration for my patient captive audience. My Japanese audiences usually treated me well, despite a dreadful, long-remembered scene when I foolishly allowed myself to lose my temper and loudly reprimanded a student in the front row, a sullen pockmarked misanthrope, aged about twenty-eight or twenty-nine, who, incapable of following a word I said, was glancing through a newspaper.

I had two classes, more and less advanced. The Bunrika Daigaku, I soon discovered, unlike the Imperial University, where I afterwards gave spare-time lectures, was primarily a teachers' college; and my students were chiefly concerned to improve their academic status, and thus gain the post on which they had set their hearts in some remote provincial school. To enrich their minds and enlarge their view of life was a secondary interest; and what they demanded were scraps of basic material they could copy out and memorize. Before long I fell into the habit of dictating every paragraph, and covering the blackboard behind my desk with an array of useful dates and names. This was the method that suited my students best; once I had turned towards the blackboard, they eagerly unscrewed their fountain-pens. Few of my attempts to reach their imaginations, or arouse some kind of personal response, by suggesting, for example, that there was perhaps a valid link between their own experience of the world, and the story or poem I discussed, had any positive result; and, during my efforts, I made a hideous mistake – one that was held against me until I left Japan.

Enjoyment, I said, was the true basis, and must always provide the starting-point, of critical appreciation; and I quoted from Baudelaire, who explains how, when he was appraising a work of art, he had set out 'to transform my pleasure into knowledge'.* They might do themselves far more good, I hazarded, by enjoying an inferior book than by wearily ploughing through a masterpiece; since, having read a second-rate work with genuine enthusiasm, and whetted their appetite for English prose and verse, they could then move on to richer fields. This was a major heresy. My invocation of the pleasure-principle struck a disconcerting

* 'Je résous de m'informer du pourquoi, et de transformer ma volupté en connaissance': *Richard Wagner et Tannhäuser à Paris*, 1860.

and alarming note. A sense of duty is the favourite Japanese virtue; and the fact that an undertaking is painfully difficult gives the task its moral worth. Thus, I earned the reputation among my students and colleagues of being an incorrigible hedonist; and the idea developed to such unpleasant proportions that I became, in other ways, a vaguely suspect character. A rumour went around, I learned at a later stage, that I had failed to take a degree and been summarily expelled from Oxford because the authorities had found me guilty of 'the same offence as that of Oscar Wilde'.

These aspersions – peculiarly unjust in the circumstances – never rose above a whisper; and, although I was well aware that the effect I produced was very often disappointing, I continued to deliver the series of lectures and talks laid down by the official programme. They covered a wide field. I have before me a bulky folder of notes, including over eighty closely-scribbled pages. Many appear to have been lost; I can see no mention of *Beowulf*, Langland, Chaucer, the Romantic poets or the mid-Victorian novelists. But those I preserved range from long lectures on the Elizabethan and Jacobean ages to critical evaluations of Strachey, Aldous Huxley, Wyndham Lewis and the Sitwells. How much did I succeed in conveying? One of the problems I faced was that even the most straightforward English poem might present images that the average Japanese reader found it almost impossible to visualize. Suppose he should open Gray's *Elegy*, the curfew bell, the 'lowing herd' and the ivy-mantled tower of an English country church formed a wholly unfamiliar background. Each detail required elucidation; and by the time I had produced it, explaining, for instance, that a Western church-bell has a pendant brazen tongue whereas a Buddhist temple-bell resounds to the measured blows of a heavy wooden beam, the imaginative spirit of the poem itself had long ago evaporated.

Nor did my problems end in the lecture-room; they extended to ordinary social life; for, although a number of the Japanese I met spoke English both grammatically and capably, they made a very different use of language. 'English', writes the modern Japanese scholar Kunituro Masao,* 'is a language intended strictly

* Quoted by Frank Gibney in 'The Japanese and their Language': *Encounter*, May 1975.

for communication. Japanese is primarily interested in feeling out the other person's mood, in order to work out one's own course of action'; to which a Western writer adds that its purpose is to establish a sense of understanding 'between two or more people, and in doing so it employs marvellous subtleties to express their relationship'. Where an Englishman states, and boldly produces a direct opinion, a Japanese suggests or hints. His hints are frequently obscure; but he expects his hearer to distinguish what he says from what he really means. The result was sometimes odd. How had he spent his evening, I would ask a student. 'I attended a lecture, sir, a most interesting and valuable lecture given by Professor X'; and, when I enquired about the subject, 'the subject, sir, was Middle English prosody'. 'I did not know that you were studying Middle English.' No, there were none of them studying it; but Professor X was a highly distinguished scholar; and they were honoured by his presence. 'I imagine he speaks well?' 'Unfortunately, the professor, sir, has a somewhat indistinct voice; and, except in the first two rows, it was difficult to hear him.' Still, he had a good reception? 'I regret, sir, that I and most of my friends were obliged to catch an early tram home . . .' From this I concluded, as of course I was meant to conclude, that Professor X's lecture had been totally disastrous, and that, after a restive quarter of an hour, his audience had gathered up their books and bundles, and left him mumbling behind his desk, to address a nearly vacant room.

From the problems I encountered at the University, a rather gloomy and neglected group of buildings, I found relief in the pleasant Japanese house into which we moved that June. It was a new house; we had watched it being built; and it smelt throughout of freshly sawn planks. The rooms were divided by sliding canvas doors; and three rows of screens, paper, glass and wood, separated us from the crowded narrow garden. The *amado*, or wooden outer screens, were only used at night; the glazed set, a Western convenience, gave us protection during wintry weather; but the paper *shoji*, beautiful at any time, though they did not exclude the cold, became particularly attractive after night had fallen. Along a Japanese street, once the lamps have been lit, each quadrangle of translucent paper-window presents a separate

shadow-play, where a group of life-sized puppets – a hunched old grandmother, a bat-eared little boy, a young woman wearing the traditional high-piled coiffure – move in delicately cut-out silhouette.

No less beautiful, and much more practical, were the *tatami* that lined our floors, long greenish slabs, that turn with age a dull gold, of finely woven rush-matting. They yield to the tread, muffle the sound of steps, and give off a faint but agreeable fragrance. We soon grew perfectly accustomed to sitting and sleeping on the floor; and the local carpenter made me a large knee-desk of silvery pawlonia wood; at which, my legs tucked up beneath me, I composed an ambitious but ill-fated novel. It is the rainy season I remember best in Japan. Then all the screens were pushed back; and, as I wrote, an almost vertical deluge glimmered down into the muddy garden, where big dark butter-flies – they appeared to have mackintosh wings – flapped disconsolately to and fro. Confronting the downpour, I drank Canadian whisky, and enjoyed the light cool breeze raised by an electric fan. Outside everything steamed and soaked; while from beyond the garden-fence came the slipper-sloppering sound of innumerable native clogs, and now and then the screech of a distant tram trundling through suburban Hongo.

Our garden, once the rain ceased, had itself an odd attraction, its chief ornaments being a tall dead tree, treasured for its pictur-esqueness, a group of large curiously shaped stones, some scarlet azaleas and a hedge of sprawling *fatsia japonica*. There two bob-tailed kittens that we had rescued in the street, when we saw a gang of children hurrying past our door to expose them, with a few grains of uncooked rice, on the nearest piece of waste ground,* climbed the tree and hunted insects. We loved them dearly, named them 'Clara' and 'Alice' after two forgotten film-stars, and, when they grew up, did all we could to protect them against a prowling tom-cat. Naturally, we failed; they conceived and gave birth; and we were shocked to notice that the larger and livelier parent had secretly devoured her own offspring. So long

* As Buddhists, we learned, the Japanese did not kill unwanted animals; and, if they exposed them, would leave a few scraps of inedible food beside an un-weaned puppy or kitten.

as we remained at 86 Kikusaka-cho, our behaviour in the garden and affectionate treatment of the cats continued to amuse our nearest neighbours, the pupils of a girls' school, a tall Western-style building that overlooked our corner house. A window would fill with round inquisitive faces; and a chorus of desperate giggles drift across the lane. My way of summoning the cats afforded them endless delight; and sometimes they would mimic my Japanese call – '*Neko! Neko!*' – sometimes squeak out '*Poo-us! Poo-us!*' Even my gardening clothes – a Japanese cotton dressing-gown and wooden clogs – had an exquisite absurdity of which they never tired.

In Tokyo the winter months are cold; and snow-drifts piled around our dead tree. We were fortunate then to be able to draw and lock our range of well-made glass screens; but an English acquaintance, the wife of a Japanese scholar, who occupied an unmodernized Japanese house, had to decide whether she should use the *shoji* alone – rice-paper admits every draught – or bolt the ponderous wooden *amado*, and endure many days of semi-darkness. Nor could she afford a modern electric fire. The whole family, she said, wearing their thickest garments, was obliged to huddle about the *hibachi*, a porcelain tub that contains a heap of ash and a single knob of glowing charcoal. Red-hot charcoal produces noxious fumes; and, as soon as the temperature fell, there were frequent cases of '*hibachi-poisoning*'. Though the Japanese cultivated the elegancies of life for nearly a thousand years, they have paid little attention to domestic comfort, which is equally disregarded in an old-fashioned middle-class house and in the Imperial Palace at Kyoto. The Emperor's attendants must have led a wonderfully aesthetic, but horribly comfortless existence; and it is not surprising that Murasaki's heroines (who inhabited a palace of similar design) should repeatedly retire to bed, where they hide away beneath heavy padded quilts, only an eye and a painted eyebrow showing.

The Japanese cult of elegance has not completely disappeared; but today its products must be sought out – in a small shop, an ancient local shrine, or, if one penetrates the concrete chasm of the Ginza, among the less obtrusive merchandise of a twentieth-century department-store. The lane that passed our house ran into another lane which climbed towards a main street; and the shops that filled it from end to end included a grocer's, a fishmonger's, a seal-cutter's and a manufacturer of artificial flowers. They displayed their goods with aesthetic economy, but to the greatest possible advantage, exhibiting only a few objects at the same time – the seal-cutter's showing two or three crystal globes and some miniature soapstone blocks, surmounted by a Chinese lion-dog; the flower shop, which catered for the funeral trade, carefully arranged sheafs of conventionalized white lotus-blossoms. Between them, the proprietor of a cheap restaurant devoted his whole window to an enchanting little *nature morte*, a clever arrangement of blue-grey bowls set against a dark background, each containing a strip of raw fish and some discs of thin-sliced pickle. Along the Ginza, too, the Japanese feeling for style survived in unexpected places. The big department-stores sold almost as much rubbish as their ugly Western prototypes; but, here and there, one came on an array of boldly printed cotton stuffs, or a bale of the figured silks with which Japanese women lined the short wide sleeves of their sober-coloured outdoor coats. These silks were particularly gay and imaginative because the pattern was intended to be half-concealed. Now the motif was a troop of galloping horses; now the calligraphic repetition of a well-known scrap of verse.*

Major works of art are seldom exhibited in Japan, except in certain palaces and temples. The private collector usually consigns his treasures to a massive concrete *godown*, earthquake-proof and fire-proof, whence he only removes them for the benefit of some honoured fellow aesthete. We saw no museums or picture-galleries of European size or scope; and our best guide to the extraordinary civilization that had vanished with the Shogunate, at least until we visited outlying shrines, was the Japanese theatre.

---

* The calligraphic design on a silk we had bought in the Ginza provided us with yet another insight into the unfailing unexpectedness of the Japanese point of view. Having asked a student to translate the poem that was repeated up and down its length, we were told that the poet described man walking under an umbrella through the rain, and inspecting the women assembled behind the windows of the brothel-quarter. We ourselves had had it made up as a quilt. How would a Japanese have used it? 'Probably to line a little girl's coat,' he unselfconsciously replied.

In the huge Kabuki-za, home of the popular chivalric drama, which many educated Japanese disdain, we admired such magnificent artists as Uzaemon, Sandanji Ichikawa, Baiko, who performed transvestite roles, and the celebrated dancer Kikugoro. Uzaemon had a masculine versatility; he excelled in stern heroic poses; while Ichikawa, a doyen of the Japanese theatre, was renowned for the superhuman dignity with which he moved across the boards. Still more remarkable was the wrinkled veteran Baiko. No actresses are permitted to appear on the traditional Japanese stage; but here the parts that, at the Elizabethan *Globe*, would have been taken by a boy-actor, are performed by grown men. Baiko was old; he had a haggard long-nosed face; but once he had settled down before his looking-glass and begun to rearrange his lacquered hair, he became a feather-headed beauty, twittering in a nasal falsetto voice, and pouting and smirking at his own reflection.

A Japanese audience already knows the story of every drama that it witnesses; and what absorbs its attention is the actor's handling of a well-known scene or incident. Even a single gesture, imaginatively executed, may be greeted with applause* – for example, when Uzaemon, in the role of a dissipated merchant's son, who has just arisen from a night's debauch, passes Baiko, playing the part of a fashionable courtesan, and, smitten by passionate love, allows his silken coat to slip gradually off his shoulder. The Kabuki's humblest patrons, if they cannot afford an ordinary ticket, will pay to watch a separate act; and this was the habit of our elderly servant, a gregarious roué named Morita San, whose bald cranium and gnarled expressive features reminded us of the head of a medieval Buddhist abbot finely carved in yellow boxwood. Kabuki is a genuinely popular art, a product of the 'Floating World', the bohemian universe of courtesans, actors and artists, which also gave birth to the Ukiyoe print. Between its members, I sometimes asked my students, and the

* '. . . The supreme moment of a dramatic performance is generally not a telling speech but a tableau. The movement of a [Kabuki] play proceeds until it culminates in an elaborate pose, taken and held by the actor, who thus creates by posture rather than by words the emotional tension': G. B. Sansom: *Japan: A Short Cultural History*, 1931.

society that, during Shakespeare's heyday, gathered around the theatres on the Bankside might there not have been a strong resemblance? One had only to imagine Essex and Southampton as a pair of cultivated daimyos, their henchmen as two-sworded samurai, and Shakespeare and his company as the performers they encouraged . . . My students looked blank; but I continued to think myself that the parallel was worth drawing. The splendid costumes and expert swordsmanship of a typical Kabuki play would certainly have delighted an Elizabethan theatre-goer; and so would the tragedians' thunderous tones and the stylized ferocity of their expressions – those savage scowls caught by the print-maker Sharaku in his wonderful dramatic series.

Kabuki, however, is said to be a 'poor relation' of the Nō plays,* which have a very different aesthetic appeal and attract a far more cultured audience. Kabuki-lovers occupy modern tip-up seats; the addicts of Nō must sit stiffly on a matted square; and, as six hours is the customary length of the performance, a visit to the Nō theatre demands some degree of resolution. But the rewards are large. Arthur Waley's volume, *The Nō Plays of Japan*, was not a book that I had yet studied; and, at the time, I knew nothing either of Seami, the great fifteenth-century Nō master,† or of his religious and philosophic background. Seami, I afterwards learned, had been devotedly attached to the Zen sect of Buddhism, and, besides composing both the musical accompaniments and the librettos of the plays that he performed, had written a learned treatise in which he set forth his aesthetic principles.

The quality he valued most was *yūgen*, or 'what lies beneath the surface'. Explained by Arthur Waley as 'the subtle . . . opposed to the obvious, the hint . . . opposed to the statement', it may distinguish 'the natural grace of a boy's movements . . . the gentle restraint of a nobleman's speech and bearing', or the 'delicately fluttering' strains of music. To watch the sun sink, wander alone through a huge forest, or 'ponder on the journey of wild geese seen and lost among the clouds' – these are the gates

* G. B. Sansom. op. cit.
† Seami Motokiyo, 1363–1444, who began his career as the boy-favourite of the art-loving Shogun Yoshimitsu. Quotations are from Arthur Waley's book, which appeared in 1921.

that lead to *yūgen*. And Seami also instructs the artist how he is to grasp 'the flower', the supreme manifestation of technical and creative ability that crowns and justifies his lifework.

While conflict usually provides the impetus of the bold Kabuki drama – blades clash; actors prance and strut and ruffle their brocaded plumage like ferocious fighting-cocks – the Nō dramatist 'recollects emotion', and is concerned with obsessive memories and dreams. 'In representing anger,' writes Seami, 'the action should yet retain some gentleness ... When the body is in violent action, the hands and feet must move as if by stealth.' The Nō play, Arthur Waley adds, 'does not make a frontal attack' upon the audience's feelings; 'it creeps at the subject warily'; and very often the action is relived by the ghost of an ill-fated character, who resurrects a terrible story from the past and brings it to life again in music, mime and words. Thus the past slowly becomes the present; the dead are reunited with the living. To heighten their unearthly effect, the characters of a Nō play glide on silent feet across the polished boards, and the chief personages wear painted wooden masks* – a pallid expressionless oval for girls and young women; for demons and ghosts, a wildly distorted visage under a mane of grey or reddish hair.

Realism is never attempted. 'In imitation,' Seami wrote, 'there should be a tinge of the "unlike" ... If imitation be pressed too far it impinges on reality ... If one aims only at the beautiful, the "flower" is sure to appear.' The roofed stage – an apron-stage projecting into the auditorium – apart from the picture of a pine-tree that decorates the rear wall, lacks any kind of scenic ornament; and along a gallery, running towards the left, squat ten or twelve immobile singers. This chorus is accompanied by a group of three musicians – two drummers and a single flautist; and, while one drummer uses his open hand on the drum, and his companion strikes it with a thimbled finger, the bamboo flute, which punctuates the actors' speeches, emits shrill sudden jets of sound. To a Western ear the result is seldom pleasing; but the Japanese audience, I noticed – many of them carried and fre-

---

* Some of these masks are very old, and now regarded by art-historians as important examples of Japanese sculpture. They are usually a little smaller than the face.

quently consulted scores – were as much interested in music and text as in the splendour of the spectacle. We, of course, could enjoy through the eyes alone; and, as we watched, the Goddess of Mountains – or so the students accompanying us helpfully identified that gaunt mysterious shape – slowly advanced and step by step materialized. Wearing a stiff robe of richly brocaded silk, she supported her gliding steps upon a twisted bough; and her voice recalled the plangent sing-song of the wind among the tree-tops, rising and falling and dying away through endless melancholy gradations. She personified, we were told, the spirit of sexual desire – but of desire unfulfilled, of solitary embittered yearning; and beneath the silvery mane that swept around her shoulders glared out a wild demonic face.

A third type of Japanese dramatic art, the Bunraku or puppet-play, is now confined to Osaka, although in popular appeal it at one time rivalled the Kabuki; and many of the scripts it employs were written by Chikamatsu Monzaemon,* regarded as Japan's greatest playwright, who served the Bunraku-za for over thirty years. Like Nō plays, the traditional puppet-dramas depend upon the combined effect of music, language and harmonious movement. The puppets are large, the size of a well-grown child, but with disproportionately small heads; and behind them crouch the puppet-handlers, black-hooded and often black-gloved, to distinguish them from the fiercely animated dolls they are putting through their paces. These handlers soon fade into obscurity; and the puppets hold the stage. Their attendants may draw their swords, flourish their fans, even assist them in a game of chess; but the illusion is so complete that every gesture they execute they appear to make unaided. They have a vivid life of their own; and their long-limbed, small-headed bodies are beautifully articulated; mouths open and shut, eyebrows lift and twitch, and eyes roll. They do not speak; but, to the right-hand side of the stage, a story-teller behind a small red lacquered desk unfolds the action of the play in high-pitched or sonorous recitative, and a musician, holding an ivory plectrum, smites a simple three-stringed instrument.

* For a scholarly appreciation of Chikamatsu Monzaemon, 1653–1724, see G. B. Sansom. op. cit.

We attended the puppet-theatre on our way home from Peking, where we had spent a memorable ten days. My curriculum at the University allowed me a good deal of leisure; and in Japan itself we found time to explore the palaces and temples of Kyoto, while the cherry trees were thick with blossom, and under striped tents sat cheerful family groups picnicking and drinking *saki*; to revisit Nara, and, best of all, make a brief pilgrimage to the secluded monastery of Horyūji, which stands alone among the rice-fields. Founded by the seventh-century Empress Suiko and her minister Prince Shōtoku, it was the birthplace of Japanese Buddhist art. There are few more elegant buildings in Japan than the little one-storeyed octagonal oratory whither the pious Prince is said to have resorted for his prayers and meditations; and the frescoed Golden Hall* and his mother's neighbouring retreat enclose an array of extraordinarily moving statues. No doubt created by Chinese or Korean artists, they represent the intercessory spirits of the crowded Buddhist pantheon. Their delicate fingers are raised towards their cheeks; and their pensive half-smiles, as they brood over mankind, reflect an infinite solicitude.

By comparison with Horyūji, the polychrome shrines of seventeenth-century Nikko have a slightly meretricious air, but, on a winter week-end, painted gateways and columns stood out brilliantly against the snow-drifts and the sombre evergreen foliage of the giant Cryptomerias. The previous August we had passed through Nikko, bound for Chuzenji in the hills above. A village beside a lake, it was the favourite summer refuge of the European diplomatic corps; and, following the ambassadors, came numerous secretaries and aides, the younger unmarried men often accompanied by the Japanese girls whom they had brought from Tokyo, and whom they were careful to keep hidden away until the hottest period of the afternoon, when they hurried their companions out into boats and briefly sculled them back and forth. Here I learned that Cyril Connolly had married – his wife, a charming young American, we had already met in Europe –

* Since my visit, many of its frescoes have been damaged or destroyed by fire. The Kondo, or Golden Hall, is probably the oldest wooden building in existence. See G. B. Sansom. op. cit.

and wrote him a letter of congratulation. Naturally, I described my own existence. Tokyo, I announced, was horrible; and 'the Japanese have a good many private virtues; but they are very dense, very slow'. I felt obliged to admit, however, that I led a fairly easy life: 'My work occupied last term just eight hours a week'; and 'I earn quite a large income, without the least intellectual effort . . .' Both Cyril and I had frequently discussed marriage, which we likened to a floating island; and I assured him, àpropos of S. and myself, that 'the floating island is still water-tight – and except for the adolescent beauty of the dancing-partners at a Chinese night-club in Shanghai . . . nothing has appeared to make me regret its continued sea-worthiness!'

Most of my admiration seems to have been reserved for Chuzenji and its landscape – 'a lake on which we are learning to sail, and steep green mountains running down to the water's edge'; I was less appreciative of certain friends we had made. There were some 'amiable young men at the different embassies – but all rather sloppy and boozed and usually suffering from clap or in trouble with their Japanese paramours'. Secretly, I think, I may sometimes have envied those more adventurous young men, their hidden girls and the quiet evening parties where they smoked a pipe or two of opium. Lake Chuzenji is long and dark and deep; and beneath its chilly surface was believed to lurk a monstrous eft or salamander. It had other perils; violent gusts of wind blew off Nantai San, the green-clad, almost perfectly conical peak that swept up smoothly from its shores; and then the foreigners' boats – racing dinghies, each carrying a tall sail and a narrow metal centre-board – would plunge and rear in wild confusion. Nearly every day we watched a new race; and the hazards of the course usually provoked a quarrel. Sailing around Formosa, an islet at the end of the run, the stepdaughter of the British Commercial Attaché had inconsiderately gybed; or the Belgian Ambassador's dinghy had been fouled by the wife of the German Chargé d'Affaires, a handsome muscular blonde, who in the boathouse loudly defended her conduct. 'Man should intensely live!' she exclaimed with Nietzschean fervour, thumping her clenched fist on her solid bronze-skinned thigh.

More peaceful were picnics beside the lake, and on such a

picnic I observed the British Ambassador, superficially a plain and awkward person, perform a miracle of diplomatic tact. The French envoy, having left his wife in Peking, had imported a middle-aged American mistress. Evidently, Sir John must greet his dear colleague and exchange a civil word or two. He did not think, however, that it was any part of his function to recognize Mrs B.'s existence; and he, therefore, ambled towards Monsieur de M. with a cordial look and outstretched hand, not so much cutting Mrs B. as, in some mysterious yet decisive fashion, rendering her temporarily invisible – a feat that was all the more accomplished since she was extremely large and wore a gaily flowered dress. Then, his duty performed, he hastened to turn about and, again circumventing Mrs B., who, despite her clumsy attempts at self-assertion, seemed yet again to melt into thin air, settled down near his own legitimate consort.

We spent our happiest days in Chuzenji; and, besides sailing and swimming and sun-bathing on lonely beaches, I scaled the forest-covered flanks of Nantai San, and gazed across the rusty rock-strewn depths of its extinct volcanic crater. If the skies darkened, one could adopt a foetal position in a wood-framed native bath, and through steam-clouds watch sheets of rain descend – as they fell, they evoked a delicious fragrance, the scent of wet earth and sodden evergreen trees – beyond the open bathroom window. To our return we did not look forward. But by the summer of 1931 we were already planning our escape, and I was meditating resignation. In London I had agreed to remain at the University for a period of three years – a demoralizing prospect. S. would occasionally shed tears when old copies of *Vogue*, battered and way-worn after their long journey, reminded her of English life; and, though I appreciated the comfortable salary I received – equivalent, I heard, to that of a Japanese cabinet minister – I had grown increasingly restive at the Bunrika Daigaku.

I had friends there who liked to discuss poetry, among them the amusing and erudite Professor Taketomo, an amateur of French verse, who said that he admired Arthur Waley's translations of Li-Po and Po-Chü-i, yet added that he considered them a little too 'free' and insufficiently '*Parnassien*'. My fellow pedagogues, as a rule, were devoted civil servants with a civil servant's shortcomings; and in Japan not only does the holder of any official post keep an apprehensive eye on his superiors, but he also pays a no less nervous attention to those immediately beneath his rank. If the atmosphere of the University was often tense and claustrophobic, what I saw of the world beyond its confines produced a similar uneasiness. Japan was preparing for war; during 1931 the Imperial army would drive deep into Manchuria; and there was already a militarist spirit abroad that overclouded the whole social scene. 'Dangerous thoughts' (which included every type of twentieth-century liberalism) were savagely repressed by an efficient police force – the slightest mention of Karl Marx caused my audiences ill-concealed alarm; and the shouts of drill-sergeants parading their squads below often penetrated my class-room; to which I retorted by reading aloud from the works of Siegfried Sassoon, Wilfred Owen and other disillusioned soldier-poets, who had portrayed the horrors of the First World War.

Thus, we both experienced an 'overwhelming relief', as I recorded in a travel-diary, when the spring vacation arrived and we left Tokyo for Peking. Our voyage began, on 14 March 1931, at the ugly modern port of Kobe; and next day, about the hour of dawn, we found that we were steaming through the Inland Sea – 'lilac-coloured water [I wrote], sailing-boats with ribbed sails, air deliciously cold and smooth'. The Inland Sea is a detail of the Japanese landscape where the relationship between art and nature appears particularly harmonious, so exquisitely attuned to the native artist's style are its islets, crags and mountains, which float above a low-lying band of mist that we recognize from innumerable prints and pictures. But, as soon as we cleared the placid Inland Sea, the unfriendly Yellow Sea continued to buffet us until we reached the Chinese coastline, and our ship dropped anchor opposite a row of desolate buildings in a muddy river-mouth.

Since early childhood I had hoped to visit China; and now, as we crossed the bar and moved upstream, I had a curious sense of déjà-vu, the sense of reviving on the plane of everyday life some dream-adventure one has half forgotten. In mid-March the Northern Chinese plain, though a few small trees were just coming into leaf, was bare and dry and tawny-brown; and along the banks of the turbid brownish river we passed groups of mud-walled, mud-roofed houses and, beyond them, endless families of grave-mounds that stretched away towards a vague horizon. Across the fields walked stout and dignified figures, wearing blue silk gowns and round black caps; while red-suited women and little girls, and old men smoking tasselled pipes, watched us gravely from their thresholds. A single cyclist, who seemed bound for infinity, sailed off down a lonely track, followed by a big-wheeled hooded cart; and the yellow-tiled eaves of a road-side temple glittered distantly through naked branches. After the bustle of overcrowded Japan, it was a calm and spacious prospect. But the powerful wake our arrogant steamer raised kept savaging the fields above, tearing out huge slabs of soil and frightening the tethered junks. A boatman cursed us, and waved angry arms. Otherwise, even the farmers themselves displayed a stoic resignation.

At Tientsin we disembarked, spent the night in a scrubbed and polished hotel, and took the train for Peking. Having traversed another bare brown landscape with the same grave-mounds and the same dry earth, we sighted the low grey crenellated wall that then enclosed the so-called Chinese City, a region of farms and cottages and desiccated water-courses between the open country and the imperial city proper. Ahead rose the far more commanding walls of the North, or Tatar City, and a noble towered and galleried city-gate. That was almost half a century ago. Most of the Peking I entered that day has now been levelled to the ground; and the massive walls have vanished. What has become of the Legation I have not heard. But there, as guests of the young British Third Secretary and wife (to whom Evelyn Waugh had given us a letter) we spent a long refreshing holiday. Our first expedition, soon after we arrived, took in Kublai Khan's 'Purple Forbidden City', which we saw, my diary notes, under a 'pale brilliant dusty light'. The substructure of the pavilions was the colour of dried blood. Grass shimmered on their yellow tiles; and a sinuous marble-lined canal, spanned by narrow hump-backed marble bridges, traversed the vast surrounding courtyard. The Palace was almost empty; paintwork was faded and scaling. Some pavilions had been roughly sealed up; but through their torn casements we glimpsed piles of debris; while others contained the miscellaneous bric-à-brac that the last Manchu emperors collected – European clocks and odd mechanical toys, gilt ballroom chairs and ugly bent-wood furniture, as well as solemn ancestor-portraits of the Sons of Heaven.

Our host was particularly interested in the collaboration of Eastern and Western artists; and from the exterior courtyards he led us to a little vaulted bathroom, that the Emperor Ch'ien Lung* had had built for his ill-fated concubine Hsiang Fei, sometimes called 'The Perfumed Princess'. It was decorated with two pictures, both executed by the Italian artist Father Giuseppe Castiglione,† one of the gifted and versatile Jesuits whom the Emperor assembled at his court; and both depict the beautiful Hsiang Fei – an oil-painting in the Western style that represents her as Minerva or Bellona, displaying a breast-plate and a feathered helmet, and a painting on silk, in an approximately Chinese style, that shows her as a European garden-girl, wearing an elegant straw hat and carrying a small hoe. Hsiang Fei was a Turki prisoner of war; and, despite the Emperor's devotion, she is said – though this seems improbable – to have refused him her embraces; for which she paid the penalty when his mother, the Dowager Empress, either advised her to commit suicide or gave orders that she should be hung.

Meanwhile, Ch'ien Lung went to extraordinary lengths to divert the homesick girl; and the Winter Palace, Yuan-ming-yuan, that Castiglione and his French assistant, Father Michel Benoist, a skilled hydraulic engineer, constructed 'in the manner of the European barbarians' six miles beyond the city's walls, enclosed a suite of rooms where she and her attendants could amuse themselves, amid suitably exotic surroundings – tapestries, *boiseries*, and looking-glasses – by adopting European modes. Yuan-ming-yuan, before a European army plundered and gutted

* This enlightened Emperor reigned years longer than Queen Victoria, from 1739 to 1796.
† For a scholarly account of the artist and his work, see Cécile and Michel Beurdeley: *Giuseppe Castiglione: A Jesuit Painter at the Court of the Chinese Emperors*, 1973. His two portraits of Hsiang Fei are now in the National Museum, Taiwan.

it,* must have been a place of visionary splendour, with baroque pavilions and serpentine flights of steps, leading down to Benoist's water-gardens, and, behind the central edifice, named the Palace of the Calm Sea, a great reservoir that fed the chief fountains and a labyrinth of cascades and wandering rills. The Emperor loved his Xanadu; and, on the Feast of Lanterns every year, he would preside over a lantern-race, in which all the young girls of the Palace joined, each holding at the end of a long staff a candle-lit water-lily made of yellow silk, so that they resembled 'myriads of stars shining among a thousand green pine trees'.

The skeleton of Yuan-ming-yuan seems to have remained intact at least until the present century. But by 1930 it had been reduced to a heap of tumbled stonework in a rough and swampy field. Thanks to the engravings of Jesuit artists, however, we could recognize its general plan – the broad terraces on which the pavilions stood, and the site of pools and fountains. Every pavilion, though its masonry was European, had a wide-winged roof of Chinese tiles; and glazed shards, yellow and bright green, could still be picked up here and there. There were sculptural relics too; beneath a terrace we found a finely moulded scallop-shell from which a rivulet had once flowed; we saw some pillars, a toppling baroque arch and the pedestals of vanished statues. Little else remained; and we heard, soon after we left Peking, that even those few poor fragments had been sold and broken up.

We explored the ruins of Yuan-ming-yuan on a cold and cloudy spring day; and, as in August we visited Peking again during the earliest stage of our journey back to England, I have a double set of memories. In March and April, except when a dust-storm blew, the country beyond the walls suggested one of Corot's Roman sketches, pallid and bare and sharply detailed beneath a cloudless, clear blue sky. In August, crops had flooded the fields, and the dense green maize stood six feet deep. Peking itself had suffered a miraculous change; and, if one looked down from the artificial mount that commands the palace-quarter, the whole city seemed almost to have disappeared amid the foliage of parks and gardens. Formerly smooth and chill, the moats sur-

* It was pillaged and partly destroyed in 1860 by Lord Elgin's Franco-British troops.

rounding the Palace were now thick with rose-pink lotus blossoms – flowers of the Chinese plant which, unlike the Japanese, supports its pointed buds upon a lengthy stem. Whatever the month, one had a glorious impression of space. It is to a damp climate that Japanese landscapes owe their peculiar two-dimensional charm; the immense prospects that open around Peking have a more enlivening beauty. I remember, for example, how we climbed the Western Hills where our friends had hired a long-abandoned temple. We reached a rocky summit, and there stretched out at our feet lay yet another huge plain, rolling off, mile after mile, towards a jagged mountain-ridge. The air was so clear that we could hear the voices of peasants, minute laborious blue-clad figures at work in the dry fields below, and the yelps of a pair of curly-tailed dogs which chased one another through wide dusty circles.

The contrast between Japanese and Chinese landscapes extended to their populations. Two races more strangely dissimilar can seldom have dwelt side by side; and, in some respects, the 'progressive', over-educated Japanese appeared to fall behind their supposedly 'backward' neighbours. Persuading a Japanese tradesman to make some shirts or a coat involved many days of talk and trouble; and, although his English-speaking aides took meticulous measurements, the result was often poor. In Peking, a gowned and slippered personage, who spoke not a word of English, visited the house itself, walked around the customer, darted a few considering glances and quietly shuffled from the room, to return, before the week had ended, bearing an inexpensive and well-finished product. There was something French, I thought, about the Chinese national character; in Paris and Peking the *client sérieux* – the man who has money, understands its value, but is prepared to spend it upon his own pleasure – was equally appreciated. The French, of course, are an intensely domestic people; and the Chinese, my English friends explained, saw the family unit as the corner-stone of the established social structure, and would thus sacrifice any other standards to the interests of the clan. Hence the political chaos into which their country had subsided. War-lords still flourished; in 1931 Peking was governed by Marshal Chang, the Young Marshal, son of the old Marshal, a former Manchurian bandit, said to have been assassinated by the Japanese; and his shabby green-uniformed troops lounged around the streets and Palace.

The Chinese, too, have a Gallic social sense; and all their Chinese friends, to whom our host and hostess introduced us, were gay, talkative and uninhibited, and often displayed a touch of straightforward cynical humour, which, after the endless obliquities of Japanese conversations, seemed particularly engaging. Once we dined at the house of a well-known actor. The food was bad; among the other unpleasant dishes we ate were balls of mincemeat wrapped in lotus-leaves – the leaves we dropped upon the littered floor. But, meanwhile, our fellow guests, a Manchu gentleman and his slender painted wife, kept up a lively flow of talk about half a dozen different subjects. Would the Young Marshal ascend the Dragon Throne; and what were the pros and cons of opium-smoking? The Manchu lady claimed it improved her figure; while her husband declared that it led ultimately to sexual impotence. When we had left the table, the actor suggested that I should try some pipes myself; and, having retired to a brass-knobbed Victorian bed – the room was crammed with oddly chosen furniture, Chinese screens, little fretwork brackets, faded photographs and tin alarum clocks – I watched him prepare the pipes and cook the raw opium over a small naked flame. The effect of a few pipes was pleasantly soothing rather than exhilarating; but I enjoyed the aroma that the drug diffused – a strong vegetable fragrance which, many years later, happening to pass through a Western addict's apartment, I immediately recognized.

No doubt the narcotic he bought had been considerably adulterated, by the addition of 'dross' scraped out of the pipe's bowl, which is thought to make it doubly powerful. The opium I smoked at the actor's house was of the best and purest kind, and had come straight across the Great Wall from the poppy-fields of Kansu. In this form, the product of the white poppy, *papaver somniferum*, is not a rapidly destructive agent. It undermines the smoker's morale by stealth; and causes neither physical nor mental collapse, but an increasing carelessness and lassitude that slowly paralyses the will. We met, for example, an ageing

Manchu princess, once a lady-in-waiting to the Empress dowager, a remarkably intelligent and entertaining woman, who spoke several European languages. She had a crippled daughter; and we learned that, when the little girl had broken her hip sliding on the frozen palace-moat, Princess D., at the time in a euphoric opium-trance, had bidden the servants, though Peking contained an excellent European hospital, to call a Buddhist soothsayer; and the only curative regime the quack adopted was to plaster sacred inscriptions over the child's chest and stomach. She had survived, but, as a result, would always limp. Since those days, the Princess had conquered her long drug-addiction. It had made her ill, she said; 'pendant deux années', she told us, 'je n'ai mangé presque rien'; and she was now again a high-spirited woman of the world, with a fine enquiring profile and neatly shingled jet-black hair.

She spoke of the Manchu Court just as her English equivalent might have described the life she had led at Victorian Osborne or Balmoral, and showed us a photograph of herself and other Manchu court-ladies surrounding the ancient Empress Tz'u Hsi seated in her state-barge, which eunuch boatmen poled across a lake. All the reports of Tz'u Hsi's cruelties, she declared, were vulgar fables. She had been devoted to her mistress, a good-natured, affectionate woman; while, as to the palace eunuchs, they had had no political significance; and she and her companions had frequently made fun of the harmless, stupid creatures. Well, all that had passed; today she seldom ventured out. 'Mes compatriotes look at me so oddly. I remember when the Palace was quite different. I should not care to see it now . . .'

Leaving the Princess's house, we found our rickshaws patiently expecting us. They could be hired by the day for a very small fee, arrived about seven or eight o'clock, and, if we announced that we needed them, remained in attendance till long after midnight. There are few pleasanter methods of locomotion; but, as one bowled along through broad and dusty avenues, past secretive lattice-windowed shops and under the carved wooden arches that during former days were an emblem of imperial patronage, one noticed the large dark patch that had begun to form between the rickshaw-coolie's shoulder-blades, where sweat soaked into his blue cotton jacket. The winter months are bitterly cold in

Peking; and coolies, who either ran and sweated, or sat and shivered on a client's threshold, soon became tubercular. Western tourists in the Hotel des Wagons-Lits would sometimes grumble that they were kept awake at night by the incessant coughing of consumptive coolies which reached them from the street below. Our own men were lucky enough to have a regularly paid job. Less fortunate were those who assembled after dusk round a restaurant or a cinema. They must fight to gain an hour's work, clashing, scuffling and shrieking; while Chinese police, armed with stout leather thongs, energetically beat them back.

The Peking I knew was a city in decline, and cruel to its poorer inhabitants as most declining cities are. '*Ça pue la merde et la mort*', said a French traveller whom the Goncourt brothers questioned about his recollections of the Middle Kingdom; and ideas of physical decay and death still haunted one at every turn. Grave-mounds roughened the fields; close to the villages stood trim white-washed cisterns, the thrifty farmers' sewage-tanks. The Palace itself was dying; grass grew thick on its eaves; and even its official custodians had begun to sell its treasures.* Other monuments were going the same way. Yet how much of the past survived! On a bastion of the old walls stood the Jesuit observatory, with the astronomical instruments, supported by a series of fantastic bronze dragons, that Father Castiglione had designed to please Ch'ien Lung; and the blue umbrella-roofs of the Temple of Heaven rose from a large leafy park. Actors and dancers rehearsed their roles in the shade; and we observed an aged ballet-master leading his pupil through the movements of the Sword Dance; while hoopoes flicked their Red Indian crests, and stilted delicately across the lawns. The greatest Chinese dancer of the period was still the famous Mei-lan-fang, as accomplished an artist on his own plane as the equally celebrated Kikugoro. I saw him only once; by then he had passed his prime; but his virtuosity remained impressive. Western dancing emphasizes the classic grace of the naked human body; the garments an Eastern dancer wears soon

*Arthur Waley told me that he had once received a learned Chinese magazine, where a writer suggested that to catalogue the contents of a museum was always inadvisable, as, if the curator understood their value, he would probably put them on the market.

become an inseparable part of the calligraphic pattern that his steps unfold; and Mei-lan-fang's wreathing and drifting scarves, and his gauzy pendant sleeves, recalled the diaphanous draperies of some airborne Buddhist seraph.

At this point, though it has no immediate relevance, I must add another image. One evening I was invited to a supper-party, to meet a Chinese girl my host knew. Her name was Rose T'ang; and a prettier, more poignantly desirable young woman I had never seen before. Whereas Japanese women were inclined to be decorative rather than physically attractive – they were often flat-chested and short-legged; and the heavy coating of viscous 'wet-white' with which they daubed their necks and faces lent them a solemn hieratic air – most middle-class Chinese women, at least in the 1930s, displayed a lively natural charm. Long-limbed, slender and small-waisted, they wore a look of gaiety and freedom and ease that, when they grow older, would develop into a formidable vivacity. Rose T'ang was a perfect product of her race, one of those transient masterpieces Nature sometimes throws up; and by any standards she would have been a beauty. Her features were unmistakably, yet not too definitely Oriental. Around her high cheek-bones there was a soft becoming glow; if she smiled, she drew back full red lips over small almond-white, beautifully even teeth; and she had the *'attaches fines'* so dear to romantic French novelists. Rose T'ang's diminutive hands and wrists were incomparably fine and supple. Whether she pointed her fan or touched a cup and spoon, every gesture she made possessed the same disturbing elegance.

She spoke little English; and, attacked by a sudden bout of timidity, so long as the occasion lasted I could only sit and stare. When Rose T'ang presently bade us goodbye, I felt an agonizing sense of loss – the pang I had already experienced in early child-hood when my mother's old nanny had snatched me away from that unforgettable transformation-scene. Two or three days later, we left Peking and caught the Japanese boat for Kobe. We were sorry to go; again the Yellow Sea proved hostile; and in Japan, we found it difficult to settle back into our circumscribed existence. I now approached the professor and, with all the diplomatic skill I could command, alleging the precarious state of S.'s health, offered him my resignation. He expressed his regret; but, despite his polite demeanour, I suspect he was less offended than relieved. Before we left Tokyo, I had committed a crowning mistake that further reduced my professorial value.

The background was an evening party given by the cultured wife of the Turkish Chargé d'Affaires. A dull evening; and, as I wandered around the room, I caught sight of S. doing her best to escape from the attentions of an unknown Japanese, who, obviously rather drunk – the Japanese have weak heads – had placed one hand on her arm to preserve his equilibrium, while, murmuring compliments in guttural French, he caressed her with the other. Whereat all my annoyance of the last few months unaccountably exploded; and, having plucked him away, I added a vigorous shove – far more vigorous than it need have been – which sent him staggering off across the floor, until he reached a table against the nearest wall and tumbled backwards amid broken plates. Next morning, I learned that my victim had been a high-born court official; and, as a result, I failed to receive an invitation to the Chrysanthemum-Viewing Ceremony, an assemblage of honourable public servants held yearly in the Palace Gardens.

I was not unduly dismayed; indeed, I was somewhat pleased, since I had neither the top-hat nor the tail-coat that every guest, I heard, must wear; and the idea of hiring or borrowing clothes – how should I find a Japanese coat to fit me? – seemed peculiarly unattractive. But for the University my exclusion from the invitation-list represented a humiliating loss of face, one bound to be noted and commented on by rival academic bodies. My colleagues were deeply shocked. Yet the scandal was never mentioned; and, when we left Tokyo, I was given a ceremonious farewell. Speeches were delivered, in which both the departing professor and his wife were personally eulogized; my kind students contributed a handsome volume of prints, reproductions of a series by Hiroshige, that I suspected they could ill afford; and I was also handed a large parchment scroll, tied with loops of red waxed twine, recording my memorable visit and enumerating the distinguished services I had rendered the Tokyo Bunrika Daigaku.

So Japan vanished; again we saw Peking; then, one sultry night, we joined the talkative crowd that filled the old-fashioned station underneath the city wall, and began the ten-day journey that, by way of Manchuria, Russia and Poland, was to take us back to London. In 1931 the leisurely broad-gauge Trans-Siberian railroad was probably the most comfortable line on earth. Our big compartment, among its other fittings, provided a writing-desk and even a modest sofa. From that vantage-point, having already caught a brief glimpse of the Outer Mongolian desert where Buryat tribesmen were cantering their little horses against a reddish sand-storm, we saw the luminous wavelets of Lake Baikal, and watched the dark-green Siberian forests filing slowly past our window.

The landscape was fresh and summery, with forest-clearings full of familiar wild flowers, snapdragon, meadow-sweet and willow-herb; and, when the train halted, which it did regularly two or three times a day, we could clamber down into the meadow beside the rails and pick as many bunches as we needed. Of European Russia the impressions I brought home were comparatively vague – incessant train-travel is apt to blunt the mind. But I remember the hours we spent in Moscow, its crumbling nineteenth-century façades, its grim-faced weary-looking people, and our visits to Lenin's glass-walled shrine and to a repulsive 'Park of Culture and Rest' that displayed Communist slogans neatly spelled out with the help of red begonias. Poland I have entirely forgotten – apart from the name 'Warsaw' on an unknown station-platform, and the sight of a tall long-legged stork following reapers through the stubble.

Any return to London, after an absence that has lasted longer than a few months, is always oddly disconcerting. It seems so much the same; whatever the builders have done, and however many agreeable old prospects they transformed and 'modernized', it retains its massive subfuse personality. A beautiful square has half vanished; yet one recognizes a shabby corner-shop at which one used to buy one's cigarettes, and hears a well-known voice from behind the counter – 'Haven't seen much of *you* lately! Thought you must have gone away.' Drab, shapeless, often colourless – except in brief spells of marvellous illumination – the great indifferent metropolis quickly reabsorbs the traveller, who again takes up his old pursuits and interests just where he had last dropped the thread. So it happened to us. Some of our friends seemed almost unaware that we had ever left London; and few could be persuaded to take a keen interest in our subsequent adventures. Meanwhile, we had to rebuild our existence; and, as our Japanese savings were not large, and the novel I had written at Kikuzaka-cho had had good reviews but unsatisfactory sales – the American edition, its publisher told me, had been blighted by the economic crisis – I soon revisited the offices of the *New Statesman* and of Desmond MacCarthy's *Life and Letters*.*

At the *New Statesman*, Kingsley Martin now occupied Clifford Sharp's chair. An energetic, intensely well-meaning man, he had a handsome haggard face, a furrowed brow and deep-set earnest eyes. Kingsley's personal habits were abstemious – to dine with him was not a pleasure; his table-manners, incidentally, were the most unpleasing I have ever had to watch; and he felt a deep puritanical suspicion of any contemporary who did not share his views. During this period he engaged a literary editor, whom he afterwards discovered to be an ardent Anglo-Catholic. Ellis Roberts occupied the room immediately above his own; and he would gaze at the ceiling with an expression that recalled my Chelsea landlady, when she looked up from her easel and imagined the allegedly unconventional relationship of her lodgers on the first floor. Though a capable editor, he was not a sound judge, and frequently adopted opinions and espoused causes that, later, having examined the circumstances of the case, he was obliged to disavow.

Once, I remember, he became unfortunately involved in the affairs of a certain Count P. I knew the Count by sight – a tall long-haired, white-robed figure, wearing a single gold earring, who used to stalk around London. He was descended, it appears, from the New Zealand branch of a noble Polish line; but he also claimed that he was the rightful King of Poland, and held his 'royal court' at Hammersmith, whence he issued grandiose patents of nobility for comparatively small sums. A poet too,

* Established for his benefit by a generous American-born peeress in 1928, it survived until 1933.

he entrusted a love-poem he had written to an unsophisticated local printer; astonished by the work's erotic imagery, the printer telephoned the police; and the author was threatened with the law. Kingsley had been carrying on a vigorous campaign against the obscurantist Home Secretary, and immediately dashed off a number of eloquent paragraphs in which Count P. was portrayed as a modern Pym or Hampden. But he had not yet studied the poem himself; and, when he read it and grasped its implications, he was thoroughly disturbed. Driving his small motor-car at breakneck speed amid congested London traffic, he explained the whole story. After that, he told me, he had to tone down his defence of Count P. 'The poem described practices of which I had never heard – it referred to something called, I believe, *soixante-cinq* . . .'

He regarded me, he later admitted, as a 'cultured individualist'. Yet, despite this damning label, he allowed the literary editor to print my various reviews and essays; and, if he objected to my treatment of a theme, it was usually more in sorrow than in anger. During the next few years I relied on weekly and monthly journalism to provide the best part of my income. But that it was not large is shown by a sentence in a letter that Cyril Connolly received. 'Oh, for six hundred a year!' I dejectedly remark. Once I married, my father had, of course, discontinued my allowance; but the books I published – my novel, a travel-book about Japan and China, and a collection of nicely polished tales – helped to lessen the financial strain. We had now moved into a rented house, a small house near Victoria Station, in one of those streets built to accommodate respectable artisans during the second half of the nineteenth century, which had since been largely taken over by young middle-class inhabitants, and acquired snowy net curtains, cheerful multicoloured window-boxes and brightly painted front doors.

S.'s decorative gifts, which had had little scope in Japan, were fully exercised upon her new surroundings. Even Brian Howard – no longer an *elegantiae arbiter* to his well-born Oxford friends, but a vagrant bohemian who talked and drank his way around Europe – was obliged to admit that they showed admirable taste. Our sitting-room curtains, I remember, were of oyster-coloured silk; the woodwork gleamed a dull purple; only my writing-room, at the very top of the house, remained a fairly bleak apartment. This I welcomed; one could have too much, I soon decided, of exemplary good taste; and S.'s perfectionism made it difficult to move a chair without spoiling her domestic pattern. Her own appearance was just as decorative and precisely organized. Never once did I see her pull off her hat and toss it down upon a sofa. She always removed it slowly and neatly after careful reference to a looking-glass.

The decorous surroundings in which we now lived – the house itself, if not the immediate neighbourhood – were naturally much approved of by our parents. Chang had given up her flat and now lived at a sombre 'family hotel'; while her husband had retired to a converted windmill in East Anglia where he tended a herd of milk-white goats. But at Berkhamsted my own father and mother were still working on their social histories – my father with keen enjoyment, my mother patiently following the line that he had laid down. From domestic troubles they were not yet free. My sister, though good-looking, brave and sweet-tempered, was inescapably unfortunate; and the misfortunes she experienced were both emotional and physical. No one had more accidents; she seemed to attract disasters; and, having first married a handsome English rake, who, although he did not desert Gillian, was apt to leave her behind, whenever and wherever he could, like an unwanted piece of luggage, she divorced him and married a considerably less personable American, to whom my parents attributed all the hard-wearing qualities that her first husband had conspicuously lacked. They were misinformed; Tom was by no means the pillar of strength that my unhappy sister needed.

Regarding me they had ceased to feel anxious; I was clearly past reform; and, now that I was married and independent, they let me go my spendthrift way. But my mother admired my books, though I suspect she seldom reached the end, and, with murmurs of gentle appreciation, would sometimes read aloud a passage for my absent-minded father's benefit. Only my brother caused them little trouble. Fresh-faced, active and strongly built, he was destined to become an architect, and would undoubtedly have raised some excellent buildings, and led a busy, useful life, had he not been killed in a horribly mismanaged skirmish – 'the battalion gained its objective, but suffered heavy casualties', ran his colonel's cryptic message – at the beginning of the last World War.

My parents esteemed S.; but marriage and its duties was among the many subjects on which the views I held disturbed them. The attitude I adopted, they thought, lacked the right degree of seriousness; and, indeed, since we had chosen to leave Japan, where 'the floating island' was a kind of raft on which we both relied for safety, my married relationship with S. was entering a new phase. Marriages can be talked to death. Ours suffered a slow process of conversational attrition. We were perpetually asking ourselves, and asking one another, if, in every respect, it was quite as successful as we felt it ought to be; and we had each of us consulted far too many books, usually written by Central European 'sexologists' or psychoanalysts, about the problems of a happy married life and the relations of the sexes. Our approach was extremely 'modern'; and, besides discussing the present state of our union, we liked to glance ahead into the future, and imagine how we should deal with such and such a crisis – for example, if either of us were to fall passionately in love – that we had not yet confronted. These solemn debates did us little real good, and our relationship some actual harm. Though jealousy, we decided, was a ridiculous failing that we must at any cost avoid, our wise decision had a very slight effect upon our subsequent behaviour.

S. was bitterly displeased when I formed a romantic devotion to the beautiful wife of an old Oxford friend. My affection was harmless enough. But I frequently visited her house, and passed an hour or two in her enchanting company. She and her husband were rich; and her drawing-room had the luxurious quietude with which the very rich surround themselves. The butler would silently appear, followed by a footman carrying a basket of logs, and quickly, silently indicate how they should be laid upon the hearth. A fine Aubusson carpet stretched from wall to wall. D.'s father-in-law, she told me, had happened to discover it while he was looking through an attic, its colours still as fresh and vivid as the day it left the maker's hands. He had made D. a present of this serendipitous treasure-trove; and, once unfolded, it had proved to be the perfect size and shape.

D. also inhabited an enviable country house in Wiltshire, where Lytton Strachey's acolyte Dora Carrington had painted an eighteenth-century maidservant peeling an apple to occupy a blank window, and, across the hilly garden, the gifted mosaicist Boris Anrep had decorated the swimming-pool. Her range of friends was wide; and she greeted all her guests with a similarly appreciative but dreamy smile. Tête-à-tête, the expression she most often assumed was one of fascinated astonishment. 'I can't *believe* it!' she would bring out, opening her large blue eyes, in which floated particularly small pupils. An enthusiast had compared him, Byron records among his private notebook-jottings, to an 'Alabaster Vase lighted up within'; and D. produced much the same impression of transparent luminosity. That she was less ingenuous than her candid charm suggested I did not learn for many months. But then I first heard of her attachment to a well-known politician, whom, although she had assured me that she herself was 'an old-fashioned liberal at heart', she already called 'the darling Leader', and I rashly questioned her about these painful stories. She received my enquiry with her usual smiling sang-froid, and agreed they might have some foundation. I noticed, however, that a wave of sharp annoyance seemed to sweep beneath the surface of her eyes, which became a colder, even paler blue; and, although the icy change lasted only a few seconds, I felt that the moment had arrived when I must end my visit.

Naturally, I bore her no grudge; and we continued to meet until she had divorced and remarried, and under the Leader's exacting influence, moved into a very different world. But S., meanwhile, had registered her dislike of our friendship by means of a dramatic gesture. On our return to London, we found that the rage for party-going was still just as strong as when we left; and, some time in 1932, John Sutro, a great purveyor of fun, decided that he would hold a Roman party, based on Cecil B. de Mille's film, *The Sign of the Cross*, that had just appeared from Hollywood. A Covent Garden costumier's version of a Roman toga was meagre, draughty and uncomfortable; and I entered a private room at the Savoy with a good deal of embarrassment. But John's champagne soon did its cheering work; and I admired D., who performed the role of the Empress Poppaea, immaculately robed and coiffed. Later that evening, a group of Roman courtiers assembled round Poppaea's throne. S. was among us; but suddenly I saw her rise; and for the next few seconds I observed the whole scene in cinematic 'slow-motion'. Near the throne stood a magnum of champagne; or perhaps it was a jeroboam. Very gradually her sandalled foot lifted; slowly her right heel touched the bottle. It tilted; and a foaming flood of wine poured out over Poppaea's silken skirts. Whereupon S. swiftly and quietly retired; and, while the other courtiers offered their consolations, and did their best to repair the irreparable damage, I angrily followed her and called a taxi.

S. was a woman of high spirit, as she had very often shown before; and at no period had I tended to undervalue either her graces or her talents. But, by this stage, we were reaching the crucial point when any real exchange has ceased, and each partner slowly draws away into a defensive isolation. At such a point rivals are bound to emerge; and my own rival was one of the oddest and most unexpected I have ever had to meet – a tall lank young man, with dark-brown spaniel eyes, a sallow complexion, a seedy Savile Row suit, and a wisp of brown moustache wandering around the corners of his large mouth, who drew and painted and designed dresses, besides taking curiously original photographs for the London fashion-papers. S. and he struck up a close friendship, based upon their common interests, which presently showed signs of developing a slightly more romantic tinge, until I had begun to assume the attitude, and acquire the inquisitorial habits, of the old-fashioned jealous husband. I need not describe the result; but, after a series of violent disputes, we did our best to make peace; and we might well have succeeded had I not happened one summer evening to walk unaccompanied through Sloane Square.

It was a warm evening; street-lamps already shone beneath a heavy roof of leaves; and the whole square bore an agreeable resemblance to an enormous green-lit room, traversed by dusky vagrant figures. Among these figures, under a single arc of light,

I saw two quickly moving girls, a tall girl whose long fair mane had a sleek and dampish look, so that I guessed she had been swimming, and a much smaller companion who trotted a little behind, like Mephistopheles, disguised as a black poodle, in the footsteps of the youthful Faust. There was something about the fair-haired girl – perhaps her air of silent remoteness – that troubled my imagination. But, as I watched her cross the square and vanish down a narrow side-street, I felt sure that she had gone for good, to join the company of luminous apparitions we glimpse, admire and never see again.

I was wrong; and only a few years later I had just the same experience – a passer-by, admired across a street, would astonishingly reappear, with results that proved no less calamitous. On this occasion, asked to a friend's studio, I recognized the unknown girl seated in a far-off corner. But, when I approached, the impressions I received were momentarily disappointing. The face I remembered had had a more mysterious charm than the face she turned towards me; and the voice I heard had a sharp and flippant tone, provocative yet faintly hostile. Still, I persisted, began an awkward monologue and, before we parted, had even proposed that next day we should lunch together. We lunched twice; and on our second and friendlier meeting, she said that I might take her home, to the flat that she and her faithful friend Irene occupied near Sloane Square.

Considering the theories we shared about modern marriage, S.'s response, when I confessed my adventure, seemed disproportionately explosive. We then agreed that we must abandon any attempt to repair our damaged union; tempers worsened; and we built a funeral pyre in the garden with all the letters that we had exchanged during the last six or seven years, and watched their floating ashes caught up into the sky and blown away above the roofs. We also decided to separate, and that S. should leave the house, while I remained until the lease was sold. The plan suited me – I felt I needed change; but its immediate results were unexpected. S.'s personal income had been devoted to furnishing the house; I had paid the rent and household bills. She, therefore, very rightly and properly, removed every object she had purchased; and, when I re-entered the building after a day's absence,

I discovered it completely naked, the windows uncurtained and the floors uncarpeted, my entire domestic equipment reduced to a small bed and, I suppose, a chair and table. So long as I stayed in the house, candles stuck into bottles were my only form of lighting.

Yet I did not repine. Indeed, I rather enjoyed my odd bohemian existence, and certainly did not regret the neat and elegant setting that had vanished never to return. My new friend willingly joined me; she was a true bohemian herself; and our love-affair seemed all the more enjoyable because it flourished in such sparse surroundings. Isabelle's big clear eyes, set wonderfully far apart, were perhaps her greatest charm; she had a broad, high forehead, a well-shaped nose and chin, and an expression that varied between mutinous energy and a look of brooding, restive sloth. About her whole appearance there was something slightly inhuman; and at nineteen – her age when we first met – she would have made a splendid Valkyrie, with her tangled yellow locks, her boldly carried head and her broad yet graceful shoulders. No one who saw her passing along a street could have thought she was an English girl. Indeed, she was completely foreign, her father being Belgian and her mother German-Jewish.

Of her parents she had numerous stories to relate, some more easily believed than others. That Isabelle did not always stick to the truth was a discovery I soon accepted. But then, fact sometimes imitates fiction (just as Nature occasionally follows Art); and, because a tale we are told has a fictitious air, it need not necessarily have been invented. For example, there was Isabelle's story about a tragic period of her childhood. A few months ago, reading Paul Léautaud's autobiographical narrative *Le Petit Ami*, I alighted on two sentences that immediately recalled her tale. He had just seen, he writes in an illustrated journal, the picture of an elegant young demi-mondaine and her charming little boy. '*Dis, maman, est-ce-que nous irons aux bains de mer avec le même papa que l'année dernière?*' was the caption placed beneath. Though Isabelle had a perfectly legitimate father, she had also a series of supposititious 'uncles', with whom she and her mother often spent their holidays; and it was her unfortunate reference over the dinner-table to one of these alleged relations – 'Wasn't Uncle

So-and-So funny when he took us to the circus?' – that had destroyed her parents' marriage. An old photograph, her only relic of her mother, showed an irregularly attractive face, sensuous, perverse and sad. Learning that her husband meant to divorce her, Madame R. committed suicide.

Less tragic, but much more sharply detailed, were the descriptions that Isabelle gave of her stern, self-righteous father. Monsieur R. held a respectable post in the Belgian diplomatic service; and, when he married for the second time, he chose a well-bred Scandinavian lady, whose treatment of Isabelle was conscientious but not demonstratively sympathetic. Meanwhile, Monsieur R., scrutinizing his daughter, seldom failed to see her mother; and, although she longed to secure his approbation – such was her own account of her childish feelings – he would customarily refuse it. 'A cold, good, honourable man' like Lord Henry Amundeville in *Don Juan*, he combined a distinguished appearance and perfect self-possession with a glacial demeanour. Towards Isabelle, an impulsive, undisciplined child, his attitude was often frigid; and she remembered a scrap of domestic dialogue that she had once found deeply hurtful. It was a cold day; and '*Mon Dieu, Isabelle, que tes mains sont rouges!*' her stepmother had commented. '*On dirait* violet,' added Monsieur R., casting a sharp glance at her reddened wrists and fingers.

The next refuge of Isabelle's wandering childhood was an English country town, where her aunt from the Rühr had married a schoolmaster and set up a peculiarly German household. Despite her Jewish blood, Mrs C. kept a leaden statuette of Hitler reverently enshrined upon a shelf; and everything about the house (to which Isabelle once took me for a cheerless week-end to meet her aunt and aged grandmother) was heavy, hideous and solid – a huge white stove, gigantic kitchen cupboards and Brobdingnagian armchairs. Mrs C. herself was an ugly loud-voiced woman, perpetually poking fun at her inoffensive English husband, whom she accused of practising schoolboy vices; even when he was reading *The Times*, she said, its pages soon began to vibrate. Here Isabelle had been brought up; and here, aged thirteen or fourteen, she had had her earliest experience of love, star-struck by an unscrupulous middle-aged actor when he visited the town on a provincial tour.

Long afterwards she arranged to introduce me to this more successful Humbert Humbert. The odd little man I encountered was so drab and commonplace that he soon disarmed my indignation; and he spoke of the spell he exercised over very young girls with a half-apologetic smile. It was scarcely his fault, he seemed to suggest, if he was desired by children and, during the run of a pantomime based on *Alice in Wonderland*, the attractive child who played the Caterpillar had at length become his mistress.

His treatment of Isabelle appeared to have been more cautious. But she had once deserted her Warwickshire home and met him in an empty London flat. He had caressed her, then, at a decisive moment, suddenly leapt to his feet, seized an apple from a bowl, driven his teeth into it, sprung through an open window – the room was on the ground floor – and, still munching, cleared a garden-hedge and vanished down the street beyond. He did not return; and she had been so distraught, she said, that she had planned to kill herself. No doubt with this early infatuation had begun her passion for the stage. As soon as she left school, she finally eloped to London, to try her luck in the theatre; but, although she attracted friends and enlarged her knowledge of life, she was too inexperienced, and perhaps too naturally idle, to make much headway in her difficult profession; and the most lucrative part she obtained was at the Windmill Theatre just off Piccadilly Circus, which provided spectacular shows vaguely imitative of the Parisian *Folies Bergères*. Isabelle's role was to stand on a towering construction that suggested the bonnet of a monstrous motor-car, where, clad in a heavy coat of silver paint, canvas wings behind her shoulders, she represented the little Art-Nouveau figure that forms the well-known Rolls-Royce emblem. The effect was much admired; she earned a handsome salary; until one afternoon, having reached the theatre straight from a tipsy luncheon, she lost her balance, tumbled headlong to the boards and was dismissed by the stage-manager. There were other mishaps; and, when I met her first, she had been for some time out of work, sharing two small basement-rooms with the industrious friend I have already mentioned, who spoiled her, loved her uncritically and, I imagine, often paid their landlord.

Hence her impulse to start a new life; and, when I had sold my lease, and moved to cheap but agreeable quarters (which S. had generously recommended, having examined but decided against them herself) high above South Audley Street, she naturally accompanied me. At Berkhamsted my parents received the news with all the dismay I had expected. Their daughter had left her husband; I was 'living in sin'; and the rare glimpses they had had of Isabelle did nothing to dispel their fears. S., meanwhile, had launched her petition for divorce, citing Isabelle, disguised under the pseudonym 'Margaret Parker' – the name of Byron's beloved cousin, whom he had described as 'one of the most beautiful of evanescent beings' – and obtained her decree absolute in May 1935. Isabelle and I were married two months later. We had a chequered honeymoon, first of all travelling to Wiltshire, where we attended a *fête champêtre* at Clouds, the big country house designed by Norman Shaw, that the painter Richard Wyndham had inherited and was now preparing to desert. It was a memorable occasion; the evening was starry and warm; and a multitude of guests arrived, picturesquely masked and travestied. We drank champagne on a grass-grown Victorian terrace or beneath stag-antlered trees; and I fell asleep, I remember, on a comfortable knoll and did not stir again till dawn was breaking.

Less harmonious were some of the days that followed. We were staying in Cornwall; and among the company we found there was a friend I both admired and liked, whom I had already described to Isabelle as an exceptionally engaging man. T., though squat and broad-built, had a noble head that deserved a taller body, and a pale distinguished clear-cut profile. He was a sculptor; but a series of complex psychological blockages often prevented him from working; and at home he was said to spend much of his time in a cold deserted studio, wearing a bowler hat and heavy overcoat, and reading through the newspapers, surrounded by unfinished statuettes, which, since he very seldom troubled to moisten the clay, one after another cracked and crumbled. His charm was his principal asset; T. could always be relied on to talk, and above all else, to sympathize. He loved to charm; he could no more refuse the temptation than an alcoholic could decline a glass of brandy; and, whenever we crossed the threshold of the local fishermen's pub, he would gravitate towards some solitary stranger, and proceed to win his heart. T.'s strongest affections, I believe, were almost always homosexual; but he distributed his powers of charming between men and women with a generous impartiality. His desire to captivate Isabelle, and Isabelle's willingness to be captivated, far too soon became apparent. Nor did she hide her interest; and I returned to our London flat that summer feeling anxious and dispirited.

VI

IN LONDON MY FEARS WERE REPLACED BY FACTS; AND, after a midnight scene of tears, reproaches, confessions, I seized on the telephone and denounced T. as 'a creeping Jesus'. He was greatly hurt; he had expected, he said, a much more liberal outlook, a more sensible and 'civilized' response, from a person of my calibre; and the harsh words I had used, which he hastened to repeat, went echoing around Bloomsbury, and aroused a good deal of good-natured amusement among our intellectual friends. My friendship with T. was broken off; but Isabelle I soon forgave. The whole episode, she managed to persuade me, if viewed in its proper perspective, had been a mere caprice, a foolish passing whim; and I chose to thrust it down, well out of sight, into the deepest dungeons of my memory. For some months, we suffered no further crises; and, meanwhile, a very different crisis was developing at Berkhamsted.

My father had accepted the idea of being old with almost schoolboyish enthusiasm; and by the time he had reached his sixtieth birthday, in June 1932, he had already begun to assume a septuagenarian attitude and way of life. Nature took its cue; he became more and more infirm; and, during the latter part of 1935, though I doubt if he suspected, or would ever suspect, that he was seriously ill, he held a party at a London restaurant – a thing he had seldom done before – that seemed to be intended as a valediction. The restaurant he chose was the Café Royal, a place he considered alarmingly expensive, but that he must have known I liked. My mother and my brother, of course, were there; and he had insisted Isabelle should join us. When we arrived, I thought he looked weak and aged. Yet he had an air of hectic gaiety, asked me to order a wine, then lifted the yet unopened bottle and did his best to fill our glasses. The astonished wine-waiter snatched the bottle away; and not only was I shocked by the waiter's roughness, but my father's unseeing awkwardness struck me with a sudden sense of doom. I felt a poignant affection for the failing elderly man that I had rarely experienced while he was still young and vigorous.

Not long afterwards my father consulted a specialist. Euston Station, before modern builders had remodelled and disfigured it, was all that a railway station ought to be – solemn, dignified, austere. Philip Hardwick's massive Doric arch triumphantly spanned the main entry; and between the large paved courtyard, built to hold Victorian carriages, and a long range of sonorous platforms lay a grandiose Waiting Room and a Refreshment Room no less immense. Each had a coffered roof and elaborate pillars and friezes; and the Waiting Room, besides its broad benches, contained a collection of model brass engines that could be made to work by pressing a finger on a polished knob beneath. The Refreshment Room, agreeably overheated, smelt of plum-cake, toast and Indian tea; and it was here, late one afternoon, in September or October 1935, that my mother asked me to meet her before she caught the train home.

My father, she said, had been attacked by arteriosclerosis, otherwise hardening of the arteries, and had not many months to live. Thereafter his physical decline was rapid; and Isabelle and I paid him a farewell visit early in December 1935. Near his bed an old grey suit was lying neatly folded up. He talked of his convalescence, which he hoped to spend abroad; and, glancing at the threadbare folded suit, I knew that he had taken it off for ever. He spoke cheerfully, though sometimes inaudibly; and I noticed the same air of acute discomfort, the same restless move-ment of the hands, that I had observed when I sat by Nelly's bed. His appearance was unalarming; until, half way through a phrase, his eyeballs rolled back and the pupils slipped away be-neath the upper lid, and left a blank discoloured orb. He died soon afterwards; only my mother and the doctor were present, and received his unexpected last words. He had been barely conscious, and my mother had ventured to interpret, for the doctor's benefit, some broken sentences that he had uttered. Then, for a moment, my father regained lucidity and raised himself against his pillows. His voice was clear and loud: 'There you go – butting in as usual!' he exclaimed, and at once relapsed into unconsciousness. Describing the occasion, my mother sighed, even faintly, sadly smiled. Wasn't it an odd goodbye? But poor C.H.B., she supposed, hadn't really known what he was saying ...

Before he died, my father had added a last volume, *The Good New Days* – an optimistic survey of contemporary social reforms – to his well-established 'Everyday Life' series, and had also found time to give me some valuable advice about the book that I was writing. I still possess a crowded foolscap page he covered on both sides with expert suggestions, recommending me to give a detailed account of my hero's political and economic background, and attaching a pencilled note: 'Let me know if there is anything else I can do – read your m.s. if you like.' I failed to take up this typically good-natured offer, which might have produced, I thought, an argumentative and somewhat inconclusive correspondence. But many of the historical points he made I accepted gratefully; and I put more solid work into *Byron: The Years of Fame* than into any of its predecessors. Since it appeared, it has twice been vigorously corrected; and it is the only book I published between 1930 and 1939 that today, at least in its amended form, I do not hesitate to reopen. Despite the pains I had taken over my novel and short stories, they are sadly artificial works; while my travel-book, though a great deal less contrived, is marred by juvenile stylistic tricks; for example, my ridiculous habit of arbitrarily inserting three dots,* no doubt to provide dramatic emphasis, after sentences and paragraphs.

Byron: The Years of Fame appeared late in October 1935; and, when I completed the final page, which describes Byron's hurried flight from England on 25 April 1816, and quotes an old friend's account of how they had parted –

> Hobhouse ran to the end of the wooden pier; 'and as the vessel tossed by us through a rough sea and contrary wind, I saw him again; the dear fellow pulled off his cap and waved it to me. I gazed until I could not distinguish him any longer. God bless him for a gallant spirit and a kind one.'

* For this bad habit I was amusingly taken to task by Robert Graves and Alan Hodge in *The Long Week-End* (1940).

– I felt unexpectedly and deeply moved. My study of Byron's youth – the sequel, *Byron in Italy*, did not appear until 1941 – was my first genuinely adult book; and, if it has merits, I can only attribute them to the compulsive subject I had undertaken. Byron possesses an extraordinary – indeed, an almost theatrical – gift of projecting his own image on to the screen of his readers' minds and hearts. There is no English poet whose personal outline now emerges more distinctly. Unlike his fellow Romantics, Byron is constantly visible, at different periods and under varying guises – as the plump bashful boy, a cricket-bat over his shoulder, his auburn hair combed straight across his forehead, whom a Southwell friend remembered; the compact and curly-headed young man, whose vivacity delighted Leigh Hunt; the exhausted exile of Venice, his greyish locks covering his coat-collar and the knuckles of his hands lost in fat; and finally, as the slender, nervous, haggard, thirty-five-year-old hero, who told Lady Blessington, when they met and talked at Genoa, that he did not expect he would return from Greece.

During my researches, I was permitted to examine the wonderful collection of Byronic archives preserved by the poet's original publishers at No. 50 Albemarle Street. The late Sir John Murray received me kindly, if a little cautiously – he was a strong upholder of the family tradition that Byron's relationship with Augusta Leigh had been altogether blameless; but his nephew and heir, the present John Murray, gave me a warm and sympathetic welcome; and after the office had closed its doors we would sit up drinking vintage port and look through the extraordinary pile of manuscripts that he heaped upon the table. Byron seemed seldom to have thrown away a single scrap of written paper; and, besides his own letters, I studied the impassioned outpourings of his male and female correspondents, who begged for his love, solicited his personal attention and even scolded him about his moral views.* Among the moralists I noted the signature of a certain H. Dubochet; and I was delighted to be able to identify

* For a much fuller account of this aspect of Byron's correspondence, see *Byron: The Years of Fame* (1935), *The Sign of the Fish* (1957) and *To Lord Byron* by George Paston and Peter Quennell (1939).

Mlle Dubochet* with the scandal-mongering courtesan Harriette Wilson, author of the well-known *Memoirs*.

No. 50 Albemarle Street, the eighteenth-century building that Byron knew, became a favourite port of call. But, should Isabelle accompany me there, she struck sometimes a slightly discordant note. On the panelled staircase stood, and still stands, Byron's solemn bust by Thorwaldson. The poet himself considered it a poor likeness; he objected that his true expression was far more unhappy! And the marble head, with clustered curls on its brow (which recall Scrope Davies's story that he once discovered Byron in bed wearing an array of curl-papers) has a vaguely petulant and sullen look. But, as I walked up and down the stairs, I often paused to gaze at it; and one evening, when Isabelle and I had spent the evening at Albemarle Street, she flung her arms around its neck, kissing it so passionately that a heavy smudge of lipstick was imprinted on its mouth and chin; and, our host having spent some fruitless hours trying to remove the stains himself, the offended bust had to be carted away and expensively purified by a firm of professional cleaners.

Otherwise, Isabelle rarely showed much enthusiasm for literature or literary men. The only writers whose works she always enjoyed reading were the English dramatists. She was never bored by a play, and would pass a contented afternoon turning the pages of a tedious comedy, a cigarette smouldering between her fingers and a glass beside the sofa. She seemed particularly attached to the minor playwrights of the Restoration period, and rehearsed their most cynical speeches with appreciative gusto. While she read, she usually occupied the sofa rather than an armchair; for she was as lazy as a lioness; and she had a strange trick of using her sharp red nails to dismember the match she had just torn from a paper book of matches, splitting it into a series of delicate slivers and scattering them across the carpet. Once dusk had fallen, she slowly became more active; and we began to think of going out. Where should we dine that night? The kind of housekeeping my mother and S. had practised was utterly beyond her scope; and, although an elderly Frenchman, summoned by telephone, now and then

* This was her original name. Her parents had been Swiss stocking-menders in Mayfair.

arrived on a bicycle carrying a basketful of cooked provisions, unless our financial problems were particularly grave, we spent the evening at a restaurant.

Very often we chose the Café Royal. The old café I had visited and admired during holidays from Oxford, with its velvet-upholstered benches, marble-topped tables, richly painted ceilings, gold-wreathed iron pillars, stately golden caryatids and tall discoloured silvery glasses – the resort of Oscar Wilde, Alfred Douglas, Max Beerbohm, Charles Conder and their generation – had already been demolished; and in its place stood an ugly modern restaurant, encircled by a spacious gallery. This part of the restaurant (which itself has since vanished) its proprietors had named the Café Gallery; and there one could continue to dine and drink until the small hours of the morning. There, too, one could always find friends – among the most agreeable being Cyril and Jean Connolly, if they happened then to be in London, and were not rusticating at a villa near Cannes, or motoring around South-Western France.

This period of Cyril's life, I think, was probably his happiest and calmest, when, with a wife he loved and the series of cherished pets, including his pair of splendid ring-tailed lemurs, he had settled down to 'live for beauty'. Marriage had changed him; he was growing somewhat solid; and, no longer a rebellious young romantic who rejected every commonplace worldly standard, he was now prepared to give the world its due. Not that he had quite abandoned his juvenile romanticism; the worldly-wise hedonist remained an imaginative perfectionist, dreaming of the perfect house he would buy in the perfect landscape, even – he had become a renowned gourmet – of the perfectly ordered and attended meal. Cyril was a born host; I am a natural guest; and again and again, while Isabelle and I were married, we enjoyed his enthusiastic hospitality. To organize a really successful party afforded him the keenest pleasure; and many successful parties were held in the Connollys' untidy rooms. The bohemian disorder of their household was its only real drawback. None of their pets had ever been house-trained; and Aldous Huxley, a fastidious next-door neighbour at the time they lived abroad, declared that he had once watched Jean Connolly, after she had distributed raw meat to their tame ferrets, wipe her blood-stained fingers down the embroidered front of the Chinese coat that she was wearing. The tale may well be true; but the story that Cyril had left a bacon-rind between the pages of a borrowed book is almost certainly apocryphal.*

Perhaps because he so often satirized his friends, and his wit was so destructive, around Cyril himself, and his remarkable doings and sayings, a host of comic legends sprang up. But, although his character had an endearingly comic side, it also had its tragic aspect. The harmonious framework of his early married life would very soon disintegrate; and *The Unquiet Grave*, surely his best book, besides lamenting his lost happiness, provides a clue to the emotional unrest that had brought about its ruin. Cyril was seldom content with what he had, and perpetually mourned over what he had been, or, granted kindlier circumstances, might be. His pursuit of beauty at length destroyed his repose – 'in one lovely place', he wrote, 'always pining for another; with the perfect woman imagining one more perfect . . .' He liked to introduce an element of fine complexity into any relationship that he had built up. He needed a problem; there must always be two faces haunting his imagination, two magnetic poles pulling at his heart and his allegiance; and before, in 1938, he published his *Enemies of Promise*, such a conflict had entered his life and excited his creative talents. The personal result of that conflict was a war-time separation, for which he tells us that he 'felt to blame', and which, in its turn, produced *The Unquiet Grave*.

The parentage and childhood of distinguished men is an endlessly absorbing topic; and I believe that Cyril's most 'Palinuroid' traits may have been derived from his conviction, right or wrong, that his mother had deserted him. Mrs Connolly, whom I once met, was a dignified, attractive woman; Major Connolly, a mildly eccentric and slightly unattractive figure, who spent his mornings at the Natural History Museum, where he classified snail-shells (on which he was a famed authority) and his afternoons at the Windmill Theatre – he had been much impressed, I heard, to learn of Isabelle's experiences there – appraising

* It found its way, however, into a gossiping obituary notice published in the columns of *The Times*.

and reappraising the same row of nearly naked chorus girls. Cyril was an only child; the elder Connollys had parted while their son was still a boy; and Mrs Connolly had gone abroad. Hence, I think, Cyril's life-long dread of desertion, which he aggravated by his tendency to provoke the crises likeliest to imperil his domestic peace of mind.

When I met him in the Café Gallery, however, or in the Chelsea house he occupied, he was usually a blithe companion. He had a marvellous sense of fun and, despite his prejudices, which were often strong and savage, a tremendous generosity. He gave noble presents; and I possess a number of valuable books allusively inscribed by him. When he published *The Rock Pool*, the nowadays rather undervalued novel that came out in 1935, he dedicated the work to me; and on the fly-leaf of *The Unquiet Grave* itself, I read the following quickly scribbled lines: 'From Cyril to Peter – who knows the places and the people. "*Surgit amari aliquid, quod in ipsis floribus angat*".'* That *amari aliquid* – that touch of something bitter – even in Café Gallery days, occasionally crept into his conversation. But it rapidly melted away; and, although, had he been offended or disappointed, he did not hesitate to show his feelings, if his mood were cheerful and the company responsive, no one could be wittier. His jokes were apt to be cruel; but then, he was equally cruel upon the subject of himself; and he was the only conversationalist I have yet encountered who could make a pun amusing.

Oscar Wilde declared that he had employed his talents in his work, and reserved his genius for his life. But Cyril's conversation and his literary work had very much the same qualities – a similar verve and penetrative insight, a wit that went straight to the heart of his theme, and briskly turned it inside out. He was my cleverest friend; and, as often as I published a book or an article, my first impulse was always to wonder what Cyril must have thought of it. I have written too many books; Cyril wrote too few; but his comparative reticence, I couldn't help feeling, gave him the superior position; and if he approved of my work, as he

* Lucretius: *De Rerum Natura*, IV. The passage from which this quotation comes has been literally translated by H. A. J. Munro: 'Out of the very wellspring of delight rises up something bitter, to pain us amid the very flowers.'

now and then did, I was invariably relieved and pleased. What he would have thought of the present book, still half-written on his death, I hardly dare to speculate; and I welcome the opportunity of turning back towards the distant 1930s, when Cyril and Jean – Cyril heavily overcoated, bearing a load of books and magazines; Jean with a fox-faced, golden-eyed lemur wrapping its black-gloved hands around her neck – both a little stout, and neither inclined to hurry, would often re-emerge in my existence. The Second World War lay several years ahead; and the guilt-ridden Palinurus had not yet been born.

The Connollys accepted Isabelle – she cut a decorative figure at their parties; but, as Cyril would afterwards confide, they had never really liked her. Elsewhere she was more admired than liked; and the kind of admiration she aroused sometimes caused me vague anxiety. Newcomers approached her with a degree of self-assurance that jarred on my suspicious nerves; and she greeted them, I noted, with an undiscerning readiness. Isabelle was an elusive companion, inclined, given the slightest opportunity, to slip away and disappear, and apt to return exhibiting the faint half-smile that seemed the reflex of a secret triumph. What had amused her I was seldom quite sure. She had a feline independence, and a feline love of stealth. How she spent her day, if I left her alone at our flat, was another question that she rarely answered; and, even before our marriage, I had adopted a daily routine that took me every morning to an office. At last I had decided I must abandon literary journalism as my major source of income. Its rewards were poor and often irregularly paid – if an article were held over for a few weeks, my whole financial structure suffered; and, since my return from Japan, I had begun to grow more and more tired of praising or disparaging other people's books. So I adopted T. S. Eliot's advice that every young writer should have a secondary employment, and looked around in search of such a job. I had few credentials; but luckily there are certain professions today that have always welcomed footloose wanderers; and, after some false starts, I found the post I sought with a London advertising agency, where a friend of Harold Monro, a one-time poet himself, was now established on the board.

This was not my first experience, however, of the advertising business. At an earlier stage, I had done occasional work for the modern Maecenas Jack Beddington, who allocated a monthly fee to any writer or artist he considered worth encouraging. Jack was then the publicity manager of the gigantic Shell Petroleum Company and, in that role, a generous patron of the arts. Edward McKnight Kauffer had revolutionized twentieth-century poster design under his enlightened influence; and I was among the various writers he commissioned to provide his copy. Jack loved life as much as he loved art; he was a golden-hearted man; and his face, which suggested the portrait of an Austro-Hungarian hussar painted on a large egg, always radiated goodwill. His fair moustaches had a bristling upward curve; and a big old-fashioned pearl tie-pin secured his neatly patterned stock. Through him I had gained an early insight into the esoteric trade of copy-writing. Some commissions were easy and pleasant enough; but one of the minor products that his organization sold was a paraffin used on chicken-farms; and at intervals the company gave away a brochure written for the chicken-farmer's benefit. This I was asked to revise and rewrite – a difficult assignment; for the author, an aged Welsh expert, possessed a barbarous English prose style, employed an old typewriter, which had many defective keys, and the cheapest, thinnest paper. To translate his text into respectable English, and subdivide it into trim coherent paragraphs, might take me half a working day; and the information I meanwhile collected about the private life of poultry – their sudden pests and horrid endemic diseases and savage behaviour towards other members of the brood – made it all the more repulsive. The chicken's existence, as it opened before me, seemed indeed 'poor, nasty, brutish, and short'.

Still, my cheque arrived at the end of every month; and a visit to Jack's well-furnished office in the enormous Shell building often wound up with luncheon *à deux* downstairs in the Café Royal. There was a great difference, I found, between this part-time work and regular employment by a busy firm. The agency I joined as a junior copy-writer was not yet many months old; and the directors who had planned and founded it formed an interesting team. Aubrey, the ci-devant poet I had met through

Harold Monro, was now a very different person. Once a slender, shy, retiring youth, he had been completely metamorphosed. It was his wife Susan, I believe, a small dark animated young woman and a far more aggressive spirit than himself, who had originally steered him into advertising; and he had long ago given up writing verses and producing pretty little woodcuts in the style of Lovat Fraser. At the same time, he had put on two or three stones, and become ebullient, large and florid. Whether he regretted his literary past I do not know; but behind his present image, the noise, the slang and the jokes, I seemed now and then to catch a glimpse of an unhappy fallen angel.

Aubrey's colleague Felix had a more uncultivated but much better balanced disposition. He was the politician of the firm, and managed his associates and subordinates alike with a skill that was evidently its own reward. A master of the confidential talk, he took a keen and unfailingly sympathetic interest in his employees' private problems. The staff, as a whole, was not very well paid – if one asked for a raise, the answer one received was customarily 'jam tomorrow' – but he was always glad to summon the motherly female cashier, and instruct her to pay out a small advance, on the condition, eagerly accepted at the time, that it would then be deducted from one's salary. Aubrey was our creative artist; Felix, our commercial genius; Bill, a third director, a bluff, good-humoured Yorkshireman, our financial figure-head. He had a rich father; and, compared with Felix, Aubrey and the jet-bright, jet-hard Susan, he led a quiet, slow-paced life.

My fellow workers were an equally various group. Opposite me, in a room on the top floor, sat an experienced senior copy-writer, a protean humorist, who had the air of a sick eaglet and a huge fund of dialect stories and fantastic personal anecdotes, and who, while I was still struggling to find my feet, became a sympathetic friend. A vivid contrast was provided by the young executive established on the ground floor, whose dramatically dissipated good looks had troubled many an innocent secretary's heart. A great Lothario and keen frequenter of night-clubs, he needed very few hours' sleep; but, although his skin was often an ashy-grey and his deep-sunk eyes were purple-ringed, an iron-clad devotion to the firm's business somehow kept him straight and steady. A retired cavalry officer occupied the same room. An alert, cheerful youngish middle-aged man, rumoured to have left his regiment after a romantic interlude with his colonel's wife or daughter, he wandered long-leggedly about the building; and among his favourite conversational subjects were the Pathan tribesmen of the Khyber Pass. Extraordinary fellows, ragged, gaunt and bearded, they'd sit round their camp-fire, keening out a high-pitched song, which included a peculiarly wild and sad refrain. He had had it translated; he remembered it even now; it concerned 'a boy across the river'. The boy had 'a bottom like a peach'. 'But' – and here came the fiercely poignant crescendo – 'alas, alas, I cannot swim!'

Besides the reminiscent Captain we had other entertaining talkers; and, except when a sudden crisis descended, and Aubrey roared or Susan shrilled, the tone of our daily office-life was garrulous and easy-going. Once an adjacent bar had opened at half past eleven, an immediate exodus took place; lift-doors began to clang; and many desks were temporarily deserted. No doubt the advertising world has changed; but, in those days, advertising and drinking were still closely linked activities, and the most ambitious campaigns floated to success upon a powerful flood of alcohol. I cannot pretend that I deeply disliked the work, or regarded myself as a misused man of talent exploited by my philistine employers. Though some of the tasks I was set were trivial, even slightly ignominious, all involved the use of words; and I was sufficiently in love with words to enjoy arranging them into concise, effective patterns. My efforts taught me a good deal. The writer of a literary article is allowed a certain freedom; two or three additional sentences may not much disturb an editor; but the exact length of a piece of advertising copy is dictated by the lay-out man, who prescribes not only the number of lines, but the number of letters, or 'letters-and-spaces', for which he thinks that he can find room; and the copy-writer must practise an almost Chinese economy while he constructs his verbal edifice.

The client, too, will sometimes demand an exasperating alteration; such-and-such a point has been neglected, or a cherished phrase omitted. These set-backs, however, were all a part of the elaborate game we played – a cynical game perhaps, but odd and difficult enough to amuse an expert player. Although I could not immediately grasp its rules, I soon acquired some basic training, and found that my prose style could be employed with advantage upon a special range of subjects. I could be as 'literary' and decorative as I pleased, writing about products that appealed to women; and in that important field, before my career ended, I had become a virtuoso. Corsets were my first theme; the type of corset we advertised had been designed by a crippled middle-aged lady; and my weekly task was to immortalize her conception of 'the body beautiful', emphasizing the fact that, if it were to remain beautiful, 'adequate support' was needed. Miss J. liked my style, appreciated my interest in her sex, and from her invalid chair would thank me for the euphonious tributes she once called my 'ripping write-ups'. She headed a bizarre procession of female clients that led eventually to Miss Elizabeth Arden.

Every occupation, unless it employs the whole mind and satisfies the human creative instinct, is to some extent absurd; and about the advertising business what I chiefly disliked was not so much the work I did as its general atmosphere of unreality. We dealt in fairy-gold – in fugitive dreams and illusions. Buy Miss J.'s corsets; and you will be permanently lithe and strong! Wear this cut-price version of the latest French model, and you may be photographed by Cecil Beaton, invited to the Café de Paris and join 'the Prince of Wales's set!' No copy-writer can make a thorough personal investigation of every product that he recommends; and I noticed myself that I wrote with particular verve of merchandise that I had never seen, or that, so far as I was concerned, merely existed in a commercial artist's flattering sketch. I had a wide choice; our accounts ranged from petroleum and house-property, on the one hand, to 'the Rag Trade', on the other; and, when Felix secured the Elizabeth Arden account, we considerably enlarged our field.

During the next two years I crossed the Atlantic every five or six months, twice accompanied by Felix and Aubrey, twice as their ambassador plenipotentiary, charged with the difficult and delicate mission of representing them at our employer's court. Our earliest visit lasted several weeks; and we travelled in those days by sea, packed into the luxurious womb-world of an old-fashioned transatlantic liner. No sooner had we emerged than an exhausting life began. Felix and Aubrey were clearly determined that we should enjoy ourselves; and, having completed our work, we circulated busily among bars and restaurants and night-clubs – the Stork Room, where we sat in a dim-blue dusk, drinking gin-fizzes and potent whisky-sours; the Twenty-One, where the countrified check table-cloths seemed strangely inappropriate, but many famous and fashionable personages were duly pointed out to us; the zebra-striped El Morocco, and a small bohemian night-club called the Onyx, at which a steel-band twanged elastic saws, or belaboured the corrugated surface of a homely zinc tub.

New York is a city I have always admired, but secretly never quite believed in – the impression it makes is too fantastic to be altogether credible; and that spring the weather was cold and clear; and an electric spark exploded beneath my finger-tip when I pressed the elevator-button. Between tawny cliffs, rising against a hard blue sky that often reminded me of Peking, we hastened towards the Elizabeth Arden office, and the appointment, arranged the day before, that she might or might not keep. Miss Arden was a small, trim woman, simply but expensively dressed by Schiaparelli, with a number of rich but unostentatious baubles pinned upon her silken breast. From a round kittenish face all the wrinkles of age seemed to have been carefully ironed away, leaving only folds and pouches. She had bright beady eyes, dark-red hennaed hair – I was once privileged to attend her levée, and watch the henna being rubbed in – and an expression that alternated between sparkling vivacity and an almost dragon-ish ferocity. The change was sudden; if a bad mood happened to overtake her, she immediately became the tyrant; and then no Roman empress could have more alarmed her courtiers or cowed and terrorized her private household.

I remember such an occasion when she had just returned from the country to welcome home her 'little sister', Madame de M., who had wedded an authentic French vicomte and now managed her Parisian salon. Miss Arden occupied a spacious duplex apartment; and, as soon as she entered the marble-paved hall, in which we were already waiting, she declared that the place was so filthy that neither she nor any sister of hers could be expected to set foot there. The black-and-white marble pavement aroused her fiercest indignation; for the white slabs had natural greyish streaks; and these, she said, were ingrained dirt. The Italian butler and his wife and family were therefore summoned to her presence, and ordered to go down upon their knees and scrub. Much later that day they were still scrubbing; while their mistress's sharp aggrieved voice rang loudly round the upper floor.

If we needed a definite decision from Miss Arden's own lips – she would never delegate authority – we ourselves must play the part of courtiers. We learned to wait, portfolios beneath our arms, hoping to intercept her in full career as she darted through an ante-room. 'Miss Arden,' we would hurriedly exclaim, 'we wonder – can you spare a minute? We've something here we want to show you.' And Miss Arden would either brush us aside with a few words and a fleeting smile, or briefly pause to grant her imprimatur. Other attendants, who also stood and waited, were very much less gently handled. She had a suspicious mind; towards every manager she engaged Miss Arden soon developed an inveterate antagonism; and the manager she employed when we first arrived, a certain crafty Mr Schwarz, confided that he was accumulating a secret war-fund against the day of his disgrace, to finance the legal hostilities that would inevitably break out once he and his employer parted.

Yet I did not resent Miss Arden. Indeed, there was much about her that I found amusing and endearing. The young Canadian girl who had invaded New York, where in a modest room, on opposite sides of a curtain, she and her sister had administered beauty treatments and cooked up preparations over a small spirit stove, could still be distinguished now and then in the regal millionairess. We got on well; I appreciated her electric vitality and unexpected bursts of gaiety, and the strain of extravagance and wild inconsequence that redeemed her from the commonplace. Fortunately, Miss Arden returned my liking; and by my second visit I had acquired some of the privileges of an established court favourite – a position that involved no embarrassing duties and, if we had important business to transact, was often highly advantageous. But being taken to the opera, to listen to *Madame Butterfly*, proved a difficult experience; for Miss Arden wept uncontrollably throughout the famous farewell aria, not because she pitied the unhappy heroine, but, as she explained between her sobs, 'it reminds me so much of my little horses!' – the precious yearlings she had recently lost in a disaster at her stables.

Miss Arden's attachment to her horses was based upon a genuine fondness; and she had convinced herself that, whatever her trainer might say, horses and women benefited equally from many of her preparations. But she also loved the race-course's social side, and enjoyed rubbing shoulders, and exchanging friendly nods, with a Mrs Astor or a Mrs Whitney. At Saratoga Springs she had built a small house; and thither I was whirled by air and bill-boarded highway one sultry summer week-end. Accustomed to English week-ends, and to the sense of leisure and freedom that English country-life produces, I felt that I had been sucked into the heart of a dizzily revolving vortex, which spewed me forth again, limp and nearly speechless, after an interminable night and day. Guests had been chosen at random – a circumspect, slow-spoken, elderly couple introduced as 'Judge and Mrs Bangs of Baltimore', an elegant New York lady, whose presence I could not explain until I noticed she had brought her lover, a curly-headed young musician, and a stout, pink, talcum-powdered executive, with whom I had to share a room, distinguished by his Agag-like gait and unfailing air of courtly deference. I had hoped to walk around the city, and examine the attractive wooden architecture of the hotels that line its main street. But Miss Arden's round of entertainments allowed us not a moment's rest – a monster luncheon-party, a strenuous afternoon's racing, a gigantic cocktail party and, finally, a motorized descent on the Piping Rock Club, at which Sophie Tucker, huge and jellified, sang some flatly sentimental songs. A glass of champagne, I thought, might restore my morale and pacify my squeamish stomach. But Miss Arden, unluckily, had just been told that champagne was a vulgar drink, and had ordered tepid sweetish hock; while the sight of a large lobster, stuffed with caviare, that a waiter dropped before me – fat grey beads oozed through every crevice – nearly drove me from the table.

Thus far I have treated my early visits to the United States as a single comic episode, and omitted any mention of my life and work at home. In fact, between my second and third voyages, I suffered an emotional catastrophe that reduced me to profound despair; my marriage broke down and, less than a week after my return to England, Isabelle abandoned me. It was a paralysing blow; and the pain I then experienced was of a kind that I had never known before – a pain that accompanied me every day and haunted my dreams throughout the night, returning to the attack with renewed ferocity the moment that my eyes had opened. On the eve of my second American journey I had had some gloomy premonitions. Otherwise, the course of our life together had been comparatively undisturbed; and a new colour had meanwhile found its way into the spectrum of my feelings. Not only had my devotion to Isabelle increased; but it was gradually taking on a different character. When we married, the motives that inspired me were by no means altruistic – I feared losing an attractive bedfellow to whose presence I had grown accustomed; and I enjoyed the idea of making an obviously imprudent move, which demonstrated a splendid disregard for ordinary common sense. Since our marriage, however, a physical affection had become an emotional infatuation; and, for me at least, our bohemian relationship was presently reborn as a romantic love-affair. In my possessive union with Isabelle I embraced her past-existence; and all the stories she had told me of her unhappy childhood and her vagrant youth, and all the pictures I had myself built up around the strange adventures of her London life, had reinforced her hold on my imagination and, through the imagination, on my heart.

Finally, my devotion to Isabelle contained an element of gratitude; we are grateful to those we love for the quality of the emotions they happen to arouse in us, and for the imaginative release they provide from the prison of the Self. My earlier marriage had involved an exchange of benefits; it was an *égoïsme-à-deux*, the quietly reasonable alliance of two self-centred human beings, each of whom had a fairly good opinion of the other's looks and talents. Such an alliance could never have existed between myself and Isabelle; and to that extent my strangely ill-fated passion had a far more disinterested warmth than the affection it succeeded. It was protective and passionate at the same time; I longed to protect Isabelle, both against her own anarchic traits, and against the dangers and difficulties she seemed to evoke by the mere fact of her existence.

Proust was my oracle; and I remembered that, in *Un Amour de Swann*, the novelist's ageing hero, when he reviews his ill-starred passion for Odette de Crécy, observes that the woman he had pursued and married had never really been *son genre*, his type; but that somehow Odette's lack of aesthetic appeal had served to strengthen his attachment. Isabelle, I admitted, was distinctly not my type – a tall, broad-shouldered Valkyrie rather than a slender, small-boned English nymph. Yet, again, this apparent lack of charm – perhaps because, as in Swann's case, it called the mind into play before the senses – had merely added to her power of charming. Isabelle was not always the difficult companion I have described on previous pages; she had sudden bursts of juvenile gaiety and fun, gleams of childish grace and humour; and, when we travelled and the summer sky was clear, we were very often happy. She liked travelling, and had even developed a moderate taste for sightseeing; and, accompanied by a friend who was writing a book about English Gothic architecture, we rambled around the English landscape and sometimes visited cathedral cities. One expedition, our only journey abroad, took us as far afield as Luxembourg, where Isabelle had spent some time at a convent, and we paid our respects to an amiable Mother-Superior, besides examining Vauban's grandiose fortifications and the ramparts and bright-painted sentry-boxes of the little ducal residence.

From Luxembourg itself we went on to the ancient town of Wasserbillig; whence a high-arched, statue-lined bridge carries the road across the Mosel into the Palatinate. There was already talk, in Luxembourg as in England, of a Second World War; 'I saw the Germans come last time,' said an old inhabitant of Wasserbillig, 'and I shall see them come again!' We had no German visas; but the prospect of entering Germany, her mother's birthplace, at once fascinated Isabelle; and she set off down the avenue of baroque statues, towards the small knot of brown-shirted guards we could distinguish on the farther bank. Me she had instructed to stay behind; and from a café in Luxembourg I watched her go, tall, elegant, striding straight ahead, her thick hair gilded by the sun, until she reached the Nazi guard-house. I had a long wait, and was beginning to feel anxious before at last she reappeared, a small military dagger stuck in the belt of her trousers, and wearing the faint smile that, with Isabelle, always signified the successful completion of some audacious enterprise. 'We talked German', she remarked; 'they were very friendly; some of them were quite attractive'; and she asked me to order her a glass of wine. Our Moselle, once she rejoined me, tasted particularly clean and fresh.

I was preparing at the time an English edition of the private letters of Princess Lieven and Prince Metternich;* and among the objects of our journey was to spend a day or two in Brussels, and turn over the collection of schoolroom copybooks, then still owned by the Lieven family, into which Madame de Lieven, after her breach with Metternich, once she had recovered her love-letters through the Duke of Wellington, had copied out the many political and social passages she was anxious to preserve. I finished my task; but, as our holiday ended, Isabelle announced that she had made a strange discovery – among the contents of her bag she had unearthed some forgotten English bank-notes, which, if I agreed, would enable her to remain in Brussels another two or three days. I agreed, though I was puzzled and disappointed, and returned alone to London; but there, once Isabelle rejoined me, looking calm and well-pleased, I found it more and more difficult to shake off a cloud of vague anxiety. Since our first meeting we had always drunk too much; at some periods of our life in South Audley Street we seldom went to bed completely sober; and Isabelle was now inclined to drink with a kind of quiet desperation, as though she were struggling to satisfy the demands of some mysterious inward void. Eventually, I felt she had reached a stage at which she ceased to drink for pleasure, and that the habit itself, rather than the results it produced, gave her the relief she sought. Through no merit of my own – thanks,

* *The Private Letters of Princess Lieven to Prince Metternich*, 1820–1826; published 1937.

233

I suppose, to some stroke of metabolic or psychological good fortune – the angel-demon alcohol has treated me far less unkindly. But, during those last months, it had a calamitous effect on my unsettled nerves and temper; and we ran into violent quarrels, usually provoked by the jealous suspicions that she did not discourage and could not help arousing.

My suspicions were ill-directed; and, while I focused my attention on some smooth young man Isabelle encountered at a nightclub, I failed to recognize a far more immediate danger. Recently we had acquired a new friend, a representative of the generation that had succeeded mine at Oxford. The crown prince of an English financial dynasty, besides his gastronomic and sporting interests he had a cultured literary taste, as I was bound to admit when he expressed his admiration for the first of my Byronic studies, and repaid the pleasure he said it had afforded him by making me a generous gift. Soon he had become our *ami de la maison*, and regularly visited us at South Audley Street or entertained us at a restaurant. We thought him an odd and amusing companion. L'Ami had the boldly curvaceous features of an Assyrian or Babylonian court-official, a prominent lower-lip and the sardonic turn of humour, self-deprecatory yet also keenly critical, so often found in members of his race. He was a lavish host, though he frequently attempted to cast doubts on his own instinctive generosity, and an addict of literature who liked to pretend that he detested modern highbrows. 'Thank God, I'm an extrovert myself,' he cried, and would peremptorily bring the conversation back to a worldlier and safer level.

A great advantage of l'Ami's friendship was that, if I had an article to finish and had decided I must stay at home, he was prepared to act as Isabelle's escort and would entertain her in the princely style to which she was not yet quite accustomed. The arrangement suited me; I preferred to work alone. Although I loved my wife, I was sometimes a little bored by our long domestic dialogues, when Isabelle occupied the sofa smoking and drinking, and casually riffling through a newspaper; and she always returned to our flat, I noted, in a mood of high contentment. Even so, my naïvety had its limits; and I did occasionally enquire of Isabelle what she and l'Ami talked about, and whether she felt quite sure that his attitude towards her was entirely that of a good-natured friend. Isabelle's reply was prompt. She readily agreed that their harmless association might look like something very different; but, however it *looked*, she could only assure me that it was nothing of the kind. She concluded with a subtle appeal to my vanity. Fond though we were of l'Ami, surely I did not suppose that he might arouse an adulterous *grande passion*?

Though I agreed that he seemed an improbable seducer, the gulf that separated us slowly widened; and I observed that Isabelle's eyes were now beginning to reflect not so much indifference, or sullen impatience, as a glint of hard dislike. I was at length both cut off emotionally and rejected physically; and before I again left England, after a wretched week-end, passed in pleas, demands and hopeless unanswered questions, I had subsided into labyrinthine gloom. Aboard the *Queen Mary* my spirits were deadly low. Then, on the second night out, having attended a bacchanalian dinner-party held by the free-spending Felix, I took a stranger to my cabin. She was neither very young nor remarkably attractive. But under the two-fold spell of despair and drunkenness I forgot the woman and forgot myself, and, better still, managed temporarily to drop the load that I had brought with me from England. Next day, pangs of black remorse aggravated the worst effects of an atrocious hangover. It would have been anguish to meet my partner again; and I spent several hours eluding her, while she doggedly pursued me, up and down endless rubber-paved passages, through saloons and reading-rooms and bars, along dismal, empty, rain-wet decks – anywhere to escape the plaintive wraith that mouthed and gesticulated far behind.

New York provided little comfort; all my doubts and fears revived, often lending an ominous significance to some ordinary sight or sound. One afternoon, seated in a board-room on the top floor of an unknown office-block, through the window I saw that the roof was supported by a lengthy succession of monumental bison-heads; and each head, with its monstrous sculptured muzzle, short thick horns and curly brow, became a symbol of disaster. The disaster soon occurred. Felix and Mr Schwarz had arranged that we were to spend an evening at the Elizabeth

Arden office after other members of the staff had left; and there I heard that a personal telephone-call was being put through to me from London. My heart thumped out a warning message as I settled down to wait; and, when I had waited some twenty or thirty minutes, a far-off bell gave tongue. But how should I find that bell? We were quite alone in the office; and I could only follow the sound across a maze of darkened rooms, until I entered the main office, equally darkened, full of telephones and tables. The problem now was to identify the instrument that continued summoning me. I had failed to discover the electric-light switch, and blundered to and fro like an imprisoned bat, hurtling against sharp-edged pieces of furniture and tripping over chairs and cords. While I groped towards it, the noise abruptly ceased. My colleagues and Mr Schwarz were already preparing to leave for a drink in his apartment; and I thereupon telephoned the operator and asked him to relay the call. It caught up with me in Mr Schwarz's bedroom, just beyond his sitting-room, a by no means private place. When I lifted the receiver, a broken tear-clogged voice came, terrifyingly loud, along the line. Isabelle, I guessed, was rather drunk. She insisted again and again that I must stay in New York and, whatever happened, not return home. Further than that she refused to explain herself; and our conversation ended.

Aubrey and Felix, in times of emotional crisis, were a sympathetic pair; and they allowed me to begin my return journey the moment I could book a passage. It seemed an interminable journey; I was wildly confused and perplexed; and Isabelle, when we met at South Audley Street, would not immediately enlighten me, but suggested we should dine out. Over dinner, she gradually told her tale, and spoke of her passion for l'Ami, and of his deep, yet honourable love for her. They would be married once she had obtained a divorce; and she hoped that I should not object to being divorced and providing the necessary evidence. After all, she said, I had very little to lose; and, naturally, the feelings of her future husband's family must so far as possible be safeguarded. From the restaurant we drove home through the rain to desolate South Audley Street; and on the doorstep an unemployed man accosted us, carrying a basketful of white heather. 'Buy some heather,' he pleaded, 'buy a sprig of white heather! Bring you luck, Sir. You can have it for a bob. Heather's bound to bring you luck!'

Our discussions, which lasted far into the night, left me still more passionately wretched. Earlier, I have described the pain I suffered during those hag-ridden weeks. It was as concrete as physical pain; and, like some lanciniating bodily affliction, it had to be anaesthetized. This I set about deliberately and carefully. I attended my office; but no sooner had the neighbouring bar opened than I began to drink champagne-and-brandy, with a sugar-lump dipped in angostura dissolving at the bottom of the glass. An admirable specific the insidious mixture proved. Slowly I slid into a state of dull quiescence; but I dreaded the afternoon hours when the friendly bar was closed and my pain came stealing back. My mind assured me that such agonies always pass; and subsequently, when I read Boswell's account of the unhappiness caused him by a Scottish gardener's daughter, I learned that he, too, was often astonished to reflect that his sufferings, even in his own estimation, one day would seem trivial indeed. Meanwhile, I found it difficult to conceive of a world where pain was not the ruling factor; and my darkest hour arrived on the night I unlocked our door and found that Isabelle had left the flat. Her clothes had gone; I opened the cupboard in which she used to keep her dresses. Only a few skeletonic wire hangers dangled from the central rod.

Explanations that might have eased my grief Isabelle could not, or obstinately would not give. There is no doubt, I think, that her feeling for l'Ami was both an emotional and a physical obsession, whereas l'Ami himself, I suspect, might have been perfectly content with a surreptitious love-affair, and was surprised and, I dare say, much disturbed by news of her telephone-call to New York. Yes, she was in love, perhaps for the first time. The origins of almost every passion ultimately defy analysis; but I believe that between Isabelle's attachment to l'Ami and her frustrated devotion to her cold reproving father there may have existed a strong unconscious link. True, l'Ami was some years younger than myself; but he had a large commanding presence, and, through the authoritative use he made of his money, could take care of any situation. Though not a mercenary character, Isabelle may have respected his wealth because it strengthened his parental image – as a very young child, I remember assuming that my father was probably among the richest men on earth; and l'Ami's riches helped him to replace the parent who had always held her love at bay.

That Christmas season Isabelle was invited to spend with l'Ami's relations in the country, while I found a consoling refuge with Georgia and Sacheverell Sitwell; and the Divorce Courts granted her a decree absolute on 31 January 1938, after a marriage that had lasted thirty months and six days. Yet she did not re-marry. L'Ami's well-wishers can scarcely have approved of Isabelle as the Heir Apparent's future wife; but, when they had met her, they may have been shrewd enough to guess that, given a sufficiency of rope, she soon would weave herself a fatal noose. This she had done before the end of Easter. L'Ami had proposed that she and a woman friend of hers should spend the holiday with him in France; but she behaved so foolishly – according to one piece of gossip reported back to me in England, she had drunk a good deal during the short flight and had had to be carried off the plane – that his emotions abruptly swung into reverse; and, once they had both regained London, he firmly broke off their engagement. She and I had not yet lost touch; and, having been summoned to a London nursing-home where she lay recovering from an overdose, I persuaded her to go abroad. An unwise suggestion; her first move, on reaching her foreign hotel, was to buy a draught of Veronal, which could then be purchased without a doctor's prescription at almost all Parisian pharmacies.

Many intended suicides, preparing their last journey, leave a small escape-route open; before she had taken the decisive step, Isabelle telephoned me in London; and the concierge, who had failed to obtain my number, presently knocked upon her door. As she did not respond, he made use of his pass-key, discovered her inanimate and called the police. Luckily, an old companion, Brian Howard, happened to be staying near. His imperative telegram brought me across the Channel, though it was difficult to persuade my recalcitrant bank-manager to cash the necessary cheque; and at length I found my way into a huge and ancient hospital, of which I have since forgotten both the name and the exact locality, but that seemed to come straight from one of Balzac's gloomiest narratives, an agglomeration of grey dilapidated buildings, with a Gothic archway here and there. I entered a long low ward, peopled by old women; a few *tricoteuses* were huddled around an iron stove; the rest sat up in their narrow beds, vaguely muttering and peering; while at the very end lay the strange distraught figure I recognized as Isabelle. Evidently the nurses had tried to pull off the night-gown she was wearing when the police had brought her in; for its silken folds still entangled one arm, and a coarse thick hospital garment half concealed the other. She embraced me desperately – twenty or thirty pairs of eager eyes followed every detail of the scene – while I promised I would very soon have her transferred to far more comfortable surroundings. She was moved later that day; and the huddled shapes round the stove awoke and craned their necks to watch her go. Isabelle must have repulsed their offers of sympathy. '*Elle ne nous aimait pas!*' they chanted in spectral chorus.

At the American clinic, cases of Veronal-poisoning attracted very little notice, so many rich unhappy patients were already being treated there; and, after a short period of rest, a reluctant visit from l'Ami and an alarming and undignified interview with the local Corsican police-inspector, a yellow, sharp-eyed, rat-faced man, who crooked his finger and beckoned her into his office, whence she emerged after a lengthy quarter of an hour wearing her familiar smile, Isabelle was free to leave. As we left the clinic, I had accepted some words of advice from a friendly middle-aged physician. 'She's a nice kid,' he remarked in calm flat tones. 'But don't you forget; she'll try again one day!' – a prophecy I bore in mind, though I preferred to discount it, until, nine years later, on January 12th 1947, it was eventually realized. That day she seemed remote and hostile; but by this time she had lost her power to hurt; and the protective emotions she had once aroused had begun to lose their hold. While we were still married, pity and desire were always closely interwoven; now that I knew I could no longer protect her, I saw her through much clearer eyes. My friends encouraged the gradual process of recovery. They had not been in the least astonished to hear that Isabelle had 'done a bunk', and even offered their congratulations on what they regarded as a merciful release, expressing the hope that, if ever I remarried, I should be a little less incautious.

Nor did the agonies I had endured throughout the winter continue far into the spring. I found many diversions – the recently deserted husband is an interesting figure; and I learned that *amour passion*, in small graduated doses, was the best of homoeopathic remedies. This treatment I kept up in New York on my next official stay. Since I was unaccompanied, I enjoyed myself far more than during either of my previous visits and, among my less discreditable adventures, spent an extraordinary evening with the poet E. E. Cummings, whom I watched tiptoe along the terrifyingly narrow parapet of his apartment-house in Greenwich Village, arms outstretched, his noble bony head silhouetted against the flickering Manhattan sky. Another night, some bohemian acquaintances persuaded me to try the effect of cocaine and heroin mixed. Secretive telephone-calls evoked a mysterious messenger, carrying supplies of both drugs – for the purposes of the transaction they were nicknamed 'hyacinth' and 'crocus' – which the company sniffed from wooden ice-cream spoons. Next day I suffered acute malaise; but the only immediate effect I experienced was that I quickly lost all sense of time; hours passed like minutes; boredom and fatigue vanished; and the most commonplace dialogue acquired an air of deep significance. Then, although the party, I thought, had scarcely begun, I noticed that the dawn had broken, and that, in the street below, a posse of tall policemen, mackintosh capes shining beneath the rain, were setting forth upon their rounds.

I remember a worse dawn. Some English friends and I were imprudently exploring Harlem, and allowed ourselves to be conducted to a brothel or *maison de passe*, that promised us 'a daisy-chain'. Its chief protagonist of this squalid and gloomy show was to have been a monstrous black man, with a disproportionately small skull and grotesquely massive limbs. But the night was advancing; he and his fellow performers, summoned from distant beds, were already over-tired; and the priapic feats that the monster was supposed to display turned out to be totally beyond his strength. The result was fiasco on a giant scale; and an uncontrollable *fou rire* convulsed the mercenary audience. No doubt we were lucky to escape unharmed; but finally we settled our bill and made our exit. In an outer room, we passed an enormous window, looking down from Harlem Heights, beyond which, across a desolate urban gulf, big damp snow-flakes slowly drifted. The room itself contained a grand piano; and at the keyboard sat two black musicians, who wore long dark coats, white silk scarves and bowler hats. Whether they were coming or going we never knew; it was nearly five o'clock; and rigid and silent, perched on their twin piano-stools, they paid us not the least attention.

Before I returned home, Miss Arden, a galaxy of small yellow orchids stuck into her russet curls, gave me a resplendent farewell party, to which she had generously invited the most beautiful young woman whom she then employed. 1938 was a definitive year in my life; and there, or thereabouts, I think I should draw a line that concludes the present story. On March 9th 1938 I was thirty-three years old. What had I so far accomplished, and how far had I fallen beneath the literary standards of my youth? Well, I was certainly no longer a poet; since I left Japan, where I abandoned my last attempt to write original verse, the poetic impulse had deserted me; but I felt I could claim to have made some progress in the art of writing prose, and, besides translations and hackwork, had published a quartet of full-length books. On the other hand, both my marriages had failed; and the second, before it collapsed, had wasted time and energy, and caused me infinite despair. I now owed my livelihood to a daily office-job that, although it amused me and had brought me moderate success, secretly I could not help despising.

My personal problems, however, in 1938, were presently overlaid by a sense of general disquietude. Nothing about one's situation, either good or bad, seemed likely to last very long; and a giant catastrophe was already projecting its shadow across one's safe, familiar landscape. Since the outbreak of the Spanish Civil War, most of my literary friends had been more or less committed to the anti-fascist struggle; and many of them had visited the Spanish front. Even Cyril Connolly, then in the midst of a difficult love-affair, had made a pilgrimage to Barcelona, where he discovered with relief that the Ritz Hotel still provided quite passable food and service; and I have a newspaper photograph that shows him striding down a sunny Catalan road, the wind ruffling his loose tweed overcoat and whipping his hair around his large round face, which looks appropriately stern and grave. I could not afford to make such adventurous journeys myself; nor, indeed, had I the inclination. I hated the idea of fascism and authoritarian government. But I am an 'idiot', an *idiōtēs*, as the Greeks originally defined the noun – 'a person in a private station', of whom Pericles declared that 'we do not say that the man who takes no interest in politics is a man who minds his own business; we say that he had no business here at all'.*

During the period of the Spanish Civil War, the 'idiot' was scarcely less unpopular among European intellectuals than he had been in Periclean Athens. This was the age of the 'socially conscious writer', of *la littérature engagée*; and I still believed – a belief I have never lost – that the writer, if he deliberately espouses a cause, is bound to curtail, and perhaps distort his vision. Some degree of engagement he obviously cannot escape, since every work that he produces must reflect the spirit of his age, and reveal his attitude towards its values; but his most effective criticisms are not expressly stated so much as subtly and quietly implied, and form part of a picture of the human condition that transcends the problems of the present day. In 1928 many young writers expressed a puritanical distaste for style; and Cyril Connolly, when he published his *Enemies of Promise*, separated the goats, the 'Mandarin' littérateurs, who looked back to the nineteenth-century past, from the 'Vernacular' revolutionaries, Hemingway, Isherwood and George Orwell. I was conscious, at the time, of being unquestionably a Mandarin; and my main preoccupation was always with words and with their proper literary use. It was only through evolving a style, I thought, that I could discover what I had to say, and give any discoveries I made the necessary shape and substance.

This preoccupation with words, I must admit in parenthesis, has since taken some fantastic turns; my love of the English language has become a superstitious cult; and, among other

* *Thucydides*, 20.40.2; translated by Rex Warner.

foibles, I go to absurd lengths to avoid repeating prepositions; the reappearance of 'by' or 'with' or 'from', unless they occur several lines apart, causes me acute dismay, and often obliges me to turn back and reconstruct a lengthy passage. I do not defend my mania. But one must write as one can; and, though far better writers would have found it highly ridiculous, the avoidance of such repetitions is a habit I can no longer shake off. Writing is a painful business; but the pleasure of building up a single lucid paragraph far exceeds the pains involved; while the conquest of a difficult sentence, which obstinately defies the author's control and struggles snakelike in his grasp, is sometimes even more rewarding. To my father, who wrote notably careless prose, I owe, not my affection for literary style, but an appetite for daily work; and industry is almost the only virtue I have ever dared to claim. Elsewhere, the example my father set has done me very little good. But, although I have long forgotten his lectures and homilies, there at least I have responded; for the memory of those long gas-lit evenings, while I watched him draw or write, so firmly concentrated and so happily self-absorbed, left a decisive mark on my imagination.

One of the main objects with which I launched the present book was to produce my father's portrait, and describe both the debt I owed him and the contrasts that divided us. By the end of 1938 he had been dead just three years. But now that he tenanted the central niche of my mother's private pantheon, his influence was still strong. No woman could have been a better assistant or a more devoted wife. Yet, despite her sorrow, I suspect that, as time passed and she grew accustomed to her isolation, she may have dreamed that, having at last been released from the orbit of his powerful personality, she might begin a new career, an existence far less subdued and passive than any she had previously known. She was disappointed; through her long attachment to 'dear C.H.B.' she had nearly lost the gift of separate living; and, because they had had so few friends, though their friendly acquaintances were always numerous, in late middle age she found it sadly difficult to discover fresh companions. While my brother lived, and shared her London household – soon after my father's death she had abandoned Berkhamsted – she had his gay and resolute support; but once he had disappeared into the hideous chaos of the Second World War, she became a lonely woman. The War, too, deprived her of her regular occupation – the curatorship of a London children's museum – that had proved engrossing and enjoyable. When the Geffrye Museum closed and my brother's death was reported, she hurried away to the United States. On her return, she found England cold and empty; and in none of the small houses she later occupied could she ever quite achieve contentment.

She survived until 1972; and I visualize her most distinctly during the twilit years of her life in her mid-Victorian house at Lewes – a handsome upright figure, and, though latterly half-crippled, still expectant and alert. Just what she expected I cannot tell; nor, I think, did she herself know; but, clearly, besides regretting the past and detesting the limitations of the present, she retained a hopeful interest in the days to come. Meanwhile, she fretted against her lameness and deafness, the sedentary routine she had perforce accepted, and the fact that her good-natured country neighbours were seldom 'really interesting people'. She welcomed the regular visits I paid her, would demand my news and eagerly absorb the scraps of gossip I had brought with me from London. But at that point silence often fell; her deafness was a barrier across which I had to raise my voice – 'You needn't *shout*, you know,' she murmured; and we were both of us sometimes unhappily aware that our long domestic con-versations were not always as spontaneous and overflowing as we felt they ought to be. Then my mother's face revealed a touch of impatience; her smile paled, and her attention wavered. She would glance off through the plate-glass window towards the tree-tops of her Sussex garden, or in the direction of the door that would presently admit her devoted housekeeper and beloved confidante Mary, who announced that dinner was awaiting us. If Mary were a minute or two delayed, my mother's finger-tips would beat a nervous tattoo upon her chair-arm or a near-by table.

To my mother I owe my social instincts (which she herself could never gratify), many of my neurasthenic failings, such as my recurrent anxieties and irrational panic fears, and my passion for imaginative art. My father had slightly distrusted artists, and preferred the unpretentious craftsman; but, though I respect craftsmanship, I have come to consider art the noblest product of the human mind, and its cultivation the only form of endeavour that is ultimately worth pursuing. Since my childhood I have been in love with pictures, from the great visions that create a whole new world of harmony, order and celestial peace, to family portraits, conversation-groups, and the type of landscapes that German art-historians call *wanderlandschaft*, where the on-looker is invited to penetrate the background of a strange romantic landscape and literally 'wander round' its details.*

My passion for visual images has determined the shape of this book. The memory works irregularly, and preserves its archives carelessly; and every student of the past who opens them is con-fronted with the same disorder. The objects that emerge are extraordinarily ill-assorted – bright imperishable fragments, in which years of feeling have been summed up, and the meanest scraps and trifles. There is no obvious reason why the mind should preserve some of the materials it receives, and rapidly discard others. I remember foolish jokes I heard half a century ago, squalid episodes and idiotic verses; but I have almost forgotten meetings and conversations that, in my youth, impressed me deeply. Much that the mind stores up is the rubbish of experience; but amid the debris certain images remain, like the marble foot planted on the flagstones of a crowded Roman street; and these significant images I have tried to link together in a continuous pictorial frieze. Each represents a separate adventure of the mind, one of those rare flashes of insight and illumination, which, if we can recapture them, and give them literary substance, may make a human life seem worth recording.

* Among masterpieces that are also *wanderlandschaft* I think of numerous works by Poussin; for example, *The Ashes of Phocion being removed from Athens*, now in a private English collection.

INDEX

INDEX